JANE AUSTEN'S *EMMA*

JANE AUSTEN'S *EMMA*

Philosophical Perspectives

Edited by E. M. Dadlez

OXFORD
UNIVERSITY PRESS

OXFORD
UNIVERSITY PRESS

Oxford University Press is a department of the University of Oxford. It furthers
the University's objective of excellence in research, scholarship, and education
by publishing worldwide. Oxford is a registered trade mark of Oxford University
Press in the UK and certain other countries.

Published in the United States of America by Oxford University Press
198 Madison Avenue, New York, NY 10016, United States of America.

© Oxford University Press 2018

Library of Congress Cataloging-in-Publication Data
Names: Dadlez, E. M. (Eva M.), 1956– editor.
Title: Jane Austen's Emma : philosophical perspectives / edited by E. M. Dadlez.
Description: New York : Oxford University Press, 2018. |
Includes bibliographical references and index.
Identifiers: LCCN 2017059876 | ISBN 9780190689414 (hbk.) |
ISBN 9780190689421 (pbk.)
Subjects: LCSH: Austen, Jane, 1775–1817. Emma. |
Austen, Jane, 1775–1817—Philosophy. | Literature—Philosophy.
Classification: LCC PR4034.E53 J376 2018 | DDC 823/.7—dc23
LC record available at https://lccn.loc.gov/2017059876

1 3 5 7 9 8 6 4 2

Paperback printed by Webcom, Inc., Canada
Hardback printed by Bridgeport National Bindery, Inc., United States of America

Dedicated to Peter Kivy, first to contribute,
to whom we give the last word.

CONTENTS

CONTENTS

SERIES EDITOR'S FOREWORD

At least since Plato had Socrates criticize the poets and attempt to displace Homer as the authoritative articulator and transmitter of human experience and values, philosophy and literature have developed as partly competing, partly complementary enterprises. Both literary writers and philosophers have frequently studied and commented on each other's texts and ideas, sometimes with approval, sometimes with disapproval, in their efforts to become clearer about human life and about valuable commitments—moral, artistic, political, epistemic, metaphysical, and religious, as may be. Plato's texts themselves register the complexity and importance of these interactions in being dialogues in which both deductive argumentation and dramatic narration do central work in furthering a complex body of views.

While these relations have been widely recognized, they have also frequently been ignored or misunderstood, as academic disciplines have gone their separate ways within their modern institutional settings. Philosophy has often turned to science or mathematics as providing models of knowledge; in doing so, it has often explicitly set itself against cultural entanglements and literary devices, rejecting, at least officially, the importance of plot, figuration, and imagery in favor of supposedly plain speech about the truth. Literary study has moved variously through formalism, structuralism, poststructuralism, and cultural studies, among other movements, as modes of approach to a literary text. In doing so, it has understood literary texts as sample instances of images, structures, personal styles, or failures of consciousness, or it has seen the literary text as a largely fungible product, fundamentally shaped by wider pressures and patterns of consumption and expectation that affect and figure in non-literary textual production as well. It has thus set itself against the idea that major literary texts productively and originally address philosophical problems of value and commitment precisely through their form, diction, imagery, and development, even while these works also resist claiming conclusively to solve the problems that occupy them.

These distinct academic traditions have yielded important perspectives and insights. But in the end, none of them has been kind to the idea of major literary works as achievements in thinking about values and human life, often in distinctive, open, self-revising, self-critical ways. At the same time, readers outside institutional settings, and often enough philosophers and literary scholars too, have turned to major literary texts precisely in order to engage with their productive, materially and medially specific patterns and processes of thinking. These turns to literature, however, thus far have not been systematically encouraged within disciplines, and they have generally occurred independently of each other.

The aim of this series is to make manifest the multiple, complex engagements with philosophical ideas and problems that lie at the hearts of major literary texts. In doing so, its volumes aim not only to help philosophers and literary scholars of various kinds to find rich affinities and provocations to further thought and work, they also aim to bridge various gaps between academic disciplines and between those disciplines and the experiences of extra-institutional readers.

Each volume focuses on a single, undisputedly major literary text. Both philosophers with training and experience in literary study and literary scholars with training and experience in philosophy are invited to engage with themes, details, images, and incidents in the focal text, through which philosophical problems are held in view, worried at, and reformulated. Decidedly not a project simply to formulate A's philosophy of X as a finished product, merely illustrated in the text, and decidedly not a project to explain the literary work entirely by reference to external social configurations and forces, the effort is instead to track the work of open thinking in literary forms, as they lie both neighbor to and aslant from philosophy. As Walter Benjamin once wrote, "new centers of reflection are continually forming," as problems of commitment and value of all kinds take on new shapes for human agents in relation to changing historical circumstances, where reflective address remains possible. By considering how such centers of reflection are formed and expressed in and through literary works, as they engage with philosophical problems of agency, knowledge, commitment, and value, these volumes undertake to present both literature and philosophy as, at times, productive forms of reflective, medial work in relation both to each other and to social circumstances and to show how this work is specifically undertaken and developed in distinctive and original ways in exemplary works of literary art.

Richard Eldridge
Swarthmore College

CONTRIBUTORS

Neera K. Badhwar is Professor Emerita of Philosophy at the University of Oklahoma and an Affiliate at George Mason University. Her articles on moral psychology, ethical theory, and political theory have appeared in *Journal of Philosophy; Ethics; Nous; Politics, Philosophy, and Economics;* and other journals. Her anthology, *Friendship: A Philosophical Reader,* was published by Cornell University Press in 1993, and her book, *Well-being: Happiness as the Highest Good,* in 2014 by Oxford University Press. She has held fellowships at the University Center for Human Values (Princeton University), Social Philosophy and Policy Center (BGSU), and Dalhousie University.

E. M. Dadlez has a PhD in Philosophy from Syracuse University and is Professor of Philosophy at the University of Central Oklahoma. Her work is mainly on the philosophy of art and literature, and on topics at the intersection (sometimes, more accurately, the collision) of aesthetics, ethics, and epistemology. She is the author of various articles on aesthetics and feminist ethics, as well as *What's Hecuba to Him? Fictional Events and Actual Emotions* (Penn State Press) and

Mirrors to One Another: Emotion and Value in Jane Austen and David Hume (Wiley-Blackwell).

David Davies is Professor of Philosophy at McGill University, where he has taught since 1987. While his doctoral research (Western Ontario, 1987) and much of his research for the following few years was on the realism/anti-realism debate in contemporary metaphysics, and on related issues in the philosophy of mind and philosophy of language, for the past twenty years his research has focused mainly on metaphysical and epistemological issues in the philosophy of art. He has also published widely on topics relating to literature, film, photography, music, performance, and the visual arts. He is the author of *Art as Performance* (Blackwell, 2004), *Aesthetics and Literature* (Continuum, 2007), and *Philosophy of the Performing Arts* (Wiley-Blackwell, 2011); editor of *The Thin Red Line* (Routledge, 2008); and co-editor of *Blade Runner* (Routledge, 2015).

Richard Eldridge is Charles and Harriett Cox McDowell Professor of Philosophy at Swarthmore College. He has held visiting appointments at Freiburg, Erfurt, Bremen, Essex, Stanford, and Brooklyn. He is the editor of *The Oxford Handbook of Philosophy and Literature*. His most recent books are *Images of History: Kant, Benjamin, Freedom, and the Human Subject* (2016) and *Literature, Life, and Modernity* (2008). He has published widely on Wittgenstein, Kant, Hegel, Romanticism, Cavell, aesthetic theory, truth in literature, and film, among other topics.

Cynthia Freeland is Professor Emerita of Philosophy at the University of Houston. She was president of the American Society for Aesthetics (2015–2017). Her publications include work on ancient philosophy, feminist theory, and aesthetics. Her book *But Is It Art?* (Oxford, 2001) has been translated into fourteen languages. She is also editor of *Feminist Interpretations of Aristotle* (1998), *Philosophy and Film* (with Thomas Wartenberg) (1995), and author of *The Naked and* *the Undead: Evil and the Appeal of Horror* (1999) and *Portraits and Persons* (Oxford, 2010). Freeland has participated in international grant projects based in Norway and Australia. She earned her BA in Philosophy at Michigan State University and her MA and PhD in Philosophy at the University of Pittsburgh.

Eileen John is an Associate Professor of Philosophy at the University of Warwick. Her research is in aesthetics, with an emphasis on philosophy of literature. She has written on broad questions concerning artistic value and the cognitive roles of literature, and on the philosophical import of particular literary works. Some of the authors her research has engaged with are Elizabeth Bishop, J. M. Coetzee, Toni Morrison, and Marilynne Robinson. She is co-editor of the Blackwell anthology *The Philosophy of Literature* and has served as Director of Warwick's Centre for Research in Philosophy, Literature and the Arts.

Peter Kivy (1934–2017) was Board of Governors Professor of Philosophy Emeritus, Rutgers University, New Brunswick. He received his BA in Philosophy at the University of Michigan in 1956 and an MA in Philosophy from that University in 1958. He then went on to receive an MA in Music History from Yale University in 1960, a PhD in Philosophy from Columbia University in 1966, and was also awarded the degree of Honorary Doctor of Music from Goldsmiths College, University of London, where he was a permanent Honorary Fellow. Professor Kivy was the author of nineteen books on aesthetics and philosophy of art, as well as over ninety articles. Books of his have been translated into Chinese, Italian, Korean, Portuguese, and Spanish. His most recent book, *De Gustibus: Arguing about Art and Why We Do It*, was published by Oxford University Press in 2015. Professor Kivy was a former Guggenheim Fellow and a past President of the American Society for Aesthetics. He passed away on May 6, 2017.

Peter Knox-Shaw is a Research Associate at the University of Cape Town. He has published widely on eighteenth-century and Romantic literature. Work on Jane Austen includes *Jane Austen and the Enlightenment* (Cambridge, 2004), and the chapters on philosophy in *Jane Austen in Context*, ed. Janet Todd (Cambridge, 2005), and in the *Cambridge Companion to* Pride and Prejudice, ed. Janet Todd (Cambridge, 2013). He is currently at work on *The Enlivenment*, a study of the impact of natural history on the philosophy and literature of the later enlightenment.

Heidi Silcox received her PhD in English from The University of Oklahoma, where she studied images of leisure and conversation in fin de siècle British fiction. She has a Juris Doctorate from The University of Akron School of Law and practiced criminal law for five years. She also holds a masters degree in English literature from the University of Central Oklahoma. She has been published in *Poe in Context, Philosophy and Literature, Analecta Husserliana, The Kipling Journal, Dungeons and Dragons and Philosophy: Raiding the Temple of Wisdom* (Open Court Publishing, 2012), *The Routledge Encyclopedia of Modernism Online*, and *The Resource Guide to American Literature: Realism and Regionalism, 1865–1919* (Facts on File, 2010).

Mark Silcox was born and raised in Toronto, Canada. He received his PhD from the Ohio State University, and presently teaches philosophy at the University of Central Oklahoma. He is the author of *Philosophy Through Video Games* (Routledge, 2008, with Jon Cogburn) and editor of *Dungeons and Dragons and Philosophy: Raiding the Temple of Wisdom* (Open Court, 2012, with Jon Cogburn) and *Experience Machines: The Philosophy of Virtual Worlds* (Rowman & Littlefield International, 2017). His science fiction novel *The Face on the Mountain* was published by Incandescent Phoenix Press in 2016.

JANE AUSTEN'S *EMMA*

Introduction

E. M. DADLEZ

Jane Austen has always been something of a philosophical favorite. Legend has it that, when asked whether he still read novels, the philosopher Gilbert Ryle responded, "Yes, all six, every year," referring to Austen's six completed works. Her novels have invited an unusual degree of explicitly philosophical attention from literary scholars and social scientists as well as philosophers themselves. And that is unsurprising, given that her writing invariably addresses questions about virtue and vice, human interaction and rivalry, motivation and commitment, presenting readers with ethical and other dilemmas set in a variety of naturalistic contexts that represent a conscious departure from gothic supernaturalism and metaphysical excesses. Questions about social and economic class and social and economic obligations are raised. Austen reflects on self-knowledge and self-awareness, considers how it is that people justify their convictions, and investigates both the nature and the effects of imagination and emotion on human conduct and choices. She dwells on the ways in which evidence is taken note of or disregarded, and the effects of biases on decision and action. Accordingly, many philosophers have a decided soft spot for Austen, and reading Austen is often held to promote philosophical reflection.

The existence of this volume, and of similar philosophical investigations and interrogations of literary works, owes a good deal to the conviction that literature engages with philosophical ideas, elicits philosophical responses, and introduces philosophically salient perspectives. The claim is not that novels, even great novels, often make explicitly philosophical pronouncements that directly contribute to our store of knowledge (permitting an efficient reader to forgo the remaining text and retain only the relevant propositions, as if internally mimicking a PowerPoint presentation). Fictions might endorse the occasional principle, of course. They might inadvertently provide us with information about the world as well, perhaps about historical periods or customs, but this is usually not their purpose. Rather, it appears that some works of fiction give rise to or reinforce or clarify insights not by stating them outright, but by illustrating particular cases, or by eliciting empathetic responses, or by inciting patterns of attention or interpretation that expand the cognitive repertoire of the reader. Some works of fiction can reconfigure formerly familiar concepts, or show us something about the nature of our own expectations. They may show us why some things are valued and others are not, or what may and may not count as evidence for a conclusion of a certain type. They may arouse our emotions in such a way as to underwrite particular value judgments or reconfigure previous assumptions.[1]

Literature, anti-cognitivists will claim, cannot be considered a thought experiment. This certainly seems true, if the latter are narrowly construed. Fictions are not deductive arguments and cannot conclusively demonstrate the truth of propositions. There

1. For a defense of the practice of reading in general along not dissimilar lines, see Sarah E. Worth, *In Defense of Reading* (MD: Rowman and Littlefield, 2017).

is, nevertheless, a certain resemblance between a splendid fictional illustration of some particular philosophical point and the familiar intuition pump or variant case argument. The former are, as Daniel Dennett puts it, "wonderful imagination grabbers, jungle gyms for the imagination. They structure the way you think about a problem.... They're not arguments, they're stories. Instead of having a conclusion, they pump an intuition. They get you to say 'Aha! Oh, I get it!'"[2] So there is a kind of informal but nonetheless philosophical exercise that, like literature, engages the imagination and orchestrates the way we attend to the situations presented for our consideration. Not unlike fiction, variant case arguments and intuition pumps, particularly in ethics, are intended to elicit reactions of approval or disapproval toward decisions to act in accordance with one or another theoretical position. Moreover, they are intended to do so prior to the adoption of the stances or principles in dispute. That is, in classic Humean fashion, the sentiment is intended to precede and possibly give rise to the judgment, or to militate in such a judgment's favor. Peter Singer's well-known example of a failure to rescue drowning children from a shallow pond (a failure that is motivated principally by a disinclination to damage one's expensive footwear) is intended to get the reader or auditor to respond with disapproval to a failure to act, to an omission. The idea that there is no morally significant difference between killing and letting die is not assumed at the outset. That idea is, instead, supposed to gain traction from the initial reaction of the reader. The disapprobation and sense of wrongness are experienced prior to consideration of any consequentialist agenda. Thus, the philosophical contemplation of variant cases or intuition-arousing scenarios is by no means an *exclusively* intellectual endeavour. The point of many of these informal

2. Daniel C. Dennett, "Intuition Pumps" (Chapter 10), *Edge* 5.7.96, http://www.edge.org/documents/ThirdCulture/r-Ch.10.html (accessed June 7, 2016).

experiments is to arouse emotional reactions in an effort to promote one claim or position over another. Further, even non-cognitivists regarding emotion will concede that emotions are—if not inevitably, then quite frequently—accompanied by evaluations of or judgments about the situations contemplated. To regard a situation fearfully is usually to consider it dangerous. To feel disapproval in response to a description of some action (or inaction, as the case may be) is usually to judge it wrong or unjust. The eliciting of emotion should thus not be taken to signal a philosophical deficit since, first, it can be employed for philosophical ends, and second, the possibility of there being an intellectual component of the experience is not ruled out simply because an emotion is involved.

Since nearly all will agree that literary works can "illustrate" philosophical points, the preceding suggestion that such illustrations can resemble intuition pumps or variant case arguments, and so may on occasion make a real philosophical contribution, doesn't seem terribly controversial. That is, there may well be more to the kind of fictional case that, say, offers an illustration of how the quality and nature of one's friendships conduces to one's happiness, than a mere footnote to the *Nicomachean Ethics*. Literary depictions of an emotion like shame, to use a different example, can tell us something about what should motivate it, what concerns its possessor might have, and how experiencing it can affect the development of one's character and one's future decisions. This does more than add color or additional emphasis to a preexisting analysis of emotion. There can be more to the illustration of a philosophical idea than the provision of the entirely disposable species of sidebar. Moreover, cognitive investment and philosophical engagement can take many forms in addition to the illustrative. Interpreting the text can present cognitive challenges, as can the exercise of the empathetic imagination.

Let us briefly consider the claim that literature helps to develop the empathetic imagination. Novels famously enable their readers to imagine what it might be like to experience something they have not as yet undergone. They orchestrate the details attended to and the perspective adopted toward events, usually with an eye to arousing particular emotional reactions. Charles Dickens and Harriet Beecher Stowe, respectively, number among notable social reformers simply because of the internal perspectives on poverty and race that were conveyed by their work and that readers were encouraged imaginatively to adopt, or at least explore. I mention these two writers, so unlike Austen, because their work was revolutionary in their era simply because of the relatively unprecedented candidates for empathy that it offered. Stowe's style does not stand the test of time as Dickens's does, but the work of both had an enormous social impact just because it insisted on commonalities between the (hitherto alien) characters depicted and the reader—ranging from the capacity to experience fear and injury to the capacity to feel love, loyalty, and hope. Austen does not shock her audience with sudden realizations of injustice in this way (criticisms of her supposed shortfall in this respect will be discussed later). Her candidates for empathy are more familiar. But the free indirect style adopted in *Emma*, coupled with the really extraordinary stream-of-consciousness passages, are more likely to arouse empathy and to foster empathetic habits just on account of the recognizability and familiarity of their targets.

Consider that typical emotional responses to fiction are thought problematic in some circles simply because they involve emotional reactions to persons and events not believed to exist. A distinction is drawn, then, between emotional reactions of pity or admiration toward real people and those toward characters, and that difference is grounded in our believing in the existence of one but not the other. Without rehearsing the enormous literature on this matter, much of which suggests that affective response to fiction may on account of the preceding distinction be considered either irrational or not genuinely emotional, it is worth noting that empathetic emotional responses are in some respects importantly similar to responses to fiction. Empathetic responses must always be responses to what one has imagined. If I empathize with an actual person, I will carefully take note of her circumstances and behavior, I will make inferences about what she may believe and feel, and then I will imagine being placed as she is and believing as she does on the basis of the behavior and situation I've observed. But empathy with a character involves a surprisingly similar procedure. On the basis of authorial information to which I pay careful attention, I take note of the character's circumstances and behavior, make inferences (mental states may be reported in the narrative, so I may have more to go on) about the probable nature of his experience, and imagine undergoing it. The object of an empathetic emotion isn't the person or character *with whom* I empathize, but rather the circumstance *I* imagine undergoing, which is, since I never really do undergo it, *always* imaginary. If I feel empathetic shame and guilt with Emma over her cruelty to Miss Bates, the object of that shame couldn't be Emma herself, for the object of such emotions cannot be a person (or indeed, a character), but must usually be actions of one's own which one regards as wrong or which one regrets performing. And the object couldn't be Emma's cruelty, for that is not conduct for which I am personally responsible. The object would have to be an imagined wrong of my own, for shame and guilt are paradigmatically self-directed. I would be imagining having been cruel to another if I cringed empathetically while reading the passage about Emma's behavior at Box Hill. This is something that is not very difficult for me to imagine. Like Emma, I find it extraordinarily difficult to resist a good one-liner and only afterward find myself regretting the heady self-indulgence. Without belaboring the point, I wish only to emphasize that literature, and especially work like Austen's, might be held quite effectively to encourage the development of empathetic dispositions simply because empathy involves the same cognitive and imaginative processes and resources, whether we contemplate fiction or reality.

The work of the contributors to this book attests that our engagement with Jane Austen's *Emma* is indeed philosophical in a variety of ways. Two contributions maintain that Austen's *Emma* illustrates and clarifies Aristotelian conceptions—both of friendship and of the effects of shame on the development of character. It isn't held that Austen was familiar with the *Nicomachean Ethics*, of course, but only that ideas about these subjects that are conveyed by the novel illustrate, supplement, and sometimes offer prospective amendments to Aristotelian positions, even providing suggestions about the resolution of theoretical disagreements. For instance, Neera Badhwar and I (in Chapter 1) believe that *Emma* is a chronicle of the heroine's friendships and their effects on her character and development. The novel offers a picture of friendship that both reflects and revises many of Aristotle's claims in the *Nicomachean Ethics*. Aristotle maintains that a rough equality of both moral and intellectual virtue is essential for the best kinds of friendships, which are in turn necessary for a happy life. However, Aristotle fails to recognize the problems inherent in his position that a virtuous wife must always be less virtuous than a virtuous husband. *Emma* illustrates Aristotle's insights while revising his conception of marital friendship. Emma's story begins with her fear of intellectual isolation, as her governess leaves to marry, and shows the effects of Emma's friendships on both her moral and her intellectual development. Once Miss Taylor has departed, Emma's overconfidence is exacerbated by the friendship she forms with the intellectually inferior and adoring Harriet Smith, whose uncritical acceptance of Emma's every pronouncement helps to validate Emma's baseless romantic speculations. When Emma realizes her mistakes, however, she becomes more skeptical of her own views and more receptive to Knightley's. Equally receptive, Knightley acknowledges Emma's influence in correcting his own ungenerous view of Harriet.

For Austen, as for Aristotle, the friendship of moral and intellectual equals, the wisdom of whose criticisms each can recognize, is a vital ingredient of the happy life. Yet for Austen, unlike Aristotle, this friendship can occur in and may even be best exemplified by a marriage between true companions.

Cynthia Freeland (in Chapter 2) also sees Austen as a source of Aristotelian insights. Freeland believes that *Emma*'s depiction of the role of shame in moral development is similar to Aristotle's, diverging from but nevertheless serving to inform debates in Aristotelian scholarship concerning the roles of pain and pleasure as stimuli of moral growth. Does a good moral upbringing instill a taste for noble actions (and corresponding distaste for ignoble ones), as some Aristotelian scholars claim? Or must one have developed appropriate habits of virtue before one can take real pleasure in the good? In the latter case, shame propels one via aversion toward good habits that are not initially pleasant and will only eventually become so. The moral development of Austen's central character can be mined for illustrations that shed light on such questions and that sometimes deviate from the Aristotelian account. Emma Woodhouse's conduct toward the unfortunate Miss Bates at the picnic at Box Hill proves an excruciating source of shame for the protagonist. This is as telling an illustration of shame as one might find, dwelling as it does not only on the obligations violated, but on personal and social aspects of the emotion. Further, just as Badhwar and I have maintained in our own investigation of friendship, Freeland takes Austen to diverge from an Aristotelian position on moral and rational female inferiority, showing that the adoption of select Aristotelian insights needn't commit one to the conclusions drawn by Aristotle himself.

Again delving into Austen's gift for illustrating philosophical issues, Eileen John (in Chapter 3) explores what *Emma* and Austen might have to say about human agency and autonomy. John considers and challenges Christine Korsgaard's use of Austen's characters (Emma Woodhouse and Harriet Smith) to exemplify a species of defective autonomous action. It is unmistakably the case that *Emma* addresses and clarifies the nature and sources of defective action. Harriet Smith's happy subordination to Emma's will, as Korsgaard maintains, is obviously problematic. But it is most often Emma Woodhouse herself, and not Harriet, whose conduct Austen presents as compromised, and Emma's behavior is not defective in such a way as to suggest an abdication of will. Moreover, it is evident that considering what another thinks one should do and allowing that to inform one's conduct do not constitute a course of action that is invariably deplored in *Emma*, whose heroine is shown eventually to profit from Knightley's counsel. John investigates the light that Austen's novel can shed on defects in action, appealing to an ideal of maturity rather than autonomy.

Richard Eldridge (in Chapter 4) regards Austen's *Emma* as a study in the nature and possibility of self-understanding. How might Emma come to recognize and to overcome the "danger, . . . at present . . . unperceived" that lies in her possessing "the power of having rather too much her own way, and a disposition to think a little too well of herself?" (5)[3] Drawing on accounts of self-knowledge and deliberation developed by Gilbert Ryle, P. M. S. Hacker, and Richard Wollheim, Eldridge traces the role that deliberation and reflection play in Emma's errors and speculations. Emma has been mistaken about Harriet, about

---

3. All examples from Jane Austen's *Emma* in this book will be derived from the Oxford World Classics edition of the novel: Jane Austen, *Emma*, ed. James Kinsley (Oxford: Oxford University Press, 2008). Page references to this edition will appear in the text in parentheses. All examples of Austen's work apart from *Emma* (in this introduction and the immediately succeeding chapter) will be derived from the following: *The Novels of Jane Austen*, 5 volumes, ed. R. W. Chapman, 3rd edition (Oxford: Oxford University Press, 1988) and *The Works of Jane Austen*, ed. R. W. Chapman, Vol. 6: *Minor Works* (Oxford: Oxford University Press, 1988). Titles will be abbreviated as is standard: SS, *Sense and Sensibility* (v. 1); PP, *Pride and Prejudice* (v. 2); MP, *Mansfield Park* (v. 3); NA, *Northanger Abbey* (v. 5); P, *Persuasion* (v. 5); MW, *Minor Works* (including *Lady Susan, The Watsons, Sanditon*; v. 6).

Mr. Elton, about Robert Martin, and about Frank Churchill. She has also, on more than one occasion, erred in her conduct. Attempts to rectify such errors create tensions. On the one hand are an agent's reflective and deliberative attempts to assess and to reconfigure dispositions and motives. On the other, there are self-centered, self-reinforcing fantasies that can preclude the recasting of problematic dispositions and that resist change. Both of these are evident in *Emma*. Austen chronicles this tension (her depiction of the simultaneous facets of which is facilitated by use of the free indirect style) and the manner in which attempts to achieve self-knowledge are conducted. She goes still further, Eldridge maintains, in showing how tentative and divided such an achievement will be. Self-understanding is not achieved in isolation. It has a social dimension that resists full agential control.

Fiction can illustrate and offer insights not only into the behavior, motivation, and internal states of individuals, but also into broader social phenomena. Jane Austen provides us with an immediate vantage point on the interaction of what David Hume might have called people's narrow (social) circles. *Emma* in particular offers us Highbury as a case study of social interaction in a more or less closed social world. Heidi and Mark Silcox (in Chapter 5) explore the two faces of gossip in *Emma*, with an eye to the diversity of philosophical opinion regarding gossip's ethical and social import, ranging from Hume's discussion of eloquence to the disparagement of idle chatter found in Heidegger. Austen, they argue, exhibits a real sensitivity to both the moral pitfalls and liabilities of gossip and its wider social significance. The latter, given the role evolutionary psychologists have ascribed to gossip, would assign it a fundamental role in the regulation of human societies and the development of more indispensable forms of linguistic communication.

Peter Knox-Shaw (in Chapter 6) considers what Austen's work can contribute to our conceptions of imagination and of romance. Contrary to those who believe that naturalism like Austen's entails the sacrifice of both imagination and romance on the altar of the quotidian, Knox-Shaw believes that, especially in *Emma*, Austen shows imagination to be integral to an apprehension of the real world, as integral to the "current of ordinary life" as oxygen is to water. Austen understands imagination as both a pervasive and a productive faculty, something underlying all perception, much in line with the account of imagination proposed by David Hume and those who followed him. In *Emma*, Austen considers the workings of the imagination, its susceptibility to stereotypes and self-deceptions, and the necessity of benevolence for its proper function, emphasizing once again the virtue of sociability and social cohesion, and undertaking a critique of romance that salvages the virtue of benevolence.

As the preceding observations indicate, *Emma* offers diverse opportunities for philosophical reflection. Indeed, such opportunities appear to present themselves even when considerations of style, rather than content, are the focus of attention. John Mullan has recently written in *The Guardian* of *Emma*'s radically experimental presentation of events "through the distorting lens of the protagonist's mind" and lauds her as a harbinger of what is now referred to as *style indirect libre*, foregrounding Austen's then-unique blending of third- and first-person points of vantage.[4] *Emma*'s susceptibility to error, to the extent that a reader enters into her interpretation of events, may expose the same susceptibility in that reader. Yet a reader's apprehension of *Emma*'s errors may equally reveal a sense of superiority not unlike that of Austen's heroine. The prospect of such perspective-shifting presents unique opportunities for insight and reflection. Among *Emma*'s manifold stylistic innovations are also the hilariously Joycean stream-of-consciousness monologues of such characters as

---

4. John Mullan, "How Jane Austen's Emma Changed the Face of Fiction," *The Guardian*, December 5, 2015, https://www.theguardian.com/books/2015/dec/05/jane-austen-emma-changed-face-fiction (accessed July 28, 2017).

the despicable Mrs. Elton and the ridiculous Miss Bates, capturing in an instant a portrait of character, state of mind, and motivations. Here, then, is fodder for philosophers who regard works of literature as thought experiments or engines of cognitive development, and for investigations of the way in which narratives can mimic states of consciousness.

The effects of the free indirect style praised by Mullan are addressed by David Davies's exploration (in Chapter 7) of Emma's susceptibility to error and her misreading of the motives and actions of others. In particular, Davies takes to task those who maintain that the free indirect style that Austen has adopted encourages the first-time reader to misconstrue events in concert with Emma. That is, such readers are held to be presented with events as they appear to Emma's consciousness and thereby are encouraged by the text to misread them along with her. Davies contests such claims, pointing out that we are not (or at least needn't be) cozened into Emma's misreading simply by being carefully presented with the particular evidence that is available to Emma (via the free indirect style). It is perfectly possible to register Emma's misreadings as the narrative unfolds. Indeed, Davies argues that the reader's experience in detecting Emma's misreadings, also made possible by the lens on Emma's consciousness that the free indirect style provides, can help to foster valuable hermeneutic dispositions that allow us to infer quite different things from the same evidence, and that encourage the development of an attention to detail crucial to our understanding and interpretation of actual events as well as fictional ones.

In Chapter 8, Peter Kivy addresses criticisms of Austen's work that also will be taken up at some length in the rest of this introduction. He proposes an informal paradox or dilemma that appears to be posed by such criticisms. On the one hand, *Emma* and Austen's other novels are regarded both as classics and as members in good standing of the Western canon. Works known as masterpieces, classics, and members in good standing of the canon are expected, at minimum, to tell a whopping good story. But a variety of complaints about *Emma*'s falling short in respect of story have been and are still being ventured. These range from claims about the novel's deficiencies in story and substance to accusations of triviality and superficiality. Are these criticisms legitimate, imperiling Austen's standing? Kivy challenges the contention that some deficiency in story can be laid at Austen's door, maintaining that these apprehensions are due, rather, to deficiencies in the imaginative capacities of the reader who makes such judgments concerning *Emma*.

Despite all the foregoing talk of achieving philosophical insight and clarification by literary means, there are still hurdles to be overcome when one considers we are talking about Jane Austen. Even given the obvious sentiments of the contributors to this book, we should concede that Austen is quite often regarded as invincibly conventional and risk-aversive. She was, in fact, buttressed in respectability by clerical and religious relations who burned her more revealing letters and represented her, repeatedly and in print, as a humble and placid old maid, content with her domestic duties, having taken up writing as a kind of feminine alternative to darning socks. The whitewash job did not begin to fade until the latter half of the twentieth century. This particular image of Jane Austen is just such a one as would appear entirely incompatible with philosophical profundity and cognitively challenging engagement. Indeed, Jane Austen herself, in a letter to James Stanier Clarke (Librarian to the Prince Regent) concerning *Emma* as well as Clarke's suggestions about a new subject for her next novel, professed to know nothing of philosophy:

> I am quite honoured by your thinking me capable of drawing such a clergyman as you gave the sketch of. . . . But I assure you I am *not*. The comic part of the character I might be equal to, but

not the good, the enthusiastic, the literary. Such a man's conversation must be on subjects of science and philosophy, of which I know nothing; or must occasionally be abundant in allusions and quotations which a woman who, like me, knows only her mother tongue, and has read very little in that, would be totally without the power of giving. A classical education, or at any rate a very extensive acquaintance with English literature, ancient and modern, appears to me quite indispensable for the person who would do justice to your clergyman; and I think I may boast myself to be, with all possible vanity, the most unlearned and ill-informed female who ever dared to be an authoress.[5]

Questions of false modesty aside, this disavowal of Austen's is reminiscent of the tone of those who take her works to be drawn on a canvas too small to afford sweeping insights. Austen does not consider herself expert enough to mimic philosophical or scientific conversation and thus pronounces herself unworthy of undertaking the task Clarke proposes. Of course, one might suspect that the self-deprecation provides a convenient way of avoiding officious and irritating interference with one's work while at the same time flattering a proponent who has connections in high places. However, though it seems reasonable to speculate that Austen was exposed to Adam Smith, for instance, and perhaps to David Hume,[6] she is clearly adamant about leaving explicitly philosophical discourse out of the purview of her characters. Then again, one needn't depict explicitly

5. *Jane Austen's Letters*, ed. D. Le Faye, 3rd ed. (Oxford: Oxford University Press, 1995), Letter 132 (D), December 11, 1815. We may note, given Austen's perhaps deliberate phrasing, that there may be *male* authors even less learned and less informed.
6. Peter Knox-Shaw and his reviewer Michael Caines speculate that Austen may have read or been exposed to Adam Smith's *Theory of Moral Sentiments*. Peter Knox-Shaw, "Austen's Reading," in Letters to the Editor, *Times Literary Supplement*, March 18, 2005, 15. Austen refers to Hume's histories in *Northanger Abbey*.

philosophical discourse in order to exhibit skepticism, to ally one-self in a practical way with eighteenth-century empiricism, to provide telling counterexamples to generalizations, or to canvas reasons that might ground moral approbation or disapproval. One cannot base one's every philosophical insight and assumption exclusively on philosophical pronouncements, in any event.

A related objection to Austen's being held up as a source of insight (or even as a contributor in good standing to the Western canon) involves not her lack of expertise as a constructor of arguments, but the narrowness of the vista with which her readers are presented. Such objections typically take one of two forms. The first directly targets Austen's subject matter and perceived insularity. One of my students, midway through *Emma*, wailed, "Nothing *happens!*" Austen certainly is not a source of adventure stories or thrillers. As any reader of *Northanger Abbey* would be aware, Austen is a consciously naturalistic writer who mocks the indulgences of melodrama. Her focus is for the most part on everyday experiences and problems. The principal matters of interest are according to some lights limited to, as Peter Kivy puts it, "who marries whom" (Chapter 8 of this volume). And several students of my acquaintance, at least, don't care. They see such concerns as trivial. One said that he couldn't relate to a situation in which someone's principal aim was to marry. Another took Austen to be endorsing that aim above all others. They were bored, they said. Some of these criticisms are, of course, based on misunderstandings. But the underlying affiliation of insularity with Austen's choice of a small arena on which to concentrate should be challenged, as should the claim that only trivial concerns are depicted (the argument being that small arenas and trivial concerns are antithetical to the eliciting of insights). Peter Kivy grapples with this accusation of triviality in Chapter 8, "The Dilemma of *Emma*." Kivy's approach suggests that he would put down the ascription of triviality to a failure of readerly imagination.

Imaginative resistance on the part of a reader can sometimes signal an authorial error, as when the author endorses some moral stance that most of her readers find unacceptable, or invites them to imagine something that can't be conceived. Here, the author might simply be held to fail: she did not elicit the response that she aspired to evoke, or failed to arouse the degree of imaginative engagement that she had intended to elicit. But imaginative resistance may also be due to an imaginative failure of the reader. Perhaps the reader is guilty of a form of imaginative parochialism. Perhaps he cannot or is unwilling to imagine how events he regards as trivial could be of great moment to someone differently placed. Perhaps the reader cannot or is unwilling to imagine how it would be to be a woman confronted with a particular, narrow range of options. Cases such as these involve an unwillingness or incapacity to adopt alternative perspectives.

Consider, for instance, the prospect that being a governess holds for Jane Fairfax in the world of Austen's *Emma*. It is not a prospect of gainful employment. It is, literally, a prospect of poorly recompensed servitude unalleviated by any possibility of improved conditions or remuneration. Her time will never be her own, her liberty will be entirely circumscribed, her resources too limited for independence. So from Jane's perspective and from that afforded by the novel, her decision to seek a position as a governess is momentous and harrowing. It (at least after certain revelations are made) shows her despair over her secret engagement with Frank Churchill, and it tells us how intolerable she finds her situation. That situation is anything but trivial for one who has entered imaginatively into the perspective of the novel. Here, the finding of triviality can be put at the door of the reader rather than that of the author. It is the reader who refuses to adopt (or perhaps is incapable of adopting) a perspective from which the problems depicted in the novel count as problems.

There is a further (though related) difficulty some critics have in looking to Austen's novels for deeper insights or in regarding them as contenders for canonization. This difficulty involves what Austen *doesn't* choose to write about, rather than what she does decide to take up. Thus, some charges of conventionality and parochialism stem from what Austen has left out. Most recently, Patricia Matthew has written for *The Atlantic* about her ambivalence concerning such lacunae, and what she may see as Austen's literary disinclination to rock the boat:

> I've long been skeptical about the politics that shape which texts are deemed canonical—works like *Emma*—and which are pushed to the margins. I remember in college reading the critic F. R. Leavis's announcement in *The Great Tradition* that "the great English novelists are Jane Austen, George Eliot, Henry James, and Joseph Conrad" and wanting to know what, exactly, made them so great. Even back then, when I had more youthful angst than critical acumen, my gut told me the 19th-century authors that scholars canonize are those like Austen, whose fiction played with, but ultimately conformed to, the social conventions of their time. Still I was surprised by what I found, what I continue to find, in literature from that period, particularly when it comes to the inclusion of people of color. I was late in my doctoral studies before I even stumbled upon my first black character in 19th-century British literature. And lest anyone think I'm casting 21st-century concerns back onto Jane and her peers, consider reading the anonymously written novel *The Woman of Colour: A Tale*, published in 1808. Unlike Austen, many of her contemporaries wrote stories about interracial marriage and biracial women (that were not tucked away in Charlotte Brontë's attic). They also used their fiction and poems to contribute to the debates about abolition, in

concert with women who circulated petitions, raised funds for the cause, and boycotted sugar from the West Indies.[7]

Most of Jane Austen's novels were written during the Napoleonic wars, *Emma* seeing publication just as the conflict reached its end in 1815. Slavery and abolitionism were topics of heated debate in Britain at that time. While the slave trade was outlawed in 1808, it wasn't until 1833 that slavery itself was abolished. Women's suffrage had yet to arise as a live possibility, wives had few rights of protection against their husbands, primogeniture was the order of the day, and women had almost no economic prospects. Indeed, economic inequalities in general were grotesque. Why is so little of this in evidence in Austen's novels? My mother, a political scientist and staunch socialist, put just such a question to me upon discovering that I was philosophizing about Jane Austen. How could Austen *not* have used her skill to call attention to injustices so egregious and unmistakable? War, want, disenfranchisement are the real issues, the important facets of the human condition that writers should deploy their skills to chronicle, thereby raising consciousness and creating awareness.

First, such expectations are unfair in a number of respects. It is rather like demanding that a still life painter immediately begin a series of works depicting urban poverty, or like criticizing a theoretical mathematician for not leaping to analyze voting patterns in gerrymandered districts. The problem at the heart of the objection seems to be that the wrong specialization has been (perversely) adopted, that one has chosen to develop one skill set rather than

---

7. Patricia A. Matthew, "On Teaching, but Not Loving, Jane Austen," *The Atlantic*, July 23, 2017,https://www.theatlantic.com/entertainment/archive/2017/07/on-teaching-but-not-loving-jane-austen/534012/?utm_source=atlfb (accessed July 25, 2017).

another. But that in itself should not be problematic. As Austen herself admitted, her talents did not lie in the direction of sweeping philosophical and political analysis. One can't hope to sway and inspire the public by employing a means of expression at which one isn't in the least proficient or by approaching a subject concerning which one's expertise is minimal. Moreover, while Austen was neither overtly political nor overtly concerned with the kinds of issues canvassed by critics such as these, she isn't given enough credit for some of the subtle but unmistakable jabs she did take at the patriarchy, primogeniture, and the lot of women in general. *Pride and Prejudice, Sense and Sensibility*, and *Persuasion* all take aim at Britain's inheritance laws, and especially the burden they impose on women. As has already been indicated, *Emma's* Jane Fairfax sees employment opportunities for women in grim terms. In the following, she responds to pressure from the interfering Mrs. Elton, who wants to secure her a position as a governess:

> "Excuse me, ma'am, but this is by no means my intention; I make no inquiry myself, and should be sorry to have any made by my friends. When I am quite determined as to the time, I am not at all afraid of being long unemployed. There are places in town, offices, where inquiry would soon produce something— Offices for the sale—not quite of human flesh—but of human intellect."
>
> "Oh! my dear, human flesh! You quite shock me; if you mean a fling at the slave-trade, I assure you Mr. Suckling was always rather a friend to the abolition."
>
> "I did not mean, I was not thinking of the slave-trade," replied Jane; "governess-trade, I assure you, was all that I had in view; widely different certainly as to the guilt of those who carry it on; but as to the greater misery of the victims, I do not know where it lies." (235)

Here there is no depiction of the horrors of slavery, but there is a clear endorsement of abolition. Even the contemptible Mrs. Elton is moved by the example of her beloved Mr. Suckling (on whom she lavishes her sycophantic attentions) to support abolition, and the estimable and intelligent Jane Fairfax considers slavery blame-worthy and wrong. She is hyperbolic in her comparisons, but the concept of wage slavery is genuine enough to take seriously, and again demonstrates Austen's willingness to emphasize the economic difficulties (and the lack of alternatives) that afflicted women in her world.

Emma is a revolutionary work in other respects as well. We are, after all, given a heroine who is emphatically not as good as she is beautiful: a protagonist with flaws, whose mistakes largely dictate the trajectory of the plot. Austen's female characters are notable for speaking truth to power and for demonstrating the courage of their convictions. But only Emma can continue to engage us despite errors and overconfidence. That is, *Emma* is also unusual in that it presents a female character with flaws more commonly considered mascu-line: boldness, overconfidence, taking charge of others' lives. Hubris. And Austen's acerbic reflections on the economic and social limita-tions to which women were subjected in the early nineteenth century are given more voice in *Emma* than in any of her other novels. It is in *Emma* that one of the few professions open to women is compared to the slave trade, in *Emma* that the heroine must explain that she will be safe from general contempt if she declines to marry: "it is pov-erty only which makes celibacy contemptible to a generous public! A single woman, with a very narrow income, must be a ridiculous, disagreeable old maid . . . but a single woman, of good fortune, is al-ways respectable, and may be as sensible and pleasant as any body else" (68–69). Comedy can convey as many insights as tragedy by means of a like reliance on reversals of expectation. Austen's ironic wit is a case in point throughout this and other novels.

20

This last point about comedy provides a final reply to the contention that Jane Austen fails to address big issues and thereby falls short of eliciting important insights or fostering useful dispositions and habits of attention. The very fact that Austen is a comic writer might be enough in some quarters to be thought to deprive her work of any prospect of profundity. All of Austen's novels are, after all, comic novels to one degree or another. If this were indeed a philosophical liability, the case would be closed. But there is nothing to say that comedy cannot be as great a source of insight or philosophical fodder for reflection as a tragedy would be, or, indeed, as would be any other work indulging more directly in the depiction of sweeping issues of rights or justice or the plight of humanity at large. I have argued elsewhere that comedy and tragedy employ remarkably similar tactics both in presenting their subject matter and in arousing characteristic emotional reactions to that subject matter.[8] Both, that is, rely on eliciting reactions to incongruity or reversal of expectations. Tragedy arouses, so Aristotle would tell us, a catharsis of pity and fear, while comedy arouses amusement. Each reaction involves or arises from a kind of clarification. That is, each depends on recognition or discovery—the type of realization allowing one to understand a tragic misapprehension or, alternatively, to "get" a joke. Aristotle's description of recognition and discovery—the revelation of the causal process that made the outcome inevitable—is not unlike the revelation of meaning in irony or satire, in which what is said is often the opposite of what is meant. Here there is a realization of the intended rather than the literal meaning.

---

8. E. M. Dadlez and Daniel Lüthi, "Comedy and Tragedy as Two Sides of the Same Coin: Reversal and Incongruity as Sources of Insight," *Journal of Aesthetic Education* 52, no. 2 (2018): 81–94.

Consider Austen's sly and splendid undermining of Emma's reliability as a judge of character, in the description of Emma's introduction to Harriet Smith:

> She was not struck by any thing remarkably clever in Miss Smith's conversation, but she found her altogether very engaging—not inconveniently shy, not unwilling to talk—and yet so far from pushing, shewing so proper and becoming a deference, seeming so pleasantly grateful for being admitted to Hartfield, and so artlessly impressed by the appearance of every thing in so superior a style to what she had been used to, that she must have good sense, and deserve encouragement. (E 19)

The key incongruity is the leap from the fact of Harriet's awe and admiration to the abrupt conclusion that Harriet is sensible and deserving. Here, a person's sense and desert are established, not on account of their own characteristics, but by their overenthusiastic approbation of those possessed by the individual conducting the character assessment. A cruder and more blatantly farcical version of such a self-interested method of character evaluation appears in *Lady Susan*, in a letter discussing the preferability of one lover over another:

> I infinitely prefer the tender and liberal spirit of Mainwaring, which, impressed with the deepest conviction of my merit, is satisfied that whatever I do must be right; and looks with a degree of contempt on the inquisitive and doubtful fancies of that heart which seems always debating on the reasonableness of its emotions. Mainwaring is indeed, beyond all compare, superior to Reginald. (MW 268–269)

There is a kind of insight at the heart of the incongruity in question, especially the subtler and more familiar inversion that we see in

Emma. And there is a form of recognition as well. Most of us are inclined to take any positive evaluation of ourselves as evidence of incisiveness and perspicacity, and we are sometimes inclined to value others, insofar as they provide flattering mirrors. (David Hume would more generously say that sympathy leads us to share the emotions of others toward ourselves and thereby to share their admiration or at least their pleasure.) This says something about the unreliability and the instability of our own ability to assess character, about our susceptibility to self-absorption, about how our estimates of traits can go wrong. It is neither narrow nor trivial. Austen is aware of this and shows it concretely, in ways we can immediately recognize and feel, and in ways that are unmatched by other writers and often ignored in abstract philosophy.

Austen's small stage proves a positive advantage for certain kinds of philosophical explorations, rather than a liability. It is the very narrowness of Austen's scope, her relentless focus on the everyday experiences of ordinary quite familiar people, that provides a spotlight on all the minutia of motive and decision and self-deception which so often supply material for philosophical speculation. It is the smaller arena that permits one to observe and track the consequences of particular choices, and it is the smaller population that enables one to observe relationships: their tensions and reciprocities and value. A description of a picnic can afford as many insights into human nature or the human condition as depictions of political upheaval; it will just do so with less fanfare and fewer corpses.

REFERENCES

Austen, Jane. *Emma*, edited by James Kinsley. Oxford: Oxford University Press, 2008.
Austen, Jane. *Jane Austen's Letters*, edited by D. Le Faye, 3rd ed. Oxford: Oxford University Press, 1995.

Austen, Jane. *The Novels of Jane Austen*, 5 volumes, edited by R. W. Chapman, 3rd ed. Oxford: Oxford University Press, 1988.

Austen, Jane. *The Works of Jane Austen*, edited by R. W. Chapman, Vol. 6: *Minor Works*. Oxford: Oxford University Press, 1988.

Dadlez, E. M., and Daniel Lüthi. "Comedy and Tragedy as Two Sides of the Same Coin: Reversal and Incongruity as Sources of Insight." *Journal of Aesthetic Education* 52, no. 2 (2018): 81–94.

Dennett, Daniel C. "Intuition Pumps" (Chapter 10). *Edge*, 5.7.96. http://www.edge.org/documents/ThirdCulture/r-Ch.10.html (accessed June 7, 2016).

Knox-Shaw, Peter. "Austen's Reading." In Letters to the Editor, *Times Literary Supplement*, March 18, 2005, 15.

Matthew, Patricia A. "On Teaching, but Not Loving, Jane Austen." *The Atlantic*, July 23, 2017. https://www.theatlantic.com/entertainment/archive/2017/07/on-teaching-but-not-loving-jane-austen/534012/?utm_source=atlfb (accessed July 25, 2017).

Mullan, John. "How Jane Austen's Emma Changed the Face of Fiction." *The Guardian*, December 5, 2015. https://www.theguardian.com/books/2015/dec/05/jane-austen-emma-changed-face-fiction (accessed July 28, 2017).

Worth, Sarah E. *In Defense of Reading*. Lanham, MD: Rowman & Littlefield, 2017.

Chapter 1

Love and Friendship

Achieving Happiness in Jane Austen's Emma

NEERA K. BADHWAR AND E. M. DADLEZ

Jane Austen's *Emma* offers a nuanced picture of the eponymous heroine's friendships that supports many of Aristotle's ideas of friendship and virtue in the *Nicomachean Ethics*. Several philosophers have noted that Jane Austen's conception of virtue is, in at least two important respects, Aristotelian: it requires a harmony of intellect, emotion, and action; and it involves a healthy, this-worldly concern for one's own happiness, or *eudaimonia*.[1] We argue that Austen's conception of true friendship in *Emma* is also Aristotelian. For Aristotle, the best kind of friendship is that of virtuous people who share their lives through conversation and common pursuits. Such sharing is possible only because they are roughly equal in virtue and intellect, and have common interests. Their equality and openness

---

1. Gilbert Ryle, "Jane Austen and the Moralists," in *Critical Essays on Jane Austen*, ed. B. C. Southam (London: Routledge & Kegan Paul, 1968), 286–301; David Gallop, "Jane Austen and the Aristotelian Ethic," *Philosophy and Literature* 23, no. 1 (April 1999): 96–106; and Anne Crippen Ruderman, *The Pleasures of Virtue: Political Thought in the Novels of Jane Austen* (Lanham, MD: Rowman & Littlefield, 1995).

with one another also enable each to help the other improve in intellect and virtue (a state that comprehends practical wisdom, and thus sound deliberation and judgment). Aristotle regards such virtue friendships as vital ingredients of the happy or flourishing life. We argue that Austen's *Emma* illustrates this conception of friendship and happiness through its depiction of Emma's friendship with Mr. Knightley and, to a somewhat lesser extent, her friendship with her governess and close friend, Mrs. Weston (née Taylor). It also illustrates the problems inherent in a friendship between people who are not intellectual or moral equals, such as the friendship between Emma and the adoring and awestruck Harriet Smith.

After introducing the reader to the characters and the major elements of the story in section I, we proceed in section II to defend our claim that Emma's friendships with Mr. Knightley and Mrs. Weston are virtue friendships of equals. We do so against critics who argue that Emma has too many faults to be considered virtuous, or to be regarded as Mr. Knightley's equal.

In section III we address two recent challenges to the Aristotelian conception of a good friendship by some philosophers. One challenge holds that, by its very nature, a good friendship is often in conflict with the demands of virtue. As the joke goes, a friend will help you move, but a good friend will help you move a body. The other challenge holds that good friends are epistemically biased, both in the way they form their beliefs about each other and in the way they interpret each other's actions, and that such bias violates epistemic virtue. In response, we argue that while these views of a good friendship might be true of friendships between bad—or what we'll call "morally casual"—people, they are not true of friendship as such. Were we to imagine Emma or Mr. Knightley or Mrs. Weston behaving as these critics imagine good friends behave, we would think much less of them and their friendships. The friendships depicted in the novel thus stand as strong counterexamples to the view that a good friendship is by its very nature often in conflict with moral and epistemic virtue. Further, if virtue is crucial to human happiness, as Aristotle and Austen both believe, then a virtue friendship is a far greater good in human life than a friendship that rides roughshod over other people's rights or well-being, or that trades in positive illusions about each other.

In *Emma*, as in all her other major novels, Austen concludes with the prospect of a marriage based on the love and friendship of equals. Austen never succumbed to the popular prejudice of the age that women were inherently irrational or, for that matter, less rational then men. Unfortunately, the same cannot be said of Aristotle, who not only succumbed to this prejudice, but even concocted a theory of reproduction to support it. This resulted in his having to give some convoluted and implausible arguments to show that, nevertheless, there could be a kind of equality even in marital friendship. In section IV we show that Emma's relationship with Knightley challenges Aristotle's conception of a good marriage, and recalls both David Hume's and John Stuart Mill's conception of marital friendship as an intimate friendship between intellectual and moral equals.

We start by introducing the reader to Emma and the other major characters in the novel.

I. *EMMA*: AN OVERVIEW

Emma Woodhouse, we are told, is "handsome, clever, and rich, with a comfortable home and happy disposition" (1). Her main fault is that she thinks "a little too well of herself," a trait born of years of being the object of her father's uncritical love and admiration. Miss Taylor's affection for Emma also tends to be somewhat uncritical, but even when Miss Taylor ventures constructive criticism, Emma tends still to abide by her own judgment: "they had been living together as friend and friend, very mutually attached, and Emma doing just as she liked; highly esteeming Miss Taylor's judgment, but chiefly directed by her own" (5). So Miss Taylor's influence is not enough to save Emma from conceit and overconfidence, and when Miss Taylor leaves the household to marry Mr. Weston, Emma is left without a close friend who can attempt guidance and offer constant companionship. Indeed, the story begins with Emma's loss of her governess to marriage and the real threat of intellectual isolation: "Emma was aware that great must be the difference between a Mrs. Weston only half a mile from them, and a Miss Taylor in the house; and with all her advantages, natural and domestic, she was now in great danger of suffering from intellectual solitude. She dearly loved her father, but he was no companion for her. He could not meet her in conversation, rational or playful" (6). Emma, remarkably, never loses patience with her father, even though he is an endlessly fussy hypochondriac, and so self-centered and unimaginative that he is incapable of adopting anyone else's point of view. Clearly, Emma cannot flourish without other company. But the village of Highbury is small and offers limited prospects for constant companionship and shared activity. And in a society that provides women with few outlets for exercising their talents and intelligence, relationships with others assume an immense importance.

The very opening of the novel thus presents us with the problem of solitude created by the absence of a close, constant companion— at least, it must be added, from Emma's point of view. For she still sees Mrs. Weston and Mr. Knightley practically every day. It's just that this is not enough for her, given her general disinterest in other pursuits. Into this void walks the beautiful, good-natured, and ignorant Harriet Smith, a seventeen-year-old girl attending Mrs. Goddard's school:

> [Emma] was not struck by anything remarkably clever in
> Miss Smith's conversation, but she found her altogether very

engaging—not inconveniently shy, not unwilling to talk—and yet so far from pushing, shewing so proper and becoming a deference, seeming so pleasantly gratefully for being admitted to Hartfield, and so artlessly impressed by the appearance of every thing in so superior a style to what she had been used to, that she must have good sense and deserve encouragement. (19)

Emma replaces the companionship of an intellectual equal (admittedly sometimes blind to her foibles) with the companionship of a kind of disciple—someone who will revere her, bolster her conceit and self-confidence, and always support any opinion or hypothesis of hers by leaping to instant agreement.

Emma undertakes to improve Harriet and find a husband for her, settling on the handsome vicar of Highbury, Mr. Elton. To this end, she manipulates Harriet into turning down Mr. Martin when he proposes, on the grounds that Mr. Martin is not enough of a gentleman for Harriet. Emma looks down on Mr. Martin for belonging to a lower class than Harriet (although Harriet's parentage is unknown, Emma's partiality leads her to decide that Harriet's father must have been a gentleman). Moreover, in Emma's eyes, Mr. Martin is neither good-looking nor well-read nor elegant enough for Harriet. Harriet must marry Mr. Elton, who possesses such sterling qualities in abundance. Emma welcomes Mr. Elton's visits, contriving to leave him and Harriet alone as often as possible. Unfortunately, it turns out that Mr. Elton is interested in Emma rather than Harriet, to Emma's dismay and Harriet's grief and chagrin.

Harriet's naïveté and lack of self-confidence, in combination with Emma's overconfidence in her matchmaking abilities and her Pygmalion project of molding Harriet into a woman who can hold her own in society, serve Harriet ill. They also serve Emma ill by reinforcing her belief that her observations of human beings are always accurate and her judgment always correct. It is only when she is

NEERA K. BADHWAR AND E. M. DADLEZ

proven wrong by Mr. Elton's declaration that she begins to question her matchmaking acumen. Everything turns out well for Harriet, however, as she soon falls out of love with Mr. Elton (as she must, after he marries someone else), in love with Mr. Knightley (a completely unsuitable match), and finally out of love with Mr. Knightley (fortunately for everyone concerned) and back in love with Mr. Martin when he proposes for a second time. Harriet has a happy knack for falling in love with anyone whom she admires or who has the good taste to be in love with her.

Fortunately for Emma, she does have a friend who is clear-sighted enough to see her motives and actions for what they are, both good and not so good, and who is close enough to her to tell her so: namely, Mr. Knightley. The two often spar good-naturedly, and it is obvious that Mr. Knightley cherishes and enjoys Emma's quick wit and ability to stand up for herself.

Emma is convinced that she'll never marry. She does not expect to be lonely, however, because she has good friends, and a sister and nephews and nieces whom she loves. In addition, she tells Harriet, she has sufficient financial resources to live comfortably and respectably. Nevertheless, she cannot help entertaining romantic notions about Frank Churchill, Mr. Weston's charming son, even before she has ever set eyes on him. Frank was adopted and raised by his childless uncle and aunt, and had never been to Highbury until his father's marriage to Mrs. Weston. However, although Frank often flirts with Emma, and Emma likes and gets along with him, she finds that she is not romantically interested in him. This is just as well, as it turns out that he's secretly engaged to Jane Fairfax. It takes Emma the length of the novel to realize that she was wrong in her opinion of Mr. Martin—and that she is in love with Mr. Knightley!

The story depicts Emma's friendships, their effects on her character and convictions, and her mistakes and misapprehensions.

Emma's errors delimit the direction of the plot, the errors being to a considerable extent byproducts of the friendships on which she relies the most.

II. EMMA'S VIRTUE FRIENDSHIPS

As is well known, Aristotle's notion of friendship is much wider than that of many contemporary philosophers, encompassing as it does not only nonfamilial relationships, but also relationships with parents, children, lovers, siblings, and colleagues. What makes them all friendships is mutual *philēsis*, that is, the affection or love or liking that is expressed in wishing and benefiting each other for each other's own sake, and not only one's own.[2] Nonfamilial friendships are grounded in utility or pleasure or virtue (Bk. VIII, Ch. 1–3). In all three types, friends like to spend time together in conversation and joint activities. What distinguishes them from each other is their ground. In utility friendships, the ground is some type of advantage, such as gaining a higher rank with the friend's help. In pleasure friendships, it is pleasure, such as the pleasure of having sex, or of playing chess together. In virtue friendships, the ground is virtue, or good character. The first two types Aristotle regards as "incomplete," because the character of the friends is incidental to the friendships. What matters in these friendships are the contingent features that make each useful or pleasurable to the other, so when these features change, the friendship ends. It is only in virtue friendships that friends love one another for what is central to their identity—namely, their character—and it is only such friendships that endure, because virtue

2. *Nicomachean Ethics* (hereafter *NE*), 1155b31–32, trans. Terence Irwin, 2nd ed. (Indianapolis: Hackett 1999). All further references to Aristotle are to this edition of the *NE*, unless otherwise noted.

is enduring. But virtue friendships are also useful and pleasurable to the friends, because such friends enjoy being together, are ready to help each other when help is needed, and inspire one another to become better.[3] They become better because they neither request nor "permit" "base actions" (1159b5ff.). Hence, should one friend become bad and beyond the other friend's efforts at redemption, the friendship must come to an end.

It is important to note that in saying that virtue is central to a person's identity and that virtue friends love each other for their virtue, Aristotle does not mean that they love each other *only* for their virtue.[4] If that were the case, then, barring time constraints (1171a1–10), a virtuous person would be able to love and befriend all virtuous people who crossed her path. But it is essential to friendship that friends find time spent together pleasurable, and their virtue doesn't guarantee that they'll enjoy each other's company. As Aristotle says, "no one could continuously endure even the Good Itself if it were painful to him" (1158a24–25).[5] And this typically requires having at least some interests in common (1166a6–7), or each being able to make some of the other's interests her own. This is why Aristotle argues that friends must be roughly equal in age (1161b34–35), wealth, or status (1158b34–1159a4), not only in virtue.

3. *NE* 1156b7–24. Similarly, at 1238a3–4 in the *Eudemian Ethics*, Aristotle states that a friend must be "not merely good absolutely but good for you, if the friend is to be a friend to you" (trans. J. Solomon, in *The Complete Works of Aristotle*, The Revised Oxford Translation, Vol. 2, ed. Jonathan Barnes, Princeton, NJ: Princeton University Press, 1984).

4. See Neera K. Badhwar and Russell E. Jones, "Aristotle on the Love of Friends," in *The Oxford Handbook of Philosophy of Love*, ed. Christopher Grau and Aaron Smuts (Oxford: Oxford University Press, 2018), 1–26. Online Publication Date: Oct. 2017. doi: 10.1093/oxfordhb/9780199395729.013.22.

5. This could be an allusion to Plato's *Philebus* 21d–e, where it is argued that wisdom without any pleasure is something that no human being would want; see Broadie in Sarah Broadie and Christopher Rowe, *Aristotle: Nicomachean Ethics, Translation, Introduction, and Commentary* (Oxford: Oxford University Press, 2002), 412.

To this we would add that they must also have similar, or complementary, personality traits. It is part of common experience that personality traits—a person's sense of humor, her manner of conversing, her way of reasoning, and even the style of her moral character—play an important role in sparking and preserving friendship. Two good individuals who share many interests might, nevertheless, fail to "hit it off" because of their personalities. Perhaps one is too chatty or not chatty enough, the other too analytic or not analytic enough, and so on. Although Aristotle doesn't talk about the importance of personality traits in friendship, his theory is perfectly compatible with acknowledging their importance.[6]

Emma's friendships with Mrs. Weston and Mr. Knightley fit Aristotle's description of virtue friendship, and illustrate also the importance of shared interests and personality traits to the pleasures of friendship. Emma is roughly equal to both friends morally and intellectually, none of them ever requests any wrongdoing from either friend, and none of them flatters either friend into thinking that he or she never does wrong. Indeed, all make both their approval or disapproval known whenever appropriate (although, as we've noted, Mrs. Weston doesn't always see Emma's faults). Mr. Knightley, in particular, holds Emma to a high standard, and lets her know his disapproval of her lack of commitment to her reading and music. He also disapproves of her making fun of poor Miss Bates at a picnic, saying gently but firmly, "How could you be so unfeeling to Miss Bates? How could you be so insolent in your wit to a woman of her character, age, and situation?—Emma, I had not thought it possible" (294). And he is more than disapproving when he realizes that Emma has manipulated Harriet into refusing Mr. Martin—he is absolutely scathing. For it was Harriet's good fortune, he thinks, to

6. See Badhwar and Jones, "Aristotle on the Love of Friends," *Oxford Handbook of Philosophy of Love*.

have attracted a man of Mr. Martin's good mind and solid character. Emma, he claims, is overestimating Harriet's worth and puffing her up with false notions about herself, to her own detriment.

In all these cases, Emma realizes (either then or later) that Mr. Knightly is mostly right, and acknowledges this. However, the correction is not all one-sided: Mr. Knightley also learns from Emma that he underestimated Harriet and was too negative in his judgments of Frank Churchill.

The novel contrasts these friendships with Emma's friendship with Harriet, and her relationship with her father, Mr. Woodhouse. Both Harriet and Mr. Woodhouse adore Emma, the latter with a doting and short-sighted father's love, the former with a child's gratitude, admiration, and willingness to learn. Both are clearly Emma's inferiors in intellect and judgment, and her father can join her neither in any of her activities nor in conversation. Harriet Smith, by contrast, is good-natured, pleasant, and talkative, but because she is naïve and awestruck, she is more inclined to provide perpetual agreement rather than anything resembling intellectual companionship. The effect of these relationships on Emma is to encourage her to put too much stock in her intuitions, treating them all as genuine insights. The absence of any critical feedback from Harriet or Emma's father serves to validate for Emma her various speculative excesses. Emma's relationship with Harriet does meet the basic requirement of a virtue friendship, namely, that the parties to it be good, that they love one another for who they are, that is, for their good character traits and personality, and that they (try to) benefit each other. But Harriet's lack of any deep understanding of Emma—or, indeed, of herself, or other people—makes it a highly unequal friendship.[7] She grows into a more observant and self-confident person toward the end of the

---

7. Cf Aristotle's discussion of friendship between unequally virtuous people (Bk. VIII, Ch. 7).

novel, but that is also when her marriage to Mr. Martin means that she and Emma will no longer spend very much time together.

Emma cannot be said to have a friendship with her father at all. She loves him as a daughter, and does her filial duty by him, but his self-absorption and total lack of understanding of Emma (or anyone else) means that his idea of her good has little to do with her good, and everything to do with what he judges to be his own good.

Our thesis that Emma has close virtue friendships with her equals might be—and has been—questioned on the ground that Emma has too many faults to be considered virtuous, at least by Aristotle's high standards, and that Mr. Knightley and Mrs. Weston are her moral and intellectual superiors (even though Mrs. Weston usually yields to her).

That Emma has faults, like everyone else, is, of course, undeniable. Her main fault, as the book itself announces in the very first chapter, is her tendency to think too well of herself. She also has trouble checking her flights of fancy, at least when it comes to match-making for Harriet. More seriously, she has a disturbing tendency to be a class snob. Instead of judging people by their character, as Mr. Knightley does, Emma shares the landed gentry's scorn of those who farm their own land and lack elegant manners, such as Mr. Martin, and those who've gained their wealth through trade, such as the Coles. She fails to see Mr. Martin's goodness until the end of the novel. It must be noted, however, that the person she spends most of her time with, and who is in the best position to enlighten her about Mr. Martin's virtues—namely, Harriet—fails to do so. This is one of the problems in a friendship with someone who is so inferior in discernment and self-confidence that she can offer no corrective to her friend's misjudgments. Further, the ease with which Harriet falls out of love with Mr. Martin and into love with Mr. Elton only strengthens Emma's judgment that she did the right thing in discouraging Harriet from accepting Mr. Martin's proposal.

Another serious flaw is Emma's jealousy of Jane Fairfax, whom she has been used to hearing praised all her life. This jealousy plays a role in preventing her from becoming friends with Jane, but is certainly not the only factor: Jane's lack of openness is also an important hindrance.[8] Even Mr. Knightley, who greatly admires Jane, remarks that "she has not the open temper which a man would wish for in a wife" (225). It turns out that her lack of openness is due to the weight of her secret engagement to Frank Churchill. After the secret is revealed, and Emma and Jane both apologize for their former unfriendliness toward one another (each insisting that the other has nothing to apologize for), Jane refers to Emma as one of those "friends, whose good opinion is most worth preserving," and says, "I know what my manners were to you.—So cold and artificial!—I had always a part to act.—It was a life of deceit!" (361). There is no reason for the reader to take Jane's coldness and artificiality less seriously than Jane herself does, or to reject her judgment of Emma as a worthy (potential) friend.

Emma's character flaws are not very surprising, given her social and personal influences, and her age. In fact, what is surprising is that, by the end of the novel, she is a remarkably mature twenty-one-year-old, aware of her flaws and well on her way to correcting them. In any case, a person doesn't have to be perfectly virtuous to be virtuous overall, or to have virtue friends, not even on Aristotle's account. For although Aristotle's conception of practical wisdom and the unity of the virtues entails that the virtuous person must be perfectly virtuous, he also frequently suggests that virtue comes in degrees (1117b9–11, 1120b9–11, 1123b26–30, 1168a33–35, 1172a10–14). And his claim that virtuous friends inspire and help each other

---

8. Here we disagree with Thomas Williams's claim that Emma's envy is the primary reason that she does not befriend Jane. He doesn't mention the secondary reasons he has in mind, or Jane's lack of openness, or the fact that Jane also made no overtures to Emma. See "Moral Vice, Cognitive Virtue," *Philosophy and Literature* 27, no. 1 (April 2003): 223–230.

to become better human beings shows that he believes that a virtue friendship is not limited to perfectly virtuous people (1170a11– 12, 1172a11ff.). What makes a friendship a virtue friendship for Aristotle, John Cooper points out, is that it is based on the virtuous qualities of the friends, even if both friends have flaws and recognize each other's flaws.[9] It is also essential, of course, for virtue friends to try to become better persons, since this aspiration is part of being an (imperfectly) virtuous person.

There is, however, one charge that, if true, calls into question our claim that Emma has virtue friendships: the charge that Emma is self-deceived across the board. For pervasive self-deception is incompatible with almost any virtue. This is why philosophers as far apart as Kant, Nietzsche, and Sartre have condemned it. And although Aristotle doesn't have a clear notion of self-deception, he does, like Socrates and Plato, praise self-knowledge, and regards truthfulness in the way we present ourselves to others in speech and action, a virtue (IV.7). The charge of pervasive self-deception is made by Jeanine Grenberg, who claims that

> because [Emma] is frightened to lose her happy situation at Hartfield, she constructs a belief that she never wants to marry. Marrying would, after all, require her to leave Hartfield, her father and visits from Mr. Knightley. She thus deceives herself into believing both that she is not in love with Mr. Knightley, and that she does not want to marry. Emma also . . . takes great pride in the belief, (sic) that she is an accomplished match-maker, a false

9. John Cooper, "Aristotle on Friendship," in *Essays on Aristotle's Ethics*, ed. Amelie Oksenberg Rorty (Berkeley: University of California Press, 1980), 301–340, at 305–307; Badhwar and Jones, "Aristotle on the Love of Friends." See also Talbott Brewer, "Virtues We Can Share: Friendship and Aristotelian Ethical Theory," *Ethics* 115 (2005): 721–758, at 738; and Nancy Sherman, "Aristotle on Friendship and the Shared Life," *Philosophy and Phenomenological Research* 47 (1987): 589–613.

belief rooted in her unwillingness to admit to herself that she is a rather lazy person, and isn't good at the sort of things—like painting or music-making—which actually do take time, hard work and discipline.[10]

But why should we believe that Emma *deceives* herself into believing that she doesn't want to marry and doesn't love Mr. Knightley, and that she does so because it would mean the end of her happy life at Hartfield? Grenberg provides two pieces of evidence for these claims, both weak. One is that Emma has to admit to herself that she loves Mr. Knightly when Harriet's confession of her love for him threatens to destroy Emma's "happy world at Hartfield," the protection of which "inspired Emma's self-deception in the first place."[11] But if Grenberg is right, why doesn't Emma "admit" to herself that she loves Mr. Knightley sooner, when Mrs. Weston confidently asserts that he is interested in Jane Fairfax, an alliance that (in the absence of any knowledge of Jane's engagement with Frank Churchill) equally threatens Emma's "happy world at Hartfield"? Not only does Emma not admit any such thing, she shows no jealousy at the thought. Emma is not particularly taken with the idea, granted, but her only apparent objection to such a match is that her nephew, Henry, will not inherit Mr. Knightley's estate. Moreover, we see Emma engaging in romantic fantasies about Frank Churchill, but never about Mr. Knightley.

10. Jeanine Grenberg, "Self-Deception and Self-Knowledge: Jane Austen's *Emma* as an Example of Kant's Notion of Self-Deception," *Contextos Kantianos: International Journal of Philosophy* 2 (November 2015): 162–176, at 165.

11. Grenberg actually says, "Mr. Knightley marrying someone else would destroy Harriet's happy world at Hartfield," but we take it that this is a typo. She also mistakenly states that Emma "tries to connect Harriet with two different men who in fact are attracted to Emma, not Harriet" (173).

Grenberg's second piece of evidence for her claim that Emma was always in love with Mr. Knightley, but had deceived herself into believing that she wasn't, is the following passage:

> To understand, thoroughly understand her own heart, was the first endeavor. . . . How long had Mr. Knightley been so dear to her, as every feeling declared him now to be? When had his influence, such influence begun?—When had he succeeded to that place in her affection . . . ? . . . —She saw that there never had been a time when she did not consider Mr. Knightley as infinitely the superior, or when his regard for her had not been infinitely the most dear. She saw, that in persuading herself, in fancying, in acting to the contrary, she had been entirely under a delusion, totally ignorant of her own heart. (324)

The statement that she had "been entirely under a delusion" *could* be taken to mean that she had deceived herself, but a delusion can also be just plain ignorance, as the words that follow indicate. From a child, Emma has loved and respected Knightley, so the affection has always been there—it just wasn't always romantic affection. Discovering that "his regard for her" had always been "infinitely the most dear" does not imply that he had always been the object of her romantic interest. After all, he was sixteen years older than she, an adult when she was only a child, with different interests and far greater maturity and knowledge of the world than Emma. Austen also informs us that until "she was threatened with its loss, Emma had never known how much her happiness depended on being first with Mr. Knightley, first in interest and affection" (326). There *is* no knowledge or belief that is suppressed, as would be the case with self-deception. Rather, Emma realizes that the decades-long fondness and familiarity and friendship have somehow, initially unnoticed, blossomed into something new. This is surely a common experience.

Not only is Grenberg's evidence for Emma's alleged self-deception weak, her theory is also psychologically implausible. We are to believe that Emma denies herself the happiness of living with the man she loves and delights in conversing with because she is too happy living with a father who offers her nothing by way of companionship. We are also to believe that Emma deceives herself into believing that she is not in love with Mr. Knightley (an idea the novel never shows her entertaining, so far is love or no-love of him from her mind until the last few pages) because she doesn't want to lose his visits to Hartfield. But the only reason she would lose his visits to Hartfield by marrying him is that she would be with him every day! It is impossible to be visited by a person you live with. So this explanation assumes that Emma prefers being visited by the man she loves over being with him all the time, a proposition that makes no sense in the context of the novel.

Further, Grenberg's charge that Emma believes that she is good at matchmaking because she doesn't want to admit that she is not very good at music or painting contradicts the passages in which we learn that Emma *is* good at music—only not as good as Jane Fairfax. It also contradicts the many passages in which Emma admits to herself and others that Jane Fairfax is much better. When she is asked to play, she does so knowing "the limitations of her own powers too well to attempt more than she could perform with credit. . . ." She then makes way for Jane Fairfax, "whose performance, both vocal and instrumental, she never could attempt to conceal from herself, was infinitely superior to her own" (178). In response to Harriet's praise of her as the better of the two singers and piano players, she says, "Don't class us together, Harriet. My playing is no more like her's, than a lamp is like sunshine" (182). In short, Emma is absolutely clear on this matter, both with herself and with others. There is no suppression of this and no failure to admit it.

Finally, Grenberg's claim that Emma deceives herself into believing that she is good at matchmaking ignores the fact that when Emma's matchmaking for Harriet fails disastrously, she immediately acknowledges that she isn't good at matchmaking, something she would have been reluctant to do had her estimate of her matchmaking abilities been rooted in self-deception.

We think that the truth about Emma is pretty clearly at odds with Grenberg's claims: she is, like many of Austen's other heroines (Elizabeth Bennet, Fanny Price, and Anne Elliot in particular), an extraordinarily self-questioning sort of person, continually examining the evidence for her judgments, the motives for her actions, and the basis and significance of her feelings.[12] Indeed, this is one of her main epistemic and moral virtues, and an integral part of her character. The fact that she doesn't always arrive at the truth doesn't undermine the fact that it is virtuous to be disposed to keep trying to reach the truth about important matters. When he declares his love for her, it is this that leads Mr. Knightley to say—no doubt, with something of a lover's hyperbole—that she has borne his lectures "as no other woman in England would have . . ." (338). She often chides herself for being jealous of Jane Fairfax, and when she hears that Jane is ill and soon to leave Highbury to work as a governess, she does her best to make up for her past coldness (306–307). She takes full responsibility for causing Harriet so much pain over Mr. Elton, and does everything she can to help Harriet overcome her infatuation. Her soul-searching over the harm she has done to Harriet leads her to become more critical and skeptical of her own judgments and (even) more receptive to Knightley's. If anything, she becomes too self-critical. For when Harriet confesses that she's in love with someone else, Emma takes care not to get entangled in her business, telling her

---

12. Anne Crippen Ruderman, *Pleasures of Virtue*, also notes this fact about Emma and Austen's other heroines (155).

NEERA K. BADHWAR AND E. M. DADLEZ

only to be guided by this person's behavior. Unfortunately, Harriet mistakes Mr. Knightley's attentions to her as Emma's friend (and possible wife of his friend, Mr. Martin) for love, and Emma blames herself for misguiding her, even though her advice was perfectly sound and the mistake was Harriet's.

Emma's analytical dispositions are not limited to her behavior. When she develops romantic feelings for the charming and high-spirited Frank Churchill, thanks largely to his outrageous flirtation with her, she doesn't conclude that she must be in love with him, as a less self-reflective person might have done. Instead, she looks at evidence for and against the supposition that she loves him and conducts mental experiments to find out how much. On the one hand, she notes, after he leaves town she feels listless and weary, and everything seems "dull and insipid about the house" (205). In addition, she thinks of him all the time and is impatient for news of him (206–208). So "I must be in love; I should be the oddest creature in the world if I were not—for a few weeks at least" (205). On the other hand, she notes, after the first morning she is as happy and busy as ever, and although she forms "a thousand amusing schemes for the progress and close of their attachment, fancying interesting dialogues, and inventing elegant letters; the conclusion of every imaginary declaration on his side was that she refused him" (206). So "I am quite enough in love. I should be sorry to be more" (207).

The counterpart of Emma's honesty with herself is her honesty with others, and a dislike of everything phony. She is quick at recognizing who is inauthentic and affected and who is genuine and genuinely warm and loving. This is why she dislikes Mr. and Mrs. Elton, and gravitates toward Harriet. After a visit with Mrs. Elton, she declares to herself that "[w]armth and tenderness of heart, with an affectionate, open manner . . . will beat all the clearness of head in the world, for attraction. . . . I have it not—but I know how to prize and respect it.—Harriet is my superior in all the charm and all the felicity it gives" (210).

Here we also see an admirable willingness to admit that a virtue that she herself doesn't possess might be a more attractive and happiness-producing virtue than a virtue that she does possess, namely, "clearness of head." It's a separate question whether she is right in her ranking of these virtues. It's also a separate question whether the two virtues are psychologically hard to combine or, worse yet, incompatible.[13] The point is that, just as she can acknowledge Jane Fairfax's superiority in musical achievement, she can acknowledge, and even take joy in, Harriet's possession of a virtue that she herself lacks.

Another striking virtue is Emma's understanding of, and patience and compassion toward, her father. Indeed, her never-failing gentleness with him, in spite of his irritating behavior and dull conversation, goes far beyond her years. She even decides to postpone her marriage to Mr. Knightley until after her father's death, because she cannot abandon him and he would never agree to moving with her to Mr. Knightley's house (341). Her compassion for and understanding of the poor also goes beyond her years, and is untinged by any class snobbery or condescension:

[T]he distresses of the poor were as sure of relief from [Emma's] . . . personal attention and kindness, her counsel and her patience, as from her purse. She understood their ways, could allow for their ignorance and their temptations, had no romantic expectations of extraordinary virtue from those for whom education had done so little; entered into their troubles with ready sympathy, and always gave her assistance with as much intelligence as good-will. (70)

13. Some philosophers have thought so, but Aristotle himself would reject the very idea.

It is easy enough to hand out money that one can afford, but not so easy to be both kind toward, and realistic about, those who need much. Although charity toward the poor is not a virtue that Aristotle recognizes, its recognition is compatible with his conception of virtue and of human nature. So it is no contradiction to say that, in her charity toward the poor, Emma is the very embodiment of the Aristotelian virtue of generosity and practical wisdom.

We believe we have given sufficient evidence for establishing that Emma is virtuous enough to count as virtuous overall, and thus to have virtue friendships. The same evidence indicates that, making allowances for her age, she is the equal of Mrs. Weston and Mr. Knightley, but we'll return to the theme of her equality with Mr. Knightley when we discuss marital friendship in section IV.

Now we turn to two radical challenges to the view of a good friendship that we see in Austen's novels and Aristotle's ethical writings. One challenge says that moral virtue is irrelevant to the goodness of a friendship, or even contrary to it. The other challenge makes the same claim about epistemic virtue and a good friendship.

III. ARE VIRTUE FRIENDSHIPS GOOD FRIENDSHIPS?

In his recent book, *On Friendship*, Alexander Nehamas argues that bad people can be good friends, so morality cannot be essential to friendship.[14] For example, two people can admire each other for their vices and be friends on account of their shared badness.

Aristotle would deny that people can love each other for their vices (Bk. IX, Ch. 3–4), but even if he's wrong about this, it doesn't

14. Alexander Nehamas, *On Friendship* (New York: Basic Books, 2016).

follow that moral virtue is irrelevant to the friendship of bad people. On the contrary, their friendship demands that they be virtuous with each other and limit their vices to other people. Even the friendship of bad, or morally casual, people requires mutual goodwill, trustworthiness, courage, kindness, and justice. This is the internal morality of friendship.[15] Austen's portrayal of the Eltons illustrates such a friendship. The Eltons are unkind, shallow, snobbish, and mean-spirited in general, but admire and love each other for these qualities, and presumably are not unkind, shallow, snobbish, or mean-spirited toward each other.[16]

Some philosophers argue that even if there is an internal morality of friendship, the non-moral reasons that arise from friendship often conflict with and override the reasons that arise from morality. Indeed, Jeanette Kennett and Dean Cocking argue that part of the value of friendship is that "it can lead us morally astray."[17] For example, "I might break a promise to give a colleague some free tickets to the movies which I have won in a raffle, when out of the blue you call me and suggest that we go" (286). The action is morally wrong, but it's still an act of friendship. Similarly, using the movie *Thelma and Louise* as an example, Nehamas argues that Thelma and Louise's "friendship is a good [to them], not despite the fact that it leads them to kill, rob, intimidate, and destroy but *because* of it" (195). Presumably, Nehamas believes this because not doing these

---

15. For discussion, see Badhwar, "Friendship, Justice, and Supererogation," *American Philosophical Quarterly* 22, no. 2 (April 1985): 123–131.

16. For Mr. Elton, Mrs. Elton's wealth seems to have been a necessary condition for marriage, but this doesn't make their marriage an example of Aristotle's utility friendship, because (i) the marriage is now based on their mutual admiration of each other's bad qualities, including their snobbery, and (ii) the loss of her wealth would not end the marriage. The Eltons' friendship cuts across Aristotle's typology.

17. "Friendship and Moral Danger," *The Journal of Philosophy* 97, no. 5 (May 2000): 278–296, at 279.

things would have meant betraying or abandoning and intentionally harming each other.[18]

Nehamas and Cocking and Kennett, however, are ignoring the fact that such acts are acts of friendship only for people who don't prize virtue, or who get trapped into acting wrongly by their own or their friends' foolish actions. People who value virtue and are attracted to others who are virtuous would not want their friends to do such things, and would not accept them as acts of friendship if their friends did do them. It's hard to imagine Mr. Knightley cheering Emma for mocking Miss Bates, or afterward having a good chuckle with her over it. Or Emma thanking Harriet for breaking a promise to Mrs. Goddard in order to spend time with her. Nor can we imagine Mrs. Weston praising Emma for being unfriendly toward Jane Fairfax out of jealousy. And it's hard to imagine liking any of them if they did have these mean or dishonest traits. So all that these arguments by Nehamas and Cocking and Kennett show is that in the friendship of bad or morally casual people, reasons of friendship often conflict with moral reasons. They do not show that reasons of friendship as such often conflict with moral reasons. Of course, if there are genuine moral dilemmas—that is, situations in which, no matter what one does, one does something wrong—then it's also possible for friends to face moral dilemmas, such that, no matter what they do,

18. But Nehamas's interpretation of Thelma and Louise's actions as acts of friendship is tendentious. Although Thelma and Louise are not wicked individuals, a series of imprudent actions by Thelma lead to Louise committing murder, and Thelma committing robbery. Louise kills the man who had threatened to rape Thelma *after* he is no longer a threat, so, contra Nehamas, her action is not in defense of her friend. The movie suggests that she might have been acting partly out of the trauma of having herself once been a rape victim. Again, Thelma robs a gas station after losing Louise's life savings through sheer carelessness, and is shown enjoying her own dare-devilry. It's true that she's trying to make up for the loss of her friend's money, but she's also trying to emulate the charming robber who robbed her after having sex with her the previous night. And Louise is shocked by her act.

they wrong either each other or someone else. But dilemmas exemplify a contingent conflict *within* morality, not between friendship and morality.

Another criticism of Austen and Aristotle's conception of a good friendship is that a good friendship requires us to see our friends not strictly as they are, but in a favorable light, even when this means being epistemically biased.[19] For example, if we hear a shocking story from a reputable source about a good friend, we do and should require far more evidence for believing it than we would in the case of a stranger. Likewise, even after we accept it as true, we do and should interpret it far more favorably by, for example, imputing honorable motives to the friend, or giving them a positive spin, than we would in the case of a stranger.

It's not clear, however, why setting a higher bar for believing a shocking story about a good friend than about a stranger, or seeking a favorable interpretation of it, is contrary to epistemic virtue. If the friend is a good person, and the story depicts her as acting out of character, that is exactly what we should do. What is contrary to epistemic virtue is doing this even when it's clear that the story is true and the friend's actions cannot plausibly be seen as morally permissible, much less honorable. But why suppose that a good friend *should* be a spin master? One reason given is that positive illusions about those we love contribute to relationship satisfaction, whereas seeing our friends as they are undermines it. But this ignores the benefits of a mutual recognition of each other's flaws in a virtue friendship: the growth in self-knowledge and virtue. Moreover, to the extent that friends deal in positive illusions, they love each other not as the persons they are, but as figments of their own

19. Simon Keller, "Friendship and Belief," *Philosophical Papers* 33 (2004): 329–351; Sarah Stroud, "Epistemic Partiality in Friendship," *Ethics* 116 (2006): 498–524.

imagination.[20] Imagine if Mr. Knightley had interpreted Emma's manipulation of Harriet as nothing but loving generosity, and her snobbishness about Mr. Martin as but evidence of refinement and elegance. We would have had to conclude that it was not the real Emma that he loved.

IV. MARRIAGE AS A FRIENDSHIP BETWEEN EQUALS

As we've already noted, on Aristotle's faulty conception of human nature, women's reason is inherently deficient, so a virtuous woman must be the inferior of her virtuous husband, and must always be guided by him in most daily affairs. At the same time, however, equality in friendship is important to Aristotle. How, then, to show that husband and wife can be equals? His solution is to argue that since the more virtuous is more lovable, the wife ought to love her husband more than he loves her. But this is hardly the kind of equality that makes for the best kind of friendship, the kind in which two equally virtuous friends share their thoughts and activities and inspire each other to become better.

Fortunately, Austen has no illusions about the natural superiority of male nature over female. Thus it is Aristotle's conception of the best kind of friendship, rather than of a good marriage, that is illustrated in her depictions of marital friendship in *Emma* and her other novels. Indeed, in *Pride and Prejudice*, Austen suggests that unequal marriages in which the husband is superior to the wife are

---

20. Badhwar, "Love," in *Oxford Handbook of Practical Ethics*, ed. Hugh Lafollette (Oxford: Oxford University Press, 2003), 42–69; and Jason Kawall, "Friendship and Epistemic Norms," *Philosophical Studies* (2013) 165: 349–370, who also argues that merely requiring more evidence and trying to give favorable interpretations doesn't necessarily mean being epistemically biased, so long as those interpretations are justified. For epistemic norms are subject to pragmatic considerations.

likely to lead to a debasement of the husband's character or intellect.[21] Unequal marriages in which the wife is intellectually and morally superior to her husband are better, for women are thought more capable of retaining meritorious traits in the face of a bad influence than are men. Hence the inferior party often proves the gainer. Sir Walter Elliot's marriage in *Persuasion* is a case in point. His wife "had humoured, or softened, or concealed his failings, and promoted his real respectability for seventeen years" (P 4). In *Emma*, Mr. Knightley reflects on the improvements that marriage to Jane Fairfax may produce in Frank Churchill: "I am very much of his opinion in thinking him likely to be happier than he deserves: but still ... I am very ready to believe his character will improve, and acquire from hers the steadiness and delicacy of principle that it wants" (352). Accordingly, unequal unions in which the wife is superior can be equalized.

The superiority in question, it should be noted, is only superiority in virtue, not in power. Just as David Hume mocks some women's taste for power, Austen mocks the domineering Mrs. Churchill of *Emma*, Lady Catherine of *Pride and Prejudice*, and Mrs. Ferrars of *Sense and Sensibility*. The ideal marriage, of course, like the ideal friendship, is a relationship of equals—a controversial position in Austen's day, in which she echoes Hume and anticipates John Stuart Mill. Hume describes the ideal marriage as one in which "there were no pretensions to authority on either side; but that every thing was carried on with perfect equality, as between two equal members of the same body."[22] Masculine sovereignty he saw as "a real usurpation" that destroys the "equality, which nature has established between the sexes. We are by nature ... [women's] lovers, their friends, their

---

21. And the more radical the disparity, the stronger the apprehension of grim consequences. See Dadlez, *Mirrors to One Another: Emotion and Value in Jane Austen and David Hume* (Chichester, UK: Wiley-Blackwell, 2009), 157–168.

22. David Hume, "Of Love and Marriage," in *Essays: Moral, Political, and Literary*, ed. Eugene F. Miller (Indianapolis: Liberty Classics, 1987), 559–560.

patrons: would we willingly exchange such endearing appellations, for the barbarous title of master and tyrant?"[23] Marriage, for Hume, "chiefly subsists by friendship, the closest possible."[24] Moved by the same sentiments, Mill calls for the establishment of a legal "principle of perfect equality that doesn't allow any power or privilege on one side or disability on the other."[25] Unequal power, he says, leads men to stay ignorant of their own wives' nature, because their wives are too afraid to be completely open with them. Yet without such openness, marriages lack intimacy and true friendship.

Although Austen never talks about legal equality, she clearly recognizes that marital friendship requires de facto equality as well as openness on both sides. This may be why, in *Persuasion*, Captain Wentworth looks askance at the union of his friend Benwick with Louisa Musgrove. Although she is "not deficient in understanding," there is still a "great . . . disparity" in their understanding (P 182). And Emma is shocked at the thought that Mr. Knightley might marry Harriet, not only because it would "debase" him socially and make him the object of disdain, but also because it seems wrong, unfitting, for "a man of first-rate abilities to be captivated by very inferior powers" (325).

In *Pride and Prejudice*, Elizabeth Bennet tells Darcy that it was her treatment of him as her equal rather than her superior that first aroused his respect: "[T]he fact is, that you were sick of civility, of deference, of officious attention. You were disgusted with the women who were always speaking, and looking, and thinking, for *your* approbation alone" (PP 380). Mr. Knightley speaks to Emma Woodhouse

23. David Hume, "Of Polygamy and Divorces," in *Essays: Moral, Political, and Literary,* ed. Eugene F. Miller (Indianapolis: Liberty Classics, 1987), 184.181–190.
24. Ibid, 190.
25. John Stuart Mill, *The Subjection of Women,* in Jonathan Bennet, *Early Modern Texts,* 1. http://www.earlymoderntexts.com/assets/pdfs/mill1869.pdf (accessed January 3, 2017).

of their "having every right that equal worth can give to be happy together" (365). Mrs. Weston, in reflecting on their match, considers that "it was all right, all open, all equal," and this is clearly intended to refer to character and intellect as well as socioeconomic status (368). "Nature gave you understanding," Mr. Knightley tells Emma, and "Miss Taylor gave you principles," so she didn't need his lectures to become his equal (363). But should we believe that they are equals, given Emma's conviction that she must become "more worthy of him, whose intentions and judgment had been ever so superior to her own"? (373). Her estimate of Mr. Knightley's superiority is also, no doubt, somewhat hyperbolic, but to the extent that it's true, its truth is surely explained by the difference in their years. Practical wisdom requires experience, not just native understanding and the right principles. Relative to her age, then, there is no difficulty in seeing Emma's character as equal to Mr. Knightley's. Mr. Knightley's recognition of the importance of equality in marriage goes beyond equality in worth. He makes what must surely be a highly extraordinary decision in those days: the decision to move into Emma's house out of concern for her father's welfare, instead of insisting that, as his wife, she must move into his. Well might Emma reflect: "Such a companion for herself in the periods of anxiety and cheerlessness before her! Such a partner in all those duties and cares to which time must be giving increase of melancholy!" (353).

The importance of openness in marriage also receives a great deal of attention in *Emma*. Mr. Knightley explicitly notes the importance of openness in marriage when he states that Jane Fairfax's only fault is that "she has not the open temper which a man would wish for in a wife" (226). He criticizes Frank Churchill for insisting on a secret engagement with Jane, because "Mystery; Finesse, pervert the understanding!" continuing, "My Emma, does not every thing serve to prove more and more the beauty of truth and sincerity in all our dealings with each other?" (350). Emma, too, hates "disguise, equivocation, mystery," and looks forward to a marriage in which she can give him "that full and perfect confidence which her disposition was most ready to welcome" (374).

In Austen's ideal marriage, as in that described by Mill many years later, equality of intellect and character allow women and men to share their interests and endeavors. We have already seen that Emma can always hold her own in conversation with Mr. Knightley, and that this is one of the traits that attracts him to her.[26] The best marriages are friendships marked by equality and mutual openness, without pretension to authority and without exploitation on either side.

Emma's story is a story about the search for the kind of companionship that is a necessary component of a fulfilling life. Recollect that the novel begins almost immediately by chronicling Emma's fear of the intellectual isolation consequent on Mrs. Weston's departure. It approaches its conclusion by making us privy to a similar but intensified fear of isolation. Emma fears the intellectual and social desert likely to be produced should Knightley marry Harriet. Indeed, Emma even compares her initial to her present prospects for companionship:

> The picture which she had then drawn of the privations of the approaching winter, had proved erroneous; no friends had deserted them, no pleasures had been lost.—But her present forebodings she feared would experience no similar contradiction. The prospect before her now, was threatening to a degree that could not be entirely dispelled—that might not be even partially brightened. If all took place that might take place among

---

26. Admiral and Mrs. Croft of *Persuasion* are also just such a couple, even treating the driving of their gig as a cooperative venture. More important, Mrs. Croft is "as intelligent and keen as any of the officers around her" when she and her husband are engaged in conversation (P 168).

the circle of her friends, Hartfield must be comparatively deserted; and she left to cheer her father with the spirits only of ruined happiness. . . . All that were good would be withdrawn; and if to these losses, the loss of Donwell were to be added, what would remain of cheerful or of rational society within their reach? Mr. Knightley to be no longer coming there for his evening comfort!—No longer walking in at all hours, as if ever willing to change his own home for their's!—How was it to be endured? (331–332)

Happily, Emma's fears are not realized, for she acquires a lifelong companion and lover in the very friend she feared to lose. Consider, however, the clear significance of the entire story's being bracketed by depictions of Emma's investment in and concern for cheerful, rational society. It is evident that love and friendship, especially in marriage, are the goods most central to Emma's achievement of happiness.

REFERENCES

Aristotle. *The Complete Works of Aristotle*, translated by J. Solomon. The Revised Oxford Translation, Vol. 2, edited by Jonathan Barnes. Princeton, NJ: Princeton University Press, 1984.

Aristotle. *Nicomachean Ethics*, translated by Terence Irwin, 2nd ed. Indianapolis: Hackett, 1999.

Austen, Jane. *Emma*, edited by James Kinsley. Oxford: Oxford University Press, 2008.

Austen, Jane. *The Novels of Jane Austen*, 5 volumes, edited by R. W. Chapman, 3rd ed. Oxford: Oxford University Press, 1988.

Austen, Jane. *The Works of Jane Austen*, edited by R. W. Chapman, Vol. 6: *Minor Works*. Oxford: Oxford University Press, 1988.

Badhwar, Neera K. "Friendship, Justice, and Supererogation." *American Philosophical Quarterly* 22, no. 2 (April 1985): 123–131.

Badhwar, Neera K. "Love." In *Oxford Handbook of Practical Ethics*, edited by Hugh Follette, 42–69. Oxford: Oxford University Press, 2003.

Badhwar, Neera K., and Russell E. Jones. "Aristotle on the Love of Friends." In *The Oxford Handbook of Philosophy of Love*, edited by Christopher Grau and Aaron Smuts, 1–26. Oxford: Oxford University Press, 2018. doi: 10.1093/oxfordhb/9780199395729.013.22. Online publication: October 2017.

Brewer, Talbot. "Virtues We Can Share: Friendship and Aristotelian Ethical Theory." *Ethics* 115 (2005): 721–758.

Broadie, Sarah, and Christopher Rowe. *Aristotle: Nicomachean Ethics, Translation, Introduction, and Commentary*. Oxford: Oxford University Press, 2002.

Cooper, John. "Aristotle on Friendship." In *Essays on Aristotle's Ethics*, edited by Amelie Oksenberg Rorty, 301–340. Berkeley: University of California Press, 1980.

Dadlez, E. M. *Mirrors to One Another: Emotion and Value in Jane Austen and David Hume*. Chichester, UK: Wiley-Blackwell, 2009.

Gallop, David. "Jane Austen and the Aristotelian Ethic." *Philosophy and Literature* 23, no. 1 (April 1999): 96–106.

Grenberg, Jeanine. "Self-Deception and Self-Knowledge: Jane Austen's *Emma* as an Example of Kant's Notion of Self-Deception." *Contextos Kantianos: International Journal of Philosophy* 2 (November 2015): 162–176.

Hume, David. "Of Love and Marriage." In *Essays: Moral, Political, and Literary*, edited by Eugene F. Miller, 559–560. Indianapolis: Liberty Classics, 1987a.

Hume, David. "Of Polygamy and Divorces." In *Essays: Moral, Political, and Literary*, edited by Eugene F. Miller, 181–190. Indianapolis: Liberty Classics, 1987b.

Kawall, Jason. "Friendship and Epistemic Norms." *Philosophical Studies* 165 (2013): 349–370.

Kennett, Jeanette, and Dean Cocking. "Friendship and Moral Danger." *The Journal of Philosophy* 97, no. 5 (May 2000): 278–296.

Keller, Simon. "Friendship and Belief." *Philosophical Papers* 33 (2004): 329–351.

Mill, John Stuart. *The Subjection of Women*. In *Early Modern Texts*, edited by Jonathan Bennet. http://www.earlymoderntexts.com/assets/pdfs/mill1869.pdf (accessed January 3, 2017).

Nehamas, Alexander. *On Friendship*. New York: Basic Books, 2016.

Ruderman, Anne Crippen. *The Pleasures of Virtue: Political Thought in the Novels of Jane Austen*. Lanham, MD: Rowman & Littlefield, 1995.

Ryle, Gilbert. "Jane Austen and the Moralists." In *Critical Essays on Jane Austen*, edited by B. C. Southam, 286–301. London: Routledge & Kegan Paul, 1968.

Sherman, Nancy. "Aristotle on Friendship and the Shared Life." *Philosophy and Phenomenological Research* 47 (1987): 589–613.

Stroud, Sarah. "Epistemic Partiality in Friendship." *Ethics* 116 (2006): 498–524.

Williams, Thomas. "Moral Vice, Cognitive Virtue." *Philosophy and Literature* 27, no. 1 (April 2003): 223–230.

Chapter 2

Emma's Pensive Meditations

CYNTHIA FREELAND

I. INTRODUCTION

Emma Woodhouse is an annoying heroine. She has so much to learn, and it takes her so long! Emma vows not to repeat her mistakes, but repeatedly meddles and misinterprets. In this chapter, I attempt to discern Jane Austen's view of what it takes for Emma to grow into virtue. At times, the author shows readers the errors of Emma's ways. Hints are dropped, both subtle and blatant, that indicate where Emma has gone wrong in acting or in assessing a situation. Often these hints are given through Austen's use of Mr. Knightley as a surrogate who voices concerns to Emma, scolding her like a child. Knightley thinks that Emma has been spoiled by her weak father and indulgent governess; she has always been "too clever" and head-strong. She needs a firmer hand to guide her, and Knightley's is the obvious one. But Emma is not all bad, and she is worth our time. She can be perceptive, loving, charitable, funny, and discerning. But in all these things she can also go wrong, and she often does: trying to arrange marriages, showing ridiculous snobbery, and pinioning victims with her wit. Again on the plus side, there are times when, even without Knightley's advice, Emma comes to realize that she has erred; she blushes and feels shame.

These episodes of shame are very significant indications of Emma's moral progress. The most important one occurs in Volume III when Mr. Knightley calls to her better nature by giving her a dressing-down for her cruelty in making a joke of poor garrulous Miss Bates during a group picnic to Box Hill. Emma is quick to retort. However, she internalizes the reprimand and admits its truth. From this point on, things move forward apace toward the book's satisfying conclusion. Emma makes a sincere gesture of apology to Miss Bates, and realizes that Mr. Knightley is the one for her. Somehow with—or in spite of—all that scolding, he has been transformed from a stern but distanced uncle figure into a desired and suitable lover. And Emma too has been transformed, from a charming child into a young woman with an adult's conscience. In this chapter I will chart how Austen depicts Emma's path to moral maturity by means of crucial moments of shame. But first I will detour by considering another intriguing discussion of the importance of shame in a youth's ethical education—from Aristotle. This will help identify some key indicators of Emma's growth into full moral virtue.

II. ARISTOTLE ON HOW VIRTUE IS TAUGHT AND LEARNED

Virtuous activity for Aristotle requires a combination of factors, including both cognitive and emotional capacities. The idea of emotional "capacities" seems odd, but on this point, Austen and Aristotle are in agreement: virtue calls for certain behaviors to be done in the right way and to stem from the right emotional sources. For Aristotle, the *phronimos*, or man of practical wisdom, has fine powers of discrimination. Moral perception is difficult and requires recognizing many details: how to act just so, in the correct situation toward the right person, and for the right reason, in the right way, and so on.[1] A person's emotions contribute to the proper sort of perception; feelings are part of the practical knowledge necessary for virtue. Austen seems to agree; virtue is an acquired ability exercised through sensitive discrimination. Young people can learn it if, like Emma, they are well-born and have good natures. But along the way they will make mistakes, causing shame. I want to consider more precisely how shame can help a young person develop true virtue.

One influential account of how people grow into virtue is Myles Burnyeat's "Aristotle on Learning to Be Good."[2] Burnyeat emphasizes Aristotle's distinctive contribution to moral theory in opposing intellectualism about morality—more specifically, by challenging Socrates' view that virtue is knowledge. According to Burnyeat, "He [Aristotle] reacted by emphasizing the importance of beginnings and the gradual development of good habits of feeling."[3] Pleasure is very significant in this path. In *Nicomachean Ethics* (*NE*) X.1, Aristotle claims that "in educating the young we steer them by the rudders of pleasure and pain" (1172a20–21).[4] Austen seems to agree with Aristotle: knowledge of principles will be part of Emma's virtue, but it is also important that she has been given a good start both by birth and by her upbringing to establish the right habits and feelings. For such a person, moral behavior is natural, habitual, and pleasant.

1. Aristotle, *Nicomachean Ethics*, translated by W. D. Ross, revised by J. O. Urmson, included in *The Complete Works of Aristotle*, ed. Jonathan Barnes (Princeton, NJ: Princeton University Press, 1984).
2. Myles Burnyeat, "Aristotle on Learning to Be Good," in *Essays on Aristotle's Ethics*, ed. Amélie Oksenberg Rorty (Berkeley and Los Angeles: University of California Press, 1980), 69–92.
3. Ibid.,70.
4. Ibid.

A fully virtuous person, for Aristotle, must have two sorts of knowledge: both *that* and *why* certain acts are just or noble. [5] On Burnyeat's account, as the young person becomes habituated to doing the right things, the reasons why those acts are right become more apparent. Drawing upon the *Politics* as well as the *Ethics*, Burnyeat says that a young person begins by learning with some certainty *that* certain things are, for example, noble or just. Thus, acquiring virtue presents a twofold challenge: learning that certain things are right, and finding those things pleasant for themselves. Aristotle holds that the young person comes to love virtue because virtuous actions are noble and pleasant *by nature*. Burnyeat tries to make this view more plausible by arguing from analogy between virtuous actions and other kinds of activities:

> There is such a thing as learning to enjoy something (painting, music, skiing, philosophy), and it is not sharply distinct from learning that the thing in question is enjoyable. . . . I learn that skiing is enjoyable only by trying it myself and coming to enjoy it. The growth of enjoyment goes hand in hand with the internalization of knowledge.[6]

For Aristotle, a crucial sign that someone is truly virtuous is not simply that they *do* what is right but that they *enjoy* doing it; they take pleasure in virtuous behavior for its own sake. Thus Burnyeat offers what commentator Marta Jimenez calls the "pleasure-centered view."[7] But his construal of Aristotle's account of moral development is not universally endorsed. Other scholars have raised what Jimenez

---

5. Here Burnyeat quotes from *Nicomachean Ethics* 1095b2–13.
6. Burnyeat, "Aristotle on Learning to Be Good," 76.
7. Marta Jimenez, "Steering the Young by Pleasure and Pain," *The Journal of Speculative Philosophy* 29, no. 2 (2015): 137–164.

calls "the priority objection."[8] *Emma* illustrates the problem: suppose, contrary to fact, that the headstrong Emma *had* taken Knightley's advice and restrained some of her matchmaking ambitions; it seems unlikely she would have enjoyed such forbearance. Can Emma learn what is prudent simply by doing what her governess or Mr. Knightley tells her to do? Does she learn to temper her pride or rein in her desire to manipulate people through finding temperance and circumspection genuinely *pleasant*? It seems more likely that she learns through what is in effect a punishment—the discovery that getting things wrong is painful and causes shame.

Skeptics about Burnyeat's version of Aristotelian moral growth similarly doubt that the process of learning virtue is enjoyable. For example, Howard Curzer writes,

> Aristotle does not say that learners take pleasure in performing virtuous acts. In fact, Aristotle says that following their pleasures leads the not-yet-virtuous astray (1104b9–12, 1109a14–16, 1113a33– b2). . . . Far from urging us to perform the acts that please us in order to learn to desire virtuous acts for their own sake, Aristotle instead urges us to steer clear of pleasure because it is likely to lead us wrong.[9]

Curzer cites other evidence from Aristotle to show that learning is not always pleasant—for example, the case of learning a difficult skill like flute-playing, as described in *Politics* 1339a29–30. Curzer doubts that learners can enjoy virtuous acts in the right way because they are not able early on to find them intrinsically valuable. "The enjoyment does not produce, but rather presupposes, the choice," he writes.[10]

8. Ibid., 138.
9. Howard J. Curzer, "Aristotle's Painful Path to Virtue," *Journal of the History of Philosophy* 40, no. 2 (2002): 141–162, 148.
10. Ibid., 149.

To sum up: there are two main ways to understand Aristotle's view of how virtue is learned. On Burnyeat's pleasure-based interpretation, Aristotle believes that someone with a good or noble nature, equipped with the right starting points, does virtuous things, presumably being told they are such. By doing them more and more, she comes to love them for their own sake. On the skeptical account, as presented by Curzer, a young person does not learn to love virtuous actions for their own sake, but must independently learn why such deeds are worthwhile. Habits or repetition alone will not provide the right kind of knowledge. Negative reinforcement and pain play a key part in helping young people realize errors. I next propose to take a closer look at how each interpretation explains the role of shame in the development of true virtue. This will also prepare us to consider what Austen would say about the debate.

III. THE ROLE OF SHAME

Scholars have had a fair amount to say about the role of shame in the process of learning virtue. First, Burnyeat quotes from Aristotle's treatment of shame in E.N. 4.9:

> Shame should not be described as a virtue; for it is more like a feeling than a state of character. It is defined, at any rate, as a kind of fear of disgrace. . . . The feeling is not becoming to every age, but only to youth. For we think young people should be prone to the feeling of shame because they live by feeling and therefore commit many errors, but are restrained by shame; and we praise young people who are prone to this feeling, but an older person no one would praise for being prone to the sense of disgrace, since we think he should not do anything that need cause this sense. (1128b10–12, 15–21)

Burnyeat calls shame a "semivirtue" for Aristotle. It helps educate the young person who will invariably make mistakes, even though aiming at doing good.

Burnyeat's explanation for the learner's feeling of shame is that a good young person who is well brought up, like our Emma, will through this upbringing have developed a taste for noble actions. She will find them pleasant, all things considered. And so if the young person chooses something ignoble because it seems pleasant at the time, he will realize this and become ashamed. "The actions pain him internally, not consequentially. He is therefore receptive to the kind of moral education which will set his judgment straight and develop the intellectual capacities (practical wisdom) which will enable him to avoid such errors."[11] We should recognize that shame here involves "internal" learning. Burnyeat's idea is that the young person can learn to recognize virtue as valuable or noble in itself, not because of consequences involving reputation or reward.

On the opposite side of the debate, factors of reward or punishment prove more central in Curzer's account of the role of shame. He quotes Aristotle's claim that people "do not by nature obey the sense of *aidos* [shame, guilt, remorse], but only fear, and do not abstain from bad acts because of their baseness but through fear of punishment. (1179b7–13)."[12] Aristotle draws a contrast between two types of moral learners: there are "the many," and also a group of people whom Aristotle calls "the generous-minded" (*eleutherios*). Such people are from youth in love with the ideals of nobility. They are not yet virtuous, however, because they do not have the right sort of knowledge or habits. They do not yet pursue the noble either as pleasant or as

---

11. Burnyeat, "Aristotle on Learning to Be Good," 79.
12. Curzer, "Aristotle's Painful Path to Virtue," 155; see also Curzer's helpful note 30 about the Greek term *aidos*, which is not an exact equivalent of the English "shame"; it also can be translated as both "guilt" and "remorse."

worthwhile for its own sake. Shame motivates the path to virtue for all prospective moral agents through negative consequences, whether external or internal. The many might choose virtue through shame, which involves fear of external punishment, but the generous-minded (and surely Emma would count among this group), for Curzer, "become able to identify virtuous acts through habituation motivated by the pain of retrospective and prospective *aidos*."[13]

Curzer's outlook is much darker than Burnyeat's. The Aristotle that Curzer portrays believes that virtue is very difficult to acquire. Even superior, generous-minded youths must be "compelled' into it by pain or the threat of pain, typically from their own concerns with what Curzer calls "prospective shame." For someone like Emma, who is presumed already to have some sort of love of the noble, the relevant forces of shame do operate *internally*. They have to do with her own feelings and developing knowledge about what is proper versus what is *aidos* or shameful. *Aidos* helps reveal the truth to someone like Emma; it serves as what Curzer calls a "salience projector."[14] Such shame involves *one's own* estimation of actions, prospective or retrospective.[15] Still, the motivation that shame provides is pain-based and not pleasure-based, as Burnyeat holds. Shame indicates that certain things are valuable for their consequences: namely, to avoid future pain.

I suspect that Austen would say that this duality between the morally educative forces of pain and pleasure is too sharp.[16] In the example that *Emma* lays out for us, Emma does learn virtue through shame, and the experiences that produce such episodes of shame are indeed quite painful for her. So far, the skeptical view seems

13. Ibid., 158.
14. Curzer, "Aristotle's Painful Path to Virtue," 160.
15. See also Curzer, "Aristotle's Painful Path to Virtue," 160–161.
16. This is not quite like the view Jimenez attributes to Aristotle; she argues for a "deflationary view" of the roles of both pleasure and pain in moral education ("Steering the Young by Pleasure and Pain," 138).

correct. But I believe that Emma, as representative of the noble, generous-minded youths who Aristotle believed were the right sorts of students of virtue, achieves moral learning not just as a matter of crude reward and punishment. Moments of shame are also moments of learning, as Austen emphasizes when she speaks of Emma's "pensive meditations," in the phrasing I have borrowed for my title. By stimulating such meditations, shame prepares the way for virtue to become its own motivation. In other words, I think that the right account of Emma's moral progress is closer to Burnyeat's view than to the skeptical interpretation of what Aristotle had in mind.

IV. EMMA'S MISTAKES AND MISADVENTURES

Many people have praised Jane Austen's narrative inventiveness in *Emma*. She both *presents* Emma's activities and thoughts, using the third person, and *implies* things about them, using the technique of free indirect discourse. That our heroine is not without flaws is evident right from the start of the book when the author says that Highbury "afforded her no equals" (7). But of course Highbury is a very small town not affording that many people to compare with Emma! After listing various positives about her looks and position, the author mentions certain defects: "the power of having rather too much her own way, and a disposition to think a little too well of herself" (5). Immediately the reader is put on alert that Emma is not always the best judge of her own situation.

Emma's misperceptions pile up, and their revelation is not always pleasant for her. The initial project she undertakes is to help guide the pretty, unsophisticated Harriet Smith into a marriage with the handsome vicar Mr. Elton. But Emma persistently misinterprets Elton's attentions as being directed toward her little friend rather than herself. Indeed, we could see the entire plot of the novel as a succession of three love stories about which Emma fails to see the truth. After her failure with Harriet and Mr. Elton, she proves again mistaken about the relationship between Jane Fairfax and Frank Churchill. And finally, she takes forever to realize that her own affection for Mr. Knightley has developed into deep love. I will examine these three stories of Emma's meddling and misperception, charting how they propel Emma into moral growth through crucial episodes of shame and recognition.

As noted, Austen alerts us at the start to Emma's shortcomings: for instance, Emma takes credit for things she has not actually done. We realize this by hearing Mr. Knightley's perspective:

> Mr. Knightley, in fact, was one of the few people who could see faults in Emma Woodhouse, and the only one who ever told her of them: and though this was not particularly agreeable to Emma herself, she knew it would be so much less so to her father, that she would not have him really suspect such a circumstance as her not being thought perfect by every body. (9–10)

Knightley functions as Emma's chief critic and moral mentor. At the very start of the book he criticizes Emma for claiming that she engineered the match between her governess and Mr. Weston. Perhaps Emma did play some role here, but she will not acknowledge any limitations or recognize that Knightley's maturity gives him a superior vantage point. Emma's actions and perceptions evolve as the story moves on.

V. LOVE MISUNDERSTOOD, CASE 1: HARRIET AND ELTON

Emma behaves like a willful child with Harriet, whom she sees as a sort of pretty doll. The narrator tells us that Emma is "quick and decided in her ways" (21), and Emma has decided that Harriet and she will become friends. But Emma can be obtuse in her observations, often made through the lens of her own self-regard. She feels that Harriet showed "no want of taste" (given her attachment to Emma!), though "strength of understanding must not be expected" (21). Emma dismisses Harriet's interest in young Mr. Martin, whom she considers unworthy by comparison to other men (to be met with in Emma's circle) who are more well-bred, such as Mr. Elton, the man she wishes to unite with Harriet. Emma draws an interesting comparison between Mr. Elton's manner and Mr. Knightley's in terms of their respective suitability to their ages. Among other things, she mentions that Knightley has a "downright, decided, commanding sort of manner" (28). These features, which might speak in his favor, are seen by Emma as somewhat negative.

Similarly, Knightley spots flaws in Emma, but the reader will find his observations more accurate than Emma's. He complains to Mrs. Weston about Emma's intimacy with Harriet because he considers it is a bad thing, observing that "they will neither of them do the other any good" (29). Harriet won't improve Emma because she is ignorant and too admiring, reinforcing Emma's high opinion of herself. When Mrs. Weston defends her former charge by saying that at least the two friends will read together, Knightley remains doubtful, commenting that "I have done with expecting any course of steady reading from Emma. She will never submit to any thing requiring industry and patience" (30). He thinks Emma has been spoiled by being so clever. Having lost her mother at an early age ("the only person able to cope with her" [30]), Emma became undisputed mistress of the house at the unlikely age of twelve, and apparently never looked back.

A comparison between the observational powers of Knightley and Elton is subtly drawn when Mr. Elton praises Emma for having improved Harriet, showing that Elton views their friendship as felicitous, in marked contrast to Knightley's negative assessment. The astute reader can see that Elton flatters Emma as a way of making up to her, but Emma in her matchmaking mode only thinks he is interested in Harriet. When Mrs. Weston voices a criticism of Emma's portrait of Harriet, and Knightley observes that "you have made her too tall" (38), Emma won't admit to any faults, though she knows the criticisms are correct.

Emma and Knightley also quarrel about Harriet's refusing Martin's offer of marriage. To prove that Harriet is the one who is beneath Martin, Knightley enumerates defects in her birth, education, station, and understanding. Emma defends Harriet's beauty and good nature, noting that Harriet is just what men want in a marriage—indeed, she would be the perfect wife for Knightley himself. "Nonsense, errant nonsense, as ever was talked!" cries Mr. Knightley (52). Although Emma is obviously upset that Knightley's opinion is so strong, she does not concede he has insight, because "she still thought herself a better judge of such a point of female right and refinement than he could be" (52). Yet it is disagreeable to her that he is so angry. This quarrel is important, as it shows us that Knightley's opinions *matter* to Emma. His remarks leave her unsettled, despite seeming so sure about her own judgment. This shows that something in Emma is open to reform. Still, she fails to grow very much here because she remains too stubborn about her own perceptions and plans: "She was sorry, but could not repent" (55).

Mr. Knightley's negative view of Elton is reinforced, providing more indications that he is right and Emma wrong, when his brother John Knightley notices during the Christmas visit how hard Elton tries to please the ladies, observing that he seems particularly interested in Emma. Again, she denies this, "Mr. Elton in love with me!— What an idea!" (89). But the error of Emma's position is shown and both Knightleys' perceptiveness confirmed, after Christmas Eve dinner at the Westons'. Emma is trapped alone in a carriage with Elton, and he proposes. Emma declares herself shocked that he is not interested in Harriet. Elton is reciprocally shocked that Emma could have imagined such a match, adducing the great inequality between himself and Harriet. This is both painful to Emma and insulting, for she feels the same superiority to Elton as he does to Harriet. She rejects him and he is very angry.

Now that she has finally perceived the disastrous failure of her matchmaking between Harriet and Elton, Emma has the decency to feel shame. She realizes that "[i]t was a wretched business indeed!" (106). And she remembers that she has been warned: "To Mr. John Knightley was she indebted for her first idea on the subject, for the first start of its possibility" (107). Emma "blushed to think how much truer a knowledge of his character had been there shewn than any she had reached herself. It was dreadfully mortifying" (107).

Many points are worth highlighting in the full passage tracing Emma's internal monologue. She realizes that "[i]t was foolish, it was wrong, to take so active a part in bringing any two people together" (108). She feels Harriet's pain almost more than her own, blushes with remorse, and resolves to change. Her admission is partly due to recognizing the greater insight of the two Knightley men: "There was no denying that those brothers had penetration" (107). These older men are playing an important role as Emma's moral tutors. Having acknowledged their greater penetration in this circumstance, perhaps Emma will now be ready to listen more willingly when they advise her in the future.

By showing for the first time that Emma both feels shame about her behavior and realizes that others have clearer perceptions than her own, this passage recounting Emma's reflections reveals her inner growth. She has new knowledge of virtue, realizing that it is wrong to play with other people's lives and emotions. Emma must act on her new awareness by admitting to Harriet the truth about what has occurred; she must "undergo the necessary penance of communication" (111). Doing the right thing is obviously painful, not pleasant. At that point, "[t]he confession completely renewed her first shame—and the sight of Harriet's tears made her think that she should never be in charity with herself again" (112). But as we shall soon see, Emma has not yet internalized her new knowledge of virtue; she soon errs again concerning Harriet.

VI. LOVE MISUNDERSTOOD, CASE 2: FRANK CHURCHILL AND JANE FAIRFAX

The next love story that Emma misjudges is that of Frank Churchill and Jane Fairfax. Since these two individuals work hard to conceal their true relationship, others are also taken in. But Emma is given clues that she fails to pick up on—just as we readers may. Emma's misperceptions are due to her feelings about the two people in question. She consistently overrates Frank because of her own fantasies about him as her perfect match. And she underrates and is cruel to Jane from jealousy over a potential rival—a young woman threatening to surpass her in almost every respect except social position.

At variance with Emma's misperceptions are the numerous narrative clues about Frank's shortcomings with which readers are presented, often through the medium of Knightley's sharp observations. However, readers may begin to doubt Knightley's perceptions by suspecting he has strong feelings for Emma. For instance, when Frank Churchill has not yet come to see his father and Mrs. Weston, Mr. Knightley holds him accountable. He claims that the younger man could get away if he wished, since he has at times gone off for his own pleasure. Frank's failure to visit the Westons is blameworthy, showing that he does not do what he knows to be his duty. After Emma defends Frank, the two have a sharp exchange:

> "I will say no more about him," cried Emma, "you turn every thing to evil. We are both prejudiced; you against, I for him; and we have no chance of agreeing till he is really here."

"Prejudiced! I am not prejudiced."

"But I am very much, and without being at all ashamed of it. My love for Mr. and Mrs. Weston gives me a decided prejudice in his favour."

"He is a person I never think of from one month's end to another," said Mr. Knightley, with a degree of vexation, which made Emma immediately talk of something else, though she could not comprehend why he should be angry. (119)

This dialogue reveals a new stage of the Emma–Knightley relationship. Emma is puzzled by the vehemence of Knightley's critique of Frank, but does not grasp what lies at the root of it: his jealousy. Similarly, even if readers believe that Knightley is probably correct in his remarks, it may seem evident that his feelings are affecting his judgments about Frank. Emma is simply puzzled by Knightley's behavior and cannot see what prompts it; she is not yet ready to credit him as being correct about Frank.

Emma's response to Jane Fairfax becomes more and more unkind. Her likely envy of Jane's many accomplishments makes her less charitable even when Mr. Knightley tries to make her appreciate Jane's position. Emma misinterprets the signs of Frank's interest in and attention to Jane, signs that Knightley observes. She wavers between imagining herself in love with Frank and her new plan to match him up with Harriet. She quarrels with Knightley once again when he tells her he suspects that Frank is somehow involved with Jane and also criticizes her behavior toward Jane. However, this time Emma does seem to learn from the quarrel, because "Mr. Knightley's words dwelt with her . . . " (228). She even concedes the correctness of his criticism:

"This is very true," said she, "at least as far as relates to me, which was all that was meant—and it is very shameful.—Of the same age—and always knowing her—I ought to have been more her friend." (228)

Emma's lack of charity will soon get her into further trouble with Mr. Knightley, who chastises her for participating in spicy word-games clearly intended by Frank to discompose Miss Fairfax. Knightley is shown to be hesitant because he realizes his own mixed feelings when seeing Emma as too invested in Frank Churchill and too cavalier about Jane Fairfax. He is anxious both on her and on Jane's behalf:

. . . he must—yes, he certainly must, as a friend—an anxious friend—give Emma some hint, ask her some question. He could not see her in a situation of such danger, without trying to pre-serve her. It was his duty. (275)

Again, this is a remarkable passage. Knightley knows he is no longer a disinterested, kindly family friend. Torn, he does not want to be seen as "interfering"—but he also does not want to be guilty of "ne-glect." He is a model of moral virtue because he is genuinely con-cerned about Emma's moral behavior. Her response is to become "extremely confused" (275). Emma has shared her suspicions with Frank about a supposed lover of Jane's, but now is "really ashamed of having ever imparted them" (275), and does not want to admit any of this to Knightley. She awkwardly tries to dismiss the situation, calling it "a mere joke among ourselves" (275). But Knightley reminds her that the target, Jane, was not in on the joke.

Knightley is worried not just about Emma's rudeness to Jane Fairfax but also that Emma will be hurt: she appears attached to Frank and has failed to notice signs that his affections are directed to-ward Jane. This is why Austen writes that "[a] variety of evils crossed his mind" (275). To Knightley, Emma's confusions and apparent plotting with Frank "seemed to declare her affection engaged." But despite worrying that his observations will not be welcome, Knightley confronts her. As Austen puts it, "He owed it to her, to risk any thing that might be involved in an unwelcome interference, rather than her welfare; to encounter any thing, rather than the remembrance of neglect in such a cause" (274–275). The conversation makes it plain that Knightley really does have Emma's interests at heart, whereas she is unable to discern what motivates his strong words to her, remaining "confused."

It is only after Frank's aunt dies that Emma (and the reader) come to know his true standing, when he reveals that he is already committed to Jane. This causes Emma even more embarrassment about her behavior to Jane. Although it is not spelled out in the text, now Emma must again admit Knightley's greater powers of observation. Much later, after everything has been resolved, she alludes to her unfair assumptions about Jane Fairfax in a conversation with the repentant Frank by commenting, "I can never think of it," she cries, "without extreme shame" (375). It seems likely that she is also conscious of not living up to Knightley's high expectations of her, and is ashamed on that account.

VII. LOVE MISUNDERSTOOD, CASE 3: EMMA AND MR. KNIGHTLEY

The third and last romantic relationship that Emma must learn to understand follows shortly after the revelations about Frank Churchill and Jane Fairfax. The underlying feelings of many more people are revealed, and so too will Emma's own be. As she begins to do less fantasizing and sees people and their relationships more clearly, Emma will discover that Knightley is the true object of her affection. When she realizes this, she fears, perhaps with reason, that his devotion might have been sidetracked onto Harriet. (After all, Emma had herself proclaimed

Harriet a good candidate for him to marry, praising her beauty and sweet nature.) Emma's progress in moral perceptiveness emerges in two crucial chapters in Volume III. These depict the town's social set venturing on some excursions. First, they travel the short distance to Donwell, Knightley's home. And second, they go on a picnic outing to Box Hill. Their ventures have mixed success, and Emma does not behave very well at either of them. The second foray leads to a climactic interaction with Mr. Knightley, when he once again feels he must step in and scold Emma for her bad behavior. In the course of these two adventures, Emma finally acquires a more mature moral vision, including more accurate views both of herself and of Knightley.

The group's visit to Donwell for strawberry picking and lunch starts out promisingly. Emma makes many approving observations about Knightley's home.

> It was just what it ought to be, and it looked what it was—and Emma felt an increasing respect for it, as the residence of a family of such true gentility, untainted in blood and understanding.— Some faults of temper John Knightley had; but Isabella had connected herself unexceptionably. She had given them neither men, nor names, nor places, that could raise a blush. (281)

Note that Emma is beginning to form a more objective picture of Knightley. She realizes that he is not simply an extension of her own family, but a responsible landowner and prominent member of the community. As she sees people and their situations more accurately, Frank Churchill suffers by comparison with Knightley. Emma is annoyed by his lateness, and she chides him for being spoiled and constantly in search of change.

In describing the second outing, Austen indicates that the picnic at Box Hill is cursed from the start. Emma is upset that

Mr. Weston has derailed her own plans for a group outing by enlisting their group in the plans of the obnoxious and vain Mrs. Elton, who accordingly takes credit for the whole thing. Emma and Frank are both out of sorts. Although by this point she no longer regards him as a serious romantic interest, she is pleased that he helps divert her by being amusing and flirtatious. But the most awful thing about the trip is Emma's extreme unkindness to Miss Bates. This garrulous woman is a repeated source of annoyance to her (and often to Austen's readers as well). Emma, feeling at her most bored and petulant, proposes a game of wits and then cannot resist a cruel joke at Miss Bates's expense. When the older woman confesses that she is bound to say only stupid things, Emma says the real issue involves the number to which those stupidities can be limited. This is genuinely unkind, and not the sort of behavior that Knightley can let pass without comment. Austen has carefully prepared us for this event by building a nuanced picture of Miss Bates at earlier points in the novel. She makes it clear when introducing Mrs. and Miss Bates that their home is humble and that Emma finds evenings with them and their friend Mrs. Goddard rather dull: "the quiet prosings of three such women made her feel that every evening so spent was indeed one of the long evenings she had fearfully anticipated" (18). But the narrator says many good things about poor Miss Bates:

> Miss Bates stood in the very worst predicament in the world for having much of the public favour; and she had no intellectual superiority to make atonement to herself, or frighten those who might hate her into outward respect. . . . And yet she was a happy woman, and a woman whom no one named without good-will. It was her own universal good-will and contented temper which worked such wonders. (17)

Lamentably, Emma shows little sympathy for Miss Bates's difficult situation in an earnest conversation with Harriet about marriage. When Emma proclaims that she will never get married, Harriet says in dismay, "But then, to be an old maid at last, like Miss Bates!" (68). Emma reveals that she regards the unfortunate Miss Bates with contempt:

> "That is as formidable an image as you could present, Harriet; and if I thought I should ever be like Miss Bates! so silly—so satisfied—so smiling—so prosing—so undistinguishing and unfastidious—and so apt to tell every thing relative to every body about me, I would marry to-morrow." (68)

Emma's remarks are mean-spirited; she holds Miss Bates at fault not just for her spinsterhood but for her character and poverty. This insensitivity should prepare us for her casual cruelty based on little more than a desire to look witty during the picnic outing.

On the whole, Emma behaves badly at the picnic. She remains insensitive to the fact that her flirting with Frank is upsetting to Jane Fairfax. And she is heedless of any damage to her own reputation, even though she realizes that this flirting has drawn the attention of others as inappropriate. All the more reason for Emma to feel both defensive and culpable when Knightley takes her aside and confronts her about her behavior.

> "Emma, I must once more speak to you as I have been used to do. . . . I cannot see you acting wrong, without a remonstrance. How could you be so unfeeling to Miss Bates? How could you be so insolent in your wit to a woman of her character, age, and situation?—Emma, I had not thought it possible."
>
> Emma recollected, blushed, was sorry, but tried to laugh it off.

> "Nay, how could I help saying what I did?—Nobody could
> have helped it. It was not so very bad. I dare say she did not un-
> derstand me." (294)

Notice that Emma has a dual reaction to Knightley's critique. On the
plus side, she blushes and is sorry; on the minus side, she laughs it
off. She next tries to dismiss the issue by saying that her insult to Miss
Bates has passed without notice. Knightley says she is wrong, but
Emma persists in defending herself. She comments, "I know there
is not a better creature in the world: but you must allow, that what
is good and what is ridiculous are most unfortunately blended in
her" (295).

Knightley has not gotten through here, any more than in previous
cases when he scolded Emma. However, things do finally progress.
Knightley gives Emma a lesson in civility, by pointing out that even
if her observation of Miss Bates is true, Emma has not taken into
account the spinster's circumstances.

> "Were she your equal in situation—but, Emma, consider how far
> this is from being the case. . . . It was badly done, indeed! . . . This
> is not pleasant to you, Emma—and it is very far from pleasant to
> me; but I must, I will,—I will tell you truths while I can; satis-
> fied with proving myself your friend by very faithful counsel, and
> trusting that you will some time or other do me greater justice
> than you can do now." (295)

Knightley's detailed critique of how Emma has gone wrong is a reminder of principles of virtue she already knows. This is no doubt just
as painful to her as he fears. Austen provides a wonderful example of
moral tutelage. A lesser student than Emma, someone irredeemably
proud or uncharitable, would reject Knightley and his "principles" at

this point. It is very much to Emma's credit that his scolding upsets her terribly. She cannot reply, but goes home in tears.

> Never had she felt so agitated, mortified, grieved, at any circumstance in her life. She was most forcibly struck. The truth of this representation there was no denying. She felt it at her heart. How could she have been so brutal, so cruel to Miss Bates! How could she have exposed herself to such ill opinion in any one she valued! And how suffer him to leave her without saying one word of gratitude, of concurrence, of common kindness! (296)

There are many important words in Austen's recounting of Emma's thoughts here. She sees the truth of her misbehavior, feels genuine pain about it, and is ashamed of her cruelty. Knightley's criticism has gone directly to her heart. She has finally learned through shame and pain and sorrow something very important about kindness, duty, and pride that she will not be able to forget soon.

This episode between Emma and Knightley is unlike their earlier quarrels because Emma concedes that he is right and stops insisting on her own superior perceptions. She is afraid of his poor opinion, not simply because she wants to impress him, but because his opinion is correct. The scolding leaves her afraid to try to make up with him. But she does resolve to make it up to Miss Bates, and does so by an early morning visit the very next day. At the Bates home, she learns that Jane Fairfax has accepted a position as a governess and that Mr. Churchill has summoned Frank home to London because of his wife's illness. Emma contrasts the status of the two women, Jane and Mrs. Churchill: one old, one young; one rich, one poor. We can see that Emma's cast of mind has been broadened. No longer preoccupied just with her own plans and social superiority, she ponders the unfairness of class-based situations and considers how someone else, Jane, must feel about the world. With this new perspective, Emma seems a better, more insightful person: ". . . the remembrance of all her former fanciful and unfair conjectures was so little pleasing, that she soon allowed herself to believe her visit had been long enough." Such thoughts continue as she walks home in "pensive meditation" (302).

Now that Emma has grown in moral maturity, the reader is likely to feel that a union with Mr. Knightley is appropriate. But we may share with Emma the worry that he will remain disapproving. Austen conveys his forgiveness beautifully by the briefest means. When Emma comes home from her visit to Miss Bates, she finds Knightley there but on the brink of departing for London. Her father inadvertently saves the day by praising her for going to visit Miss and Mrs. Bates. As Knightley looks at her, seeing her "heightened colour" (303), he realizes the truth, that she has gone to make amends: "and all that had passed of good in her feelings were at once caught and honoured" (303). He takes her hand (or was it Emma who offered it?) with a meaningful look (and even the intention of kissing it?).

Emma now wishes that she had been a better friend to Jane, but not surprisingly, her advances are rebuffed. Emma is saddened by this: "it mortified her that she was given so little credit for proper feeling . . . or esteemed so little worthy as a friend" (308). Still, when she considers how Knightley would view things—if he saw into her heart and her true motives, Mr. Knightley "would not, on this occasion, have found any thing to reprove" (308). Notice how, here, Knightley's judgment represents an objective standard by which she measures what is right and wrong in her feelings and actions.

With this altered perception, Emma realizes how much Knightley really matters to her. She worries that his affections might be directed toward Harriet, and suddenly realizes that *she* is the one who should marry Knightley! Once again, Emma has reason to regret her role in building Harriet up to a point at which the young woman could even dream of a union with Knightley. Austen writes that Emma is "ashamed of every sensation but the one revealed to her—her affection for Mr. Knightley" (324). Her self-scrutiny is scathingly honest:

> With insufferable vanity had she believed herself in the secret of every body's feelings; with unpardonable arrogance proposed to arrange every body's destiny. She was proved to have been universally mistaken; and she had not quite done nothing—for she had done mischief. She had brought evil on Harriet, on herself, and she too much feared, on Mr. Knightley. (324)

Emma's maturity is indicated in a subtle passage in which she reflects on the dim prospects awaiting her in future winters if Harriet marries Knightley. There will be no more gaiety if she loses his company, at the same time losing that of the Westons to understandable absorption in their new baby. Sighing, she can only draw comfort from "the resolution of her own better conduct," which will find her "more rational, more acquainted with herself, and leave her less to regret" (332). Emma shares this newfound wisdom, along with her increased capacity for self-criticism, at the first opportunity she has to speak alone with Mr. Knightley after his return from London. They converse about the impending nuptials between Frank Churchill and Jane Fairfax, with Emma admitting "I have not forgotten that you once tried to give me a caution... but... I seem to have been doomed to blindness" (334). Knightley is more than gallant in his response, speaking of her "own excellent sense" (334) and promising that she will recover from what he interprets as her illusions about Frank. Emma hastens to correct him by explaining that her shame stems from actions "that may well lay me open to unpleasant conjectures" (334). Several pages later, Knightley finally speaks to her the words of love she feared were not coming, and Emma is overwhelmed with happiness; "this one half hour had given to each the same precious certainty of being beloved" (339).

VIII. AUSTEN AND ARISTOTLE ON LEARNING VIRTUE: CONCLUSIONS

I hope to have shown, then, that Emma does learn moral virtue. Often she learns in a direct way, by feeling shame and great pain at her mistakes. But she also learns more indirectly and truly internalizes moral virtue: she comes to feel pleasure at changing and behaving better. Austen's account of Emma's progress does not seem to settle on either pleasure or pain as the determining factor in her improvement. In some of the many cases of mistakes that cause Emma's shame, she regrets not living up to expectations, especially Knightley's. But often she feels the direct pain of remorse at hurting someone, whether Harriet, Jane Fairfax, or Miss Bates. This indicates not just concern about her pride but genuine respect for others. Emma is also smart and honest enough to realize that someone, usually Mr. Knightley, has been closer to the mark than she has. So she learns that other people, typically her elders, are capable of finer and better perceptions (at least at times) than she has been.

Virtue in *Emma*, as in Aristotle's ethics, requires a combination of feelings, perceptions, and actions. This is clearest in the crucial example of what Emma does after being ashamed to the core about her treatment of Miss Bates at the picnic. Knightley's scolding causes Emma to have many *feelings*. She is agitated and mortified, wondering how she could possibly have been so "cruel" and "brutal" to poor Miss Bates. She *perceives* the rightness of Knightley's criticism and cringes at how she hurt Miss Bates, mainly from a kind of pride in cleverness and verbal dexterity. Emma's terrible shame about the incident is not simply (though it is partly) a matter of how Knightley is judging her—she is truly sorry she hurt the poor older woman. And very quickly she *acts* to make amends, by going to visit Miss Bates the next morning.

Since Mr. Knightley is the seeming voice of Jane Austen on many occasions of Emma's enlightenment, we should take seriously what he says to Emma when she confesses her shortcomings and gratitude to him for the things he has taught her. Driven by remorse, she maintains that she has no sense of her own: "But I had the assistance of all your endeavours to counteract the indulgence of other people. I doubt whether my own sense would have corrected me without it." But Knightley says otherwise, and what he says confirms his wisdom in loving her. He remarks, "Nature gave you understanding:—Miss Taylor gave you principles. You must have done well." Knightley's love carries him away, though, into denying he has done her any good. Emma hastens to correct him: "I am sure you were of use to me," cried Emma. "I was very often influenced rightly by you—oftener than I would own at the time. I am very sure you did me good" (363).

Note that Knightley grounds his expectations of Emma on two things: her natural understanding and the principles taught her by Mrs. Weston. The understanding he refers to is probably her natural attraction to what is right and noble and her concern for others, shown especially by care for her father. But Knightley also mentions "principles." This echoes the account of virtue in Aristotle. Remember that for him, the best young people, those whom Aristotle called the "generous-minded," begin with a noble nature, being attracted to what is right. Added to this, an education about principles forms the guide to virtuous actions. Noble youths feel shame when they violate principles, and this is how they can learn virtue. For example, when Emma violated the principle of being generous to those of lesser social position by cruelly teasing Miss Bates, and Knightley reminded her of the relevant principle, Emma's natural feelings led her to agree with him, to feel shame, and to resolve to make amends.

Where, then, does the account of Emma's progress fit within the alternative descriptions of moral growth in Aristotle that I described earlier? Is virtue a matter of learning to love good actions for their own sake, and hence driven by appropriate *pleasures*? Or is it instead learning not to do things that will evoke *pain* (prospective or retrospective)? I am not sure Austen would see the alternatives so sharply.[17] In *Emma* our heroine lacks some of the requisite aspects of virtue, but she gradually acquires them over the course of the story and improves into something close to full virtue. Moments of shame are crucial to her progress, and so pain is important. But each time Emma feels shame, she reflects on what she has done wrong and why it was wrong. She learns after the Harriet–Elton fiasco that toying with others by trying to arrange their lives is wrong. In her shame over her poor treatment of Jane, she realizes that more mature, less self-centered people have clearer perceptions of the truth. And in her "pensive meditations" about wronging Miss Bates, she remembers what she should have known before: a moment's pleasure in the exercise of her wit should not outweigh duties owed to people with fewer resources than her own. It is cruel to hurt people who have always loved and respected her. In other words, shame operates not simply like an electric shock teaching an animal to avoid something. If internalized through reflection in a generous-minded young person, like our Emma, it helps teach her that being virtuous and acting nobly offer the more pleasant and worthwhile course in life. Virtue is the right thing to do for its own sake—not simply to uphold a reputation before others.

A final note: Feminists have criticized Aristotle for his view that women are less rational than men and hence require moral guidance

17. Jimenez argues that there are two important ways in which pleasure functions to enable young people to learn virtue: by confirming that what they have done, if virtuous, is correct, and by encouraging them to perform virtuous actions. But she does not spend much time on the role of shame, and so it is difficult to comment further on how Jimenez's interpretation of Aristotle compares with my construal of Austen's view here.

from fathers and, ideally, husbands.[18] A modern reader might worry similarly about Emma's indebtedness to Mr. Knightley. Given the age difference between these two and Knightley's self-designated role as Emma's moral educator, Austen might be endorsing this kind of sexist attitude. But I think we need not infer from this case to a more general principle. Austen makes it clear that Knightley has stepped in out of concern for Emma because he sees a gap in her upbringing. Her father is a hypochondriac of weak character, and her governess has a little bit too much affection, coupled with too little power, to control the headstrong girl. Remember Knightley's comment that, had her mother lived, Emma would have been reined in properly. It is not his gender, but rather his character and the situation that determine the role he will play for Emma. (John Knightley does not similarly appear to be Isabella's moral tutor, as Austen portrays them as weaker versions of their siblings in insight and, presumably, overall virtue.)

The world of Austen's novels is one with very distinct social classes and correlative gendered divisions of labor, and in this respect it does have parallels to the Athens that formed the background for Aristotle's ethical theory. Privileged women would take care of the household and domestic realm, while men handled business, property, and worldly activities. Although we may consider ourselves superior in having achieved or valuing more equality, we should remember, too, that for both Aristotle and Austen the family and household are very significant spheres. These realms facilitate the development and exercise of a myriad of specific virtues: friendship and love, filial duty, generosity, truthfulness and wittiness, and

---

18. For discussion, see Martha C. Nussbaum, "Aristotle, Feminism, and Needs for Functioning," in *Feminist Interpretations of Aristotle*, ed. Cynthia Freeland (University Park: Penn State Press, 1998), 248–259.

justice.[19] Even if the sphere of activity may to us seem restricted, we can still appreciate the effort that it takes a young person like Emma to master it, and can find in her growth admirable lessons for our own cases in wider spheres, where we still place great value on accurate perceptions, kindness to others, honest self-awareness, and devotion to principles of virtue.

REFERENCES

Aristotle. *Nicomachean Ethics*, translated by W. D. Ross, revised by J. O. Urmson, in *The Complete Works of Aristotle*, edited by Jonathan Barnes. Princeton, NJ: Princeton University Press, 1984.

Burnyeat, Myles. "Aristotle on Learning to Be Good." In *Essays on Aristotle's Ethics*, edited by Amélie Oksenberg Rorty, 69–92. Berkeley and Los Angeles: University of California Press, 1980.

Cooper, John M. *Reason and Emotion: Essays on Ancient Moral Psychology and Ethical Theory*. Princeton, NJ: Princeton University Press, 1998.

Curzer, Howard J. "Aristotle's Painful Path to Virtue." *Journal of the History of Philosophy* 40, no. 2 (2002): 141–162.

Jimenez, Marta. "Steering the Young by Pleasure and Pain." *The Journal of Speculative Philosophy* 29, no. 2 (2015): 137–164.

Nussbaum, Martha C. "Aristotle, Feminism, and Needs for Functioning." In *Feminist Interpretations of Aristotle*, edited by Cynthia Freeland, 248–259. University Park: Penn State Press, 1998.

19. For more on the importance and development of these virtues, see John M. Cooper's discussions of Aristotle on friendship in Chapters 14–16 of *Reason and Emotion: Essays on Ancient Moral Psychology and Ethical Theory* (Princeton, NJ: Princeton University Press, 1998).

Chapter 3

Emma and Defective Action

EILEEN JOHN

What can we learn about defective action from *Emma*? This question was raised for me by the following hypothetical example, in which Christine Korsgaard alludes to "the persuadable Harriet Smith in Jane Austen's novel *Emma*":

> Imagine a person I'll call Harriet, who is, in almost any formal sense you like, an autonomous person. She has a human mind, she is self-conscious, with the normal allotment of the powers of reflection. She is not a slave or an indentured servant, and we will place her—unlike the original after whom I am modelling her—in a well-ordered modern constitutional democracy, with the full rights of free citizenship and all of her human rights legally guaranteed to her. In every formal legal and psychological sense we can think of, what Harriet does is *up to her*. Yet whenever she has to make any of the important decisions and choices of her life, the way that Harriet does that is to try to figure out what Emma thinks she should do, and then that's what she does.
>
> This is autonomous action and yet it is defective as autonomous action. Harriet is self-governed and yet she is not, for

she allows herself to be governed by Emma. Harriet is heteronomous, not in the sense that her actions are caused by Emma
rather than chosen by herself, but in the sense that she allows
herself to be governed in her choices by a law outside of herself—
by Emma's will.[1]

On this account, Harriet's willing surrender to the governance
offered by Emma makes Harriet's actions heteronomous and defective as action.

In some respects, this appeal to *Emma* makes perfect sense.
Austen's Harriet explicitly turns to Emma for advice and lets herself be guided by Emma to nearly disastrous effect, several times
over. During their excruciating conversations about Harriet's suitor
Robert Martin, Harriet assures Emma that "'I do not mean to set up
my opinion against your's'" (25) and eventually pleads for Emma's
guidance: "'What shall I do? What would you advise me to do?
Pray, dear Miss Woodhouse, tell me what I ought to do?'" (41–42).[2]
Harriet's attempts to speak from her own experience of Martin and
to defend him against Emma's ill-informed objections are feeble. But
encountering Korsgaard's example made me pause because it leaves
unmentioned what seems to be the more central question of the
novel: What is wrong with Emma's action? It is Emma who receives
Mr. Knightley's blistering rebuke at Box Hill: "'It was badly done,
indeed!'" (295). Korsgaard is not trying to do justice to the novel,
so thinking about Emma is not her burden. But I want to consider
what makes Emma's actions problematic, initially with Korsgaard's
ideas in mind. It is not obvious that Emma's problems as an agent can
be understood as a failure of autonomy. The novel is philosophically

1. Christine Korsgaard, *Self-Constitution* (Oxford: Oxford University Press, 2009), 162.
2. All examples from Jane Austen's *Emma* will be derived from the Oxford World Classics
   edition of the novel: Jane Austen, *Emma*, ed. James Kinsley (Oxford: Oxford University
   Press, 2008).

challenging in part because of the complex way in which it does not promote autonomous action as an ideal. Ryle suggests *Influence and Interference* as an alternate title for *Emma*, taking the novel to pose the question, "What makes it sometimes legitimate or even obligatory for one person deliberately to try to modify the course of another person's life, while sometimes such attempts are wrong?"[3] Perhaps defective action cannot in general be the result of being, and letting oneself be, influenced, because that is so basic to human social contact. Can we diagnose the defects of action in another way?

As a preliminary point, the term "defective action" can be used in two ways. It can be used to refer to things that fall short of being action or that count as action only to a degree—the status as action is what is in question. Or it can refer to actions that are indeed actions but are problematic by some standard applicable to actions. These issues can converge, if you think that actions lose, perhaps by degrees, their "action-status" when what is done is wrong or bad.[4] As I will sketch briefly in the following, Korsgaard has a view of this kind. One can also keep these issues separate, allowing that someone can act fully but badly. Although this discussion will not offer a deep enough exploration of how to situate Austen on this question, I will read *Emma* as leaving room for acting fully but badly. It seems likely that Austen would agree with Korsgaard that there is an ideal of action that combines the goodness of what is done with the agent's independent agency, and that conception of action can be understood within the space of her fiction. But I think this ideal is ultimately sidelined, as not

3. Gilbert Ryle, "Jane Austen and the Moralists," *The Linacre Journal* 3 (1999) 3: 85–99, at 89. He there notes the presence of these terms in a conversation between Emma and Knightley (363).

4. See Bernard Williams for the idea that categories of defective action, such as *akrasia*, can shift in their point from identifying defective control of behavior to ethical evaluation. Bernard Williams, "Voluntary Acts and Responsible Agents," *Oxford Journal of Legal Studies* 10, no. 1 (1990): 1–10, p. 3.

staking out the most relevant or perspicuous ideal for understanding the conditions and achievements of agents in her fiction.[5] I think a distinction that Bernard Williams makes between responsibility for action and an "ideal of maturity," involving "responsibility for self," is more apt in relation to Austen.[6] It is more illuminating to look for failures of maturity than autonomy, in understanding the defects of Emma's and others' actions.

Let me begin with some of Emma's low points as an agent. I have sought out passages that make me cringe, recoil, or feel anticipatory dread. Here Emma's thoughts about her plans for Harriet are articulated:

> Encouragement should be given. Those soft blue eyes and all those natural graces should not be wasted on the inferior society of Highbury and its connections. The acquaintance she had already formed were unworthy of her. The friends from whom she had just parted, though very good sort of people, must be doing her harm. . . . they must be coarse and unpolished, and very unfit to be the intimates of a girl who wanted only a little more knowledge and elegance to be quite perfect. *She* would notice her; she would improve her; she would detach her from her bad acquaintance, and introduce her into good society; she would form her opinions and her manners. It would be an interesting, and certainly a very kind undertaking; highly becoming her own situation in life, her leisure, and powers. (19–20)

---

5. See E. M. Dadlez's defense of Anne Elliot's rejection of Wentworth in *Persuasion*, even though Anne both defers to another's judgment and does the wrong thing. Dadlez, *Mirrors to One Another: Emotion and Value in Jane Austen and David Hume* (Malden, MA: Wiley-Blackwell, 2009), 154–156.

6. Williams, "Voluntary Acts and Responsible Agents," 7–8.

Not too long after, having gotten Harriet to dismiss the perfectly suited Robert Martin, Emma leads Harriet to expect a marriage proposal from Mr. Elton. She lays out the advantages of this future.

> "This is an attachment which a woman may well feel pride in creating. . . . It will give you every thing that you want— consideration, independence, a proper home—it will fix you in the centre of all your real friends, close to Hartfield and to me, and confirm our intimacy for ever. This, Harriet, is an alliance which can never raise a blush in either of us."
>
> "Dear Miss Woodhouse" – and "Dear Miss Woodhouse," was all that Harriet, with many tender embraces could articulate at first; but when they did arrive at something more like conversation, it was sufficiently clear to her friend that she saw, felt, anticipated, and remembered just as she ought. Mr. Elton's superiority had very ample acknowledgment.
>
> "Whatever you say is always right," cried Harriet, "and therefore I suppose, and believe, and hope it must be so; but otherwise I could not have imagined it." (60)

Austen sets up Emma's eventual humiliation over the Mr. Elton scheme with awful sharpness, as Emma blithely ignores her brother-in-law's word of caution (to the effect that Elton is courting Emma): "she walked on, amusing herself in the consideration of the blunders which often arise from a partial knowledge of circumstances, of the mistakes which people of high pretensions to judgment are for ever falling into" (89). Maybe there is some amusement to be had in Emma exposing her own pretensions, but it is hard to keep a safely amused distance when the blunder she perpetrates is so destructive and reckless.

Korsgaard could draw on these passages for reinforcement, as Harriet inarticulately defers to Emma's construal of her situation and acts on Emma's judgment. But for the moment consider what is going wrong with Emma. Assuming my reactions are rather typical, why is Emma's conduct such as to make a reader recoil? As far as whether she is doing something bad or wrong, a cascade of interlocking criticisms come to mind. Emma judges and dismisses people without knowing them. She pretends to give Harriet a chance to speak her mind, without genuinely expecting Harriet to have consequential views and desires. She does not give Harriet a chance to weigh in on *Harriet's* important life prospects. She turns Harriet's important life prospects into a chance to show her own kindness, talents, and power. She affirms that the friendship will last forever, on the shallow basis of securing a socially acceptable position for Harriet. Emma's attempts to manage Harriet's love life are a fertile field for criticism of their moral and prudential defects.

More generally, it seems straightforward to say that, whatever is going wrong, it is not that Emma fails to act as such, in Korsgaard's terms. Unlike Harriet, Emma revels in independent reflection, planning, and strategic action in her social world. She appears to act with striking autonomy, forming an ambitious plan, pursuing values she explicitly embraces, and not deferring to others' judgments, not even to Knightley's vehement objections. She and Harriet seem to be, at least for narrative and philosophical purposes, a well-matched pair who exemplify opposing tendencies as agents.

Perhaps we could say, however, that there is an autonomy problem here, in the way Emma fails to grasp the relations between one's own actions and another's potential for action. Is Emma's action defective because she does not acknowledge or facilitate Harriet's autonomy? Does genuine autonomy require, for consistency, acting with respect for others' autonomy? In a Kantian spirit, let every rational being propose her own ends! Emma fails to let Harriet be whatever Harriet wants and decides to be. The novel addresses this general issue in a very interesting way, but I will just note here some of the complications in this case. Harriet herself seems to be excessively limited in her capacities for independent critical judgment and decision-making, and if that is what she brings to the table, it is not clear that Harriet is wrong in turning to Emma for advice. Harriet can tell that Emma has greater intelligence, somewhat wider experience, and more social privilege. It seems not unreasonable to expect Emma to have better judgment. Harriet's docility further seems to enable some of her friend's defective actions, in that what Emma injects into the friendship does not receive proper resistance and scrutiny, like hitting a tennis ball into a pillow. Emma's efforts are tremendously misguided, but the precise diagnosis of the problem does not seem to be that Harriet should be left to judge matters for herself; the novel does not seem to hold out hope that Harriet will ever be especially "good at autonomy." In the end, it is not so obvious how Emma can be a good friend to Harriet, with such an imbalance of strengths.

The novel counters the principle of respecting others' autonomy perhaps most obviously in Emma's treatment of her father. Emma persistently deflects or thwarts her father's stifling worries about health and life beyond Hartfield, and this is arguably her only form of consistently constructive action. She is disciplined and ingenious about how to prevent his concerns from spoiling familial relations and social occasions. After Emma's most bleak episode of self-scourging reflection, she nonetheless spends the evening keeping him company: "he could only be kept tolerably comfortable by almost ceaseless attention on his daughter's side, and by exertions which had never cost her half so much before" (331). Poirier calls another such intervention on Emma's part "a heroic effort."[7] The novel will not serve straightforwardly to champion mutual respect for

---

7. Richard Poirier, *A World Elsewhere: The Place of Style in American Literature* (London: Chatto and Windus, 1967), 157.

autonomy; the capacities and limitations of one's companions must be taken into account.

Returning to Emma's claim to autonomy, Korsgaard in fact has a more complex, demanding view that would allow her to find defects in Emma's supposed autonomy. Drawing on Plato and Kant, Korsgaard argues that in acting autonomously, a person is fully unified, acting on a principle that is "for the good of the soul as a whole." Meanwhile "bad action is action governed by a principle of choice which is not reason's own."[8] Bad action issues from the impact of fragmented rivals for control of the person. If acting on "reason's own principle" means, for instance, that the categorical imperative is operative and reason governs the passions and appetites, and only actions so governed are fully owned by the agent, then we have plenty of ammunition for disputing the autonomy of Emma's behavior.[9] As was evident earlier, her operative principles and motivations are simply not defensible by such strong standards. However, it would be odd if we could dissolve the difference between Emma and Harriet as agents by showing that Emma makes moral mistakes and so fails to act as such. Perhaps we would even have to say that Harriet is a *more* successful agent because she does less that is wrong. It seems that Korsgaard too would want to maintain an interesting contrast between Emma and Harriet and would be unlikely to say that Harriet acts *less* defectively than Emma. Emma's activity seems at least more her own, less vulnerable to the charge of heteronomy than Harriet's. Trying to understand the contrast between Harriet and Emma reveals a tension between prioritizing independent governance and prioritizing doing the right thing.

8. Korsgaard, *Self-Constitution*, 175.
9. With support from Plato and Kant, "that principle, the one that really unifies us, and renders us autonomous, is also the principle of the morally good person" (Korsgaard, *Self-Constitution*, 176). "[A]gents must act justly and on the categorical imperative, if they are to act at all" (Korsgaard, *Self-Constitution*, 158).

So far I have taken something that is narratively and humanly crystal clear—the contrast between Harriet and Emma—and have suggested that it looks less clear if we approach it with a certain conception of action in mind. Austen more generally does not seem to embrace a conception of agency that requires unifying the agent around a moral principle. Austen is interested, I think, in something less restrictive and more open to what counts as agency from the perspective of the agent. Her characters reflect on their situations and act for what they take to be reasons, but those reasons encompass the range of concerns and self-oriented or radically local "principles" that matter to happiness-seeking, limited, prejudiced, passionate, socially constrained people.[10] Even if falling away from the categorical imperative or another ideal of impartial reason is indeed relevant to the meaning of her characters' actions, I think Austen would want to preserve the action-status of behavior, marked by thinking that one knows what one is doing and why. I take a character such as Frank Churchill to be an exemplar of agency within *Emma*, planning for his future and maneuvering deftly within his social context, but certainly not embodying universalizable rational principles. As a novelist, aiming to absorb her readers in an imagined social world, it seems Austen has reason to embrace a conception of action that lets characters such as Churchill, Mr. Elton, and Emma be agents responsible for crucial wrong moves. If we tie responsibility to agency, and agency lessens as we depart from moral and rational requirements, it becomes less obvious how to assign responsibility for wrongdoing (the wrongdoer is not fully *acting*). That aspiration—to present human figures as not responsible or decreasingly so, the worse they behave—*could* drive a

---

10. See Dadlez on Austen's work not exemplifying central tenets of Kantian moral theory: "There is too much in Austen that resists the kind of estrangement of choosing from desiring, or of choice from emotion, on which the Kantian distinction [between duty and happiness] depends" (Dadlez, *Mirrors to One Another*, 37–46, quoted at 46).

work of fiction, but it seems clear it is not Austen's aspiration. The defining crises and transformations in the novel, which emerge as painful and thrilling within the sedate confines of the plot, turn primarily on the character Emma's assessment of her responsibilities. "The first error and the worst lay at her door" (108). So there is a literary-artistic reason for Austen not to make agency and responsibility too hard to come by. But it seems further that the ideal of autonomous, rationally principled action just is not the ideal that Austen finds relevant to her portrayal of human social life. .

Some of the novel's suggestions about action and its potential defects and merits show up in conversations between the characters. Here is Mr. Knightley responding early on to Emma's boast about her matchmaking success with Miss Taylor and Mr. Weston.

> "I do not understand what you mean by 'success;' said Mr. Knightley. "Success supposes endeavour. . . . But if, which I rather imagine, your making the match, as you call it, means only your planning it, your saying to yourself one idle day, 'I think it would be a very good thing for Miss Taylor if Mr. Weston were to marry her,' and saying it again to yourself every now and then afterwards,—why do you talk of success? where is your merit?—what are you proud of?—you made a lucky guess; and *that* is all that can be said." (11)

He further notes that in this case, there was no need to do anything:

> "A straight-forward, open-hearted man, like Weston, and a rational unaffected woman, like Miss Taylor, may be safely left to manage their own concerns. You are more likely to have done harm to yourself, than good to them, by interference." (11–12)

We might take this as the "deliberately doing nothing" model of successful social agency. You may have a promising idea about what would improve your social world, but if the change involves other people, you should simply wait and see if it happens. Emma takes Mr. Knightley to be oversimplifying the kinds of endeavor that are called for: "You have drawn two pretty pictures—but I think there may be a third—a something between the do-nothing and the do-all," and she cites the importance of little encouragements and easings of social opportunities (11). But later, after her painful awakening to Mr. Elton's hopes, Emma seems to endorse the do-nothing model:

> It was foolish, it was wrong, to take so active a part in bringing any two people together. It was adventuring too far, assuming too much, making light of what ought to be serious, a trick of what ought to be simple. She was quite concerned and ashamed, and resolved to do such things no more. (108)

Emma, of course, qualifies this immediately, insisting to herself that she was "quite right" to persuade Harriet to reject Robert Martin: "That was well done of me; but there I should have stopped, and left the rest to time and chance. . . . I have been but half a friend to her" (109). The do-nothing model, at least with respect to others' decisions and future prospects, might cohere well with concern for others' autonomy: do nothing because if you intervene you will not respect others' autonomous status within their own lives. However, as briefly suggested earlier in relation to Emma and her father, this does not seem to be a deep commitment of the novel. Mr. Knightley notes the qualities of Miss Taylor and Mr. Weston that show why they can be "safely left to manage their own concerns"; this leaves it open that others do not have relevantly "safe" qualities. In the novel overall, the demands of friendship do not ultimately show up as amounting to a hands-off policy.

Before moving further beyond the do-nothing model, consider another model that sounds rather similar and is also suggested in conversation between Mr. Knightley and Emma. When Emma complains somewhat playfully that in their disagreements she is always wrong, Mr. Knightley explains this in terms of his having lived longer. He grants that her twenty-one years have brought her nearer, but notes, "'I have still the advantage of you by sixteen years' experience, and by not being a pretty young woman and a spoiled child'" (79). Knightley introduces complications (the looks, gender, and upbringing that Emma could not choose), but his central claim is that Emma will judge and act well once enough time has passed. Long-term patience with respect to the adequacy of one's own judgment is urged. This is not equivalent to the do-nothing model in that it in no way rules out that the experience that eventually generates good action includes actively trying and failing to act well. In one sense, a person has to wait passively for experience over time to do its work, but it seems plausible that a good deal of ill-guided, socially influential action would contribute to that process. As an answer to the question of what counts as good or defective action, this is not immediately helpful. It is a sort of procedural account: let life nudge, pummel, and polish people for a long time and they will eventually act well or at least better. As a descriptive generalization, it is probably not true in the world of this novel, as characters such as the Eltons and Mr. Woodhouse seem either not to improve or to worsen over time. But it is not a model that is obviously repudiated by the novel. It seems more like a general principle with many variables that make its application a subtle matter. The long-term pressures under which people develop, such as the insecurities of one's class background or, as Emma notes about Frank Churchill, conditions of material and social dependence, might only be tempered after very long, and somewhat lucky, experience of countering pressures.[11] This model further displaces the individual deliberate action as the locus

11. Emma defends Churchill due to his long dependence on his adoptive parents: "'You are the worst judge in the world, Mr. Knightley, of the difficulties of dependence. . . . where

of concern. I may know what I am doing and why right now; I am also contributing to long-term trends I may only occasionally notice and understand.

While I am persuaded that *Emma* loosely endorses this wisdom of Mr. Knightley,[12] and offers a very long temporal frame for assessing the discrete decisions and actions of agents at a given time (mistakes now often producing a better agent later), the novel is still intensely interested in assessing those discrete activities in their temporal moment. Even if the novelist and reader have the luxury of waiting for the fruits of experience to unfold, the novel nonetheless aims to be illuminating about the steps that characters take along the way, helping us grasp what makes them promote or impede maturity.

On the more temporally located do-nothing/do-something alternatives, while the novel strongly promotes the value of caution in one's other-directed action, it makes the do-nothing model itself seem like an immature fantasy. Maybe, if we could point to a perfect record of not having intervened in others' choices and actions, we could pat ourselves on the back for not having harmed anyone. But it is hard to imagine such a record amounting to a human life, on Austen's conception of human life. Social contact is constantly influential, and her characters are constantly tested by this contact, as small and large choices ripple through conversations, visits, meals, friendships, marriages, and neighborly relations.[13] There are junctures

little minds belong to rich people in authority, I think they have a knack of swelling out, till they are quite as unmanageable as great ones. . . . you would have no habits of early obedience and long observance to break through. To him who has, it might not be so easy to burst forth at once into perfect independence, and set all their claims on his gratitude and regard at nought'" (115–116).

12. Knightley's prediction for the Westons' newborn daughter is that "'[s]he will be disagreeable in infancy, and correct herself as she grows older'" (363).

13. See W. J. Harvey on *Emma*: "One of the powers we do not understand is the incredibly complex pressure put upon us by the actions and interests, dreams and desires—the mere existence, even—of our contiguous or remote fellow human beings." Harvey, "The Plot of *Emma*," *Essays in Criticism* 17 (1967): 48–63, at 56–57.

when characters deliberately "do nothing," as when, toward the end, Emma and Harriet make sure they do *not* talk (341–342). But assuming that avoiding impact and influence is not a realistic option, the novel is specifically astute about action within the constraints of that assumption.

One point that is interestingly pressed is that, within such socially attuned action, intending to do well by others is insufficient. The unassailably good Miss Taylor had been to Emma

> a friend and companion such as few possessed, intelligent, well-informed, useful, gentle, knowing all the ways of the family, interested in all its concerns, and peculiarly interested in herself, in every pleasure, every scheme of her's;—one to whom she could speak every thought as it arose, and who had such an affection for her as could never find fault. (6)

The value of this friendship, and the true affection and goodwill shared by the friends, are great and uncontested. Nonetheless, Mr. Knightley baldly criticizes the now-married Mrs. Weston for having been a poor governess to Emma, as *Miss Taylor* learned to submit to Emma's will (30). Miss Taylor, in her affection for Emma, did not intervene critically but acquiesced to Emma's whims and schemes. Even Isabella, Emma's innocuous, warm-hearted sister, is said to have a partially negative influence on her husband, as she does not intervene to curb his mild ill-temper: "indeed, with such a worshipping wife, it was hardly possible that any natural defects in [his disposition] should not be increased. The extreme sweetness of her temper must hurt his" (74). Mrs. Weston and Isabella, though attentively immersed in their social relationships and aiming only to do well by others, fail to do some of the good things they could be held responsible for. Mr. Knightley does not particularly blame Mrs. Weston for her defects as a governess, since he takes education, critique, and .

guidance of Emma to be very difficult, and she was simply not the right person for the job—he thinks it would take a person with specific powers to have an impact on Emma.[14]

Ryle adds, to goodwill, the condition that acceptable, socially intervening action, as portrayed in Austen but also in life, be transparent and aboveboard.

> Where is the line between Meddling and Helping? Or, more generally, between proper and improper solicitude and unsolicitude about the destinies and welfares of others? Why was Emma wrong to try to arrange Harriet's life, when Mr. Knightley was right to try to improve Emma's mind and character? Jane Austen's answer is the right answer. Emma was treating Harriet as a puppet to be worked by hidden strings. Mr. Knightley advised and scolded Emma to her face. Emma knew what Mr. Knightley required of and hoped for her. Harriet was not to know what Emma was scheming on her behalf. Mr. Knightley dealt with Emma as a potentially responsible and rational being. Emma dealt with Harriet as a doll. Proper solicitude is open and not secret.... [Frank Churchill] is not wicked, but he is not aboveboard, so many of his actions affecting others belong to the class of interference, and not of legitimate intervention.[15]

Here Ryle is concerned with the demands of behaving in a morally solicitous way; I am working with a broader category of action that includes prudential, not morally anchored action that nonetheless

---

14. " 'In her mother she lost the only person able to cope with her. She inherits her mother's talents, and must have been under subjection to her' " (30). Valerie Wainwright discusses personality types and their impact on action, including wrongdoing, in Austen: Wainwright, "Jane Austen's Challenges, or the Powers of Character and the Understanding," *Philosophy and Literature* 38, no. 1 (2014): 58–73.

15. Ryle, "Jane Austen and the Moralists," 89–90.

takes influence on others into account. But even in the model of Mr. Knightley, who does fairly well in combining the moral and the prudential, this account oversimplifies what the novel suggests. As in some passages quoted earlier, Emma is at times distastefully explicit to Harriet about what she is planning and why. " 'The misfortune of your birth ought to make you particularly careful as to your associates. . . . I want to see you permanently well connected' " (25). Meanwhile, Mr. Knightley takes a very long time to be transparent to Emma about what he wants for her and from her. It is suggested that he was slow to be clear to himself about this, but he knows well enough by the time of the novel's central action (340). Other behind-the-scenes efforts include Robert Martin consulting Knightley about marriage to Harriet, and Knightley's misunderstood attentions to Harriet, as he is of course not explicit to *her* about observing her for Martin's sake (373). Built into the very scene of mutual revelation of love between Emma and Knightley is Emma's tremendous relief at having concealed Harriet's stake in the situation. "Seldom, very seldom, does complete truth belong to any human disclosure" (339). Back to more mundane activities, Knightley is Emma's best ally in maintaining her father's congeniality, both disguising their intentions and strategies in doing so. Mr. Woodhouse is indeed treated more like a child than a potentially responsible and rational adult.

Hidden strings are thus pulled fairly regularly without appearing worthy of criticism, either prudentially or morally. This is not to say that being aboveboard and direct in one's dealings with others is not valued within *Emma*. Both characters and readers appreciate the occasions on which characters speak their minds and act clearly. But transparency to others is not always right, and not always socially or psychologically viable, as we see in Jane Fairfax's predicament. Transparency may need to be prepared for slowly, including some false pretenses and omissions, as seems appropriate in Knightley's gradually transforming friendship with Emma.

What does seem necessary and crucially valuable to an Austen-style ideal of agency is the effort to be transparent to oneself. Many commentators note that Emma, unwillingly, is on a journey toward self-knowledge.[16] She begins by assuming she already knows herself well, and the novel proceeds to assault this arrogant assumption. This progress chimes well with philosophical accounts of agency that emphasize relations between self-understanding and responsibility. Bernard Williams, drawing on ideas of Charles Taylor and Harry Frankfurt, is concerned to distinguish what he calls an ideal of "deliberative control" from an "ideal of maturity," where the latter notion calls for deeper self-understanding. The agent with deliberative control merely acts deliberately on a desire. This is a form of self-transparency, and Williams presents this notion as useful to us in various contexts, such as the law when we assign responsibility for actions. In these contexts we want each other to be "adult, non-defective" persons who are able to control their actions and respond to "public requirements."[17] The ideal of maturity, in Williams's account, brings in further aspirations that are not (normally) relevant to public life: "The maturity or self-understanding of the well-formed agent never attains a necessary claim on the attention of the public."[18] I think the notion of maturity is a good one to associate

16. "Emma's most radical failure" is "her lack of self-knowledge" (Harvey, 1967, 52). "She is deficient both in generosity and self-knowledge" according to Wayne Booth in *The Rhetoric of Fiction*, 2nd ed. (London; Chicago: University of Chicago Press, 1983), 244. "All through the novel she has sought better acquaintance with herself," says Lionel Trilling, "*Emma* and the Legend of Jane Austen," in *Jane Austen: Emma*, edited by David Lodge (London: MacMillan, 1968), 148–169, at 160.
17. Williams (1990), 5–9, phrases quoted from 9.
18. Williams (1990), 10. Williams deals with issues relevant to this discussion in *Shame and Necessity*, but with a distinct argumentative agenda considering ancient Greek agency; I note the following passage as suggestive for Austen's characters: "the necessity that Ajax recognised, was grounded in his own identity, his sense of himself as someone who can live in some social circumstances and not others." Bernard Williams, *Shame and Necessity* (Berkeley: University of California Press, 1993), 101.

with Austen, with some qualifications. Alan Goldman, focusing on *Pride and Prejudice*, makes the project of moral maturity, including self-knowledge, central to that novel: "To feel and judge in the right way, one must also have an accurate self-image, a healthy sense of one's own fallibility and biases."[19] Though not trying to capture specifically moral maturity in Austen, I am following Goldman's emphasis on maturity.

Williams sums up what he means by the ideal of maturity as "responsibility for self."[20] The mature agent "tries to make sense of his or her life," and this requires having "a certain understanding of himself or herself."[21] Williams refers to Harry Frankfurt on persons' distinctive capacity for second-order desires. We can importantly identify with certain desires: "It is no longer unsettled or uncertain whether the object of that desire . . . is what he really wants. . . . the person, in making a decision by which he identifies with a desire, *constitutes himself*."[22] Charles Taylor frames the project, of taking on responsibility for the kind of desires one has and the kind of person one is, via the notion of the "strong evaluator": one who not only acts reflectively on desires but "judges the worthiness of one's desires." Motivations and desires are to be assessed "in virtue of the kind of life and kind of subject that these desires properly belong to."[23] Strong evaluation is "a struggle of self-interpretations," as the person tries to articulate

---

19. Alan Goldman, *Philosophy and the Novel* (Oxford: Oxford University Press, 2013), 110. Goldman reads *Pride and Prejudice* as showing that "such maturity comes about through interaction with ever-expanding circles of individuals considered as equals even though differing in perspectives or values" (Goldman, 115). I do not use precisely this approach, in part because *Emma* involves rather confined expansions of perspective and acknowledges certain kinds of inequality.

20. Williams, "Voluntary Acts and Responsible Agents)," 7.

21. Ibid., 6, 7.

22. Harry Frankfurt, *The Importance of What We Care About* (Cambridge: Cambridge University Press, 1998), 170.

23. Charles Taylor, *Human Agency and Language: Philosophical Papers*, Vol. 1. (Cambridge: Cambridge University Press, 1985), 18, 25.

"which is the truer, more authentic, more illusion-free interpretation, and which on the other hand involves a distortion of the meanings things have for me."[24]

Williams, Frankfurt, and Taylor develop these ideas differently, for somewhat different philosophical purposes, but all seek a notion of responsible agency that is less concerned with "deliberative control" and more concerned with having a deeper understanding of and commitment to the meanings and values embodied in one's actions. Having responsibility for what I do does not just or even necessarily mean that I act deliberately on a desire (Williams in particular emphasizing nondeliberated action[25]), but that I know what is important to me, endorse its importance, and assess my actions and their outcomes in that light. The mature agent is responsible for what she does in this broader sense: she has taken responsibility for understanding and being able to endorse the life she is leading. Defective action, then, might issue from an immature self or might reflect the fact that a mature self does not endorse the desire acted on or the meaning an action turns out to have.

This approach seems helpful in thinking about Emma. The kinds of self-knowledge she acquires commonly have this structure: she becomes clearer about what she has wanted or does want and about whether she can endorse those desires and the conception of herself they fit into. What she wanted in her matchmaking efforts with Harriet and her flirtation with Frank Churchill, and that she cannot be proud of those desires, become clear to her. That she does want to be "*first* with Mr. Knightley" is a life-changing realization that includes a larger endorsement of what her life would mean if fully allied to his

24. Ibid., 27.
25. "The mature agent . . . will recognize his relation to his acts in their undeliberated, and also in their unforeseen and unintended aspects" (Williams, "Voluntary Acts and Responsible Agents," 10).

(326). She recognizes the "precious intercourse of friendship and confidence" that she has had and the "cheerful" and "rational society" that she and Mr. Knightley can offer each other (327, 332). Her acceptance of his proposal is supported by a sense of self that has been tested and has substantially matured. My claim here is in part that Austen allows the intuitively self-governing, reflective moves made by Emma, even in her early blunders, to count as actions as such—she controls her resources in a way that suffices for her to own her actions. But they can also be defective as actions if they emerge from an immature self, whose commitments and sense of what she wants to be have not been adequately explored, tested, and affirmed.

Let me now qualify the extent to which the novel embraces precisely this ideal of maturity. The qualifications draw on the preceding discussion of the socially influential web of action. Austen's characters, even Emma in her hard-won maturity, in some ways fail to be the kind of strongly evaluating, self-interpreting, self-transparent, self-responsible agents that I have just tried to evoke. One qualification is that this account of maturity understates the importance of knowledge of others. Many of Emma's mistakes arise as much from her difficulties in understanding others and what they desire, as from misunderstanding herself. Emma's mistakes about Mr. Elton are indeed about him, as much as they are about mistaking her own investment in Harriet's future. She fails to understand what he wants and what he disguises about his own motives and values. These kinds of self- and other-focused knowledge are entwined. To know that Harriet is not cut out to be Emma's genuinely intimate friend requires knowing important things about both of them and about how they are likely to interact. This is what Mr. Knightley attempts to prove to Mrs. Weston:

> "I have not half done about Harriet Smith. I think her the very
> worst sort of companion that Emma could possibly have. She

knows nothing herself, and looks upon Emma as knowing every thing. She is a flatterer in all her ways; and so much the worse, because undesigned. Her ignorance is hourly flattery. How can Emma imagine she has anything to learn herself, while Harriet is presenting such a delightful inferiority? And as for Harriet, I will venture to say that she cannot gain by the acquaintance. Hartfield will only put her out of conceit with all the other places she belongs to. She will grow just refined enough to be uncomfortable with those among whom birth and circumstances have placed her home." (31)

Certainly the novel presses us to see not only that forming friendships requires self-knowledge, but also that it takes complex knowledge of the likely mutual influence of the two (or more) potential friends. Achieving such complex knowledge has to contend with others' misleading self-presentations, including active deception, protective concealment, and sensible omission. This qualification is not incompatible with Williams's ideal of maturity, but it does shift the focus in an interesting way. As an Austen character matures, she comes to know what others are like and hence what she could feasibly and acceptably want from her relations with them. The relevant others may or may not offer anything congenial to the desires and kind of life a given character would like to endorse.

The importance of knowing others, and the importance of others' influence on oneself, leads into a stronger kind of divergence from the ideal of maturity sketched in the preceding. First, there may be a willing deference to others' understanding of oneself. It seems that part of Emma's mature self-awareness is that she wants her life to have Mr. Knightley's constant influence. She accepts that she needs his critical judgment and willingness to contest her own. Similarly, it is hoped that Jane Fairfax will be a good influence on Frank Churchill. The achievement of Emma (and potential achievement of Frank

Churchill) is to embrace a partnership that will put steady pressure on her attempts at strong evaluation and self-interpretation. Even though Williams's ideal of maturity is intended to weaken the centrality of the individual's discrete exercises of rational control, it does not obviously weaken it in this direction, toward committing oneself to a life adapting to the influence of another.

Second, Austen highlights accommodation to others' judgment, and to the collective practices of one's social community, in the ways the characters reckon with the options available to them. An unusual conversation in which Harriet probes Emma's self-conception shows the difficult prospects for the single woman in this society. When Emma claims to be content about never marrying, Harriet—the example of Miss Bates in view—cannot help but cry out,

> "But still, you will be an old maid! And that's so dreadful!"
>
> "Never mind, Harriet, I shall not be a poor old maid; and it is poverty only which makes celibacy contemptible to a generous public! A single woman, with a very narrow income, must be a ridiculous, disagreeable, old maid! the proper sport of boys and girls; but a single woman, of good fortune, is always respectable, and may be as sensible and pleasant as anybody else." (68–69)

Emma is presumably speaking slightly for humorous effect, but the sharp, ugly point is not disguised. Emma might come up with a self-interpretation of her single future that she finds satisfactory, but she is quite clear that the acceptability of this future would turn crucially on having wealth. Jane Fairfax's ability to make sense of her life, and to form desires she can identify with wholeheartedly, hangs terribly in the balance as she waits for Frank Churchill's circumstances to change. Miss Bates is in this respect exceptional, as Emma almost sympathetically reflects, since she has not been soured by her poverty (69). Poirier takes *Emma* to have "behind it a confidence that

English society gives everyone a chance ... to find a place that can be called 'natural.'" Such a society "requires a sensitivity to 'differences,' and therefore actually protects people like Harriet from being the victim of standards they cannot meet or from being exploited in the interest of other people's fancies."[26] While I think the novel tempers this confidence substantially with the role of chance or luck, Poirier's casting of English society as a central player, ideally offering people a niche they can safely inhabit, is compelling.[27] It seems that the maturation of an agent has to accommodate these social constraints and opportunities. On this model, social expectations that one does not choose and possibly would not reflectively endorse contribute in a fairly non-negotiable way to self-interpretation and assessment of desires. Yes, acting well requires maturity, but maturity is importantly social and is not adequately accounted for as a matter of strongly evaluating one's individually, independently formed desires and self-conception.

Finally, there is a sense in which Austen lets her central character plumb some depths of self-understanding but not others, and perhaps not for very long. Emma faces clearly the rightness of her being matched with Mr. Knightley, and the wrongness of him marrying Harriet. But when Emma assesses the latter potential alliance "as most unequal and degrading" (338–339), it seems that this is a truth that should only surface briefly at a moment of crisis. That she and Mr. Knightley are importantly superior beings who belong together can be affirmed, but it also seems to need to be submerged for purposes of engaging with friends and neighbors with ease and lack of pretension. Or consider that Emma can dwell on the wonderfully cheerful,

---

26. Poirier, *A World Elsewhere*, 163.
27. Fortunately Harriet "would be placed in the midst of those who loved her, and who had better sense than herself; retired enough for safety, and occupied enough for cheerfulness. She would be never led into temptation, nor left for it to find her out. She would be respectable and happy" (379).

rational company she and Mr. Knightley provide for each other, but the significance of her bringing wealth to the match, and having a claim to equality on that score, is probably best not thought. The lower social status of Robert Martin remains a problem at the end of the novel, in the sense that Austen has exposed its unreasonableness to her readers, but Emma, while significantly reversing her view of him, does not deeply question his assigned status. She is allowed not to strongly evaluate the worth of the social ranking she implicitly accepts. Schorer comments that "the heroine comes into partial self-recognition, and at the same time sinks more completely into that society."[28] This point, that Austen lets her characters be subtle and flexible in how they manage the insights they reach in maturing, is perhaps more procedural than substantive, since it does not deny the importance of self-knowledge, self-interpretation, and strong evaluation to maturity. Nonetheless, I think Austen is cautious about the impact and role of the insights that punctuate the maturation process. Emma makes enormous progress in understanding herself and her social world; it seems that some of this understanding should slip into the unreflective background.

To sum up, *Emma* is a novel about action and its rich potential for going wrong. The ideal that is implicitly developed, especially through understanding the transformation of Emma, does not insist on autonomously governed and morally principled action. It requires knowledge of self and other, astute awareness and embrace of social influence and constraint, and a sense of self that has been tested by these factors. There is an ideal of maturity that will be realized differently within different lives (as Mrs. Weston, Emma, and Miss Bates can, arguably, all claim maturity), and it provides the needed, complex context for assessing the defects of action.

28. Mark Schorer, "The Humiliation of Emma Woodhouse," in *Jane Austen: Emma*, edited by David Lodge (London: Macmillan, 1968), 170–194, at 185.

REFERENCES

Austen, Jane. *Emma*, edited by James Kinsley. Oxford: Oxford University Press, 2008.

Booth, Wayne. *The Rhetoric of Fiction*, 2nd ed. London; Chicago: University of Chicago Press, 1983.

Dadlez, E. M. *Mirrors to One Another: Emotion and Value in Jane Austen and David Hume*. Malden, MA: Wiley-Blackwell, 2009.

Frankfurt, Harry. *The Importance of What We Care About*. Cambridge: Cambridge University Press, 1998.

Goldman, Alan. *Philosophy and the Novel*. Oxford: Oxford University Press, 2013.

Harvey, W. J. "The Plot of *Emma*." *Essays in Criticism* 17 (1967): 48–63.

Korsgaard, Christine. *Self-Constitution*. Oxford: Oxford University Press, 2009.

Poirier, Richard. *A World Elsewhere: The Place of Style in American Literature*. London: Chatto and Windus, 1967.

Ryle, Gilbert. "Jane Austen and the Moralists." *The Linacre Journal* 3 (1999): 85–99.

Schorer, Mark. "The Humiliation of Emma Woodhouse." In *Jane Austen: Emma*, edited by David Lodge, 170–194. London: Macmillan, 1968.

Taylor, Charles. *Human Agency and Language: Philosophical Papers*, Vol. 1. Cambridge: Cambridge University Press, 1985.

Trilling, Lionel. "*Emma* and the Legend of Jane Austen." In *Jane Austen: Emma*, edited by David Lodge, 148–169. London: Macmillan, 1968.

Wainwright, Valerie. "Jane Austen's Challenges, or the Powers of Character and the Understanding." *Philosophy and Literature* 38, no. 1 (2014): 58–73.

Williams, Bernard. *Shame and Necessity*. Berkeley: University of California Press, 1993.

Williams, Bernard. "Voluntary Acts and Responsible Agents." *Oxford Journal of Legal Studies* 10, no. 1 (1990): 1–10.

Chapter 4

"A Danger at Present Unperceived"

Self-Understanding, Imagination, Emotion,
and Social Stance in Emma

RICHARD ELDRIDGE

On the first page of the novel, we are told that Emma Woodhouse, though "handsome, clever, and rich, with a comfortable home and happy disposition," also suffers from the "real evils" of possessing "the power of having rather too much her own way, and a disposition to think a little too well of herself." These evils constitute, we are further told, a "danger . . . at present . . . unperceived" both to her own enjoyments and to the enjoyments of others (5). This danger is then consistently realized throughout the novel, as Emma repeatedly acts out her dispositions to fantasy and self-centeredness by meddlesomely and ineptly scripting the affairs of others. The catalogue of her errors includes at least her attempt to match Harriett to Mr. Elton, her vanity-feeding insults to Miss Bates on Box Hill, her flirtations with Frank Churchill, her imagining an affair between Jane Fairfax and Mr. Dixon, and her misunderstanding the objects of Harriett's interest (first Robert Martin, later George Knightley). In each case, what Emma is in fact doing—what her actions objectively mean—is not what she thinks she is doing, as she mistakenly supposes, variously, that she is being helpful to Harriett, amusing her audience, ferreting out secrets, and so on. Jane Austen herself famously described Emma as "a heroine whom no one but myself will much like."[1] If for many readers that prediction has turned out to be false, it is nonetheless not easy to say why Emma is, after all, likable. One might suppose that she learns from her errors and so is educated into being a proper grownup with concern for others as well as vivacity, so that she earns her entry into what is supposed to be a happy marriage as the seal of completed maturity. But then it is not quite clear either how Emma changes or how much—her errors are persistent—and it is not clear how any of us ever manage to overcome or to curb persistent tendencies to self-centeredness, vanity, and fantasy. Emma's character constitutes, then, in its fitful, incomplete, but genuine development, a study in the nature and possibility of self-understanding, for creatures such as us who share her tendencies.

Frequently philosophers have conceived of self-understanding as in one way too easy (and irrelevant to practical life) or in another way too difficult (and alienating from practical life). Within a broadly Cartesian tradition that focuses on occurrent thoughts, emotions, and qualitative states, self-understanding, conceived as a matter of introspective awareness, is too easy. Surely, it seems, I cannot fail to be wrong about what I am currently thinking or feeling (no matter how the world itself is): I am thinking about a dancing pink elephant or experiencing anger or the taste of lemons if and only if I know that I am doing so. Despite appearances, however, this account of self-understanding is open to a number of objections. First, I must know what a claim (publicly assessable as true or false) or anger *at* an insult or the taste *of* a lemon *is* in order to have such forms of awareness,

1. James Edward Austen-Leigh, *A Memoir of Jane Austen*, ed. R. W. Chapman (Oxford: Clarendon Press, 1967), 159.

and in order to know these things I must already know something about what is in fact true or false in the world, what in fact an insult is, and what is in fact a lemon. Absent such kinds of knowledge in general, I am left only with a stream of unstructured sensory inputs that lack clear discursive representational content.[2] Hence introspective knowledge of distinct discursive representational contents cannot be primitive and independent of knowledge of the world, and about the way the world is I can sometimes be wrong. The introspectionist picture of self-understanding mistakenly takes knowledge of discursive representational contents to be automatic and infallible.

Second, this kind of self-knowledge—knowledge of occurrent episodes of thinking, feeling, and sensing—is in any case not central to what we care about when we care about self-knowledge or self-understanding. Quassim Cassam has recently usefully distinguished between *trivial* self-knowledge, including the cases of self-knowledge favored in the introspectionist tradition as well as, for example, your awareness "that you are wearing socks," and *substantial* self-knowledge, that is, "knowledge of your deepest desires, hopes, and fears, knowledge of your character, emotions, abilities, and values, and knowledge of what makes you happy."[3] Only this latter, substantial form of self-knowledge, Cassam rightly insists, is what we care about when we care about self-understanding, and it is frequently hard to come by.

In developing his own view, however, Cassam casts self-understanding as both too difficult to come by and too impersonal. Drawing on cases of implicit, unacknowledged bias, but overgeneralizing from them, Cassam argues that substantial

2. Arguments about the incoherence of introspectionist self-knowledge of thought contents, itself conceived as primitive, immediate, and infallible, are legion, those of Collingwood, Wittgenstein, Austin, Ryle, and Sellars being among the most prominent.
3. Quassim Cassam, *Self-Knowledge for Humans* (Oxford: Oxford University Press, 2015), vii.

self-knowledge *"is* normally based on evidence and *is* inferential."[4]
That is, I must, for example, *infer* from my behavior that I am cow-
ardly, that I desire to eat a peach, or that I love my children. While this
view has some plausibility in the case of cowardice, it is less plausible
as an account of desiring peaches or loving children. Surely, it can't be
all that difficult to know these things.

Second, the existence of these kinds of facts about oneself is *not*
a matter entirely of just how things in the world happen to be, but
rather also significantly of what I *decide on* or *set myself* to do. No
doubt I sometimes fail in my resolutions, and no doubt I am sometimes unclear about what I have resolved, what I am in fact doing,
and what motivates my behavior. But that is not normally the case.
In Matthew Boyle's elegant phrase, the issues of what I have resolved
to do, what I am doing, and what I count as my motivations are normally "mine to settle."[5] It is significantly up to me to *count* my peach-
eating urges as reasons for action (thence to eat a peach) and to *count*
my children as to be loved (and so to love them). Yes, there is a significant background of feelings and urges that I do not control behind
such countings and doings, but I am not wholly or even normally the
passive victim of them, as if they hydraulically moved me to act of
their own power.[6] Were that so, I would not be the agent I normally
am in being responsive to complex norms and in taking responsibility

4. Ibid., viii.
5. Matthew Boyle, "Critical Study: Cassam on Self-Knowledge for Humans," *European Journal
   of Philosophy* 23, no. 2 (June 2015): 337–348, at 341. Boyle is building on and defending
   Richard Moran's work on one's commitments, including one's beliefs, as things over which
   one normally has authority in his *Authority and Estrangement: An Essay on Self-Knowledge*
   (Princeton, NJ: Princeton University Press, 2001).
6. This point is well developed by T. M. Scanlon in *What We Owe to Each Other* (Cambridge,
   MA: Belknap Press, 2000), and it has a long tradition within Kantian and post-Kantian philosophy in the treatment of the relation between *Willkür* (choice) and *Wille* (the moral law,
   a fundamental norm of rational willing).

for what I do (and believe and, in many cases, feel); I would instead be deeply alienated from my own practical life.

Yet while this latter, anti-introspectionist view that emphasizes responsibility for self and for one's own stances, epistemic and practical, is surely right, it is also easy to overemphasize our volitional power and possibilities of success in agentive navigations of our worlds, come what may.[7] Where, after all, are the boundaries between my normal enough control of my commitments and actions in familiar enough cases and my bumbling in one way or another elsewhere? What about all the liabilities to which action is vulnerable that J. L. Austin famously noted under the heading of excuses,[8] all the things I do out of inadvertence, negligence, hastiness, self-centered failure of due consideration, or just plain sloppiness?[9] Human agents do sometimes get into trouble, do sometimes fail to take responsibility effectively for their commitments and thus for their actions, and we had better have an account of that as well as an account of rational and volitional powers. Emma's valetudinarian father, Mr. Woodhouse, for example, is pretty much unable to take any effective action at all; he relies on Emma, especially, to see to the running of the household, while his dependence on others, as Richard Jenkyns has noted, in fact disguises a rapacious manipulativeness. His genuine surface amiability both masks and expresses the unconsciously assumed stance of

---

7. Arguably, this kind of overemphasis appears in Sartre in both *Being and Nothingness* and "Existentialism Is a Humanism," where Sartre mistakenly holds that something being a reason at all *for me* and a course of life being meaningful *for me* are things that are altogether within my personal power simply to decide.

8. See J. L. Austin, "A Plea for Excuses," in Austin, *Philosophical Papers*, 3rd ed. (Oxford: Oxford University Press, 1979), 175–204.

9. To his great credit, Moran does not ignore this topic, as he treats the cases of Fred Vincy in George Eliot's *Middlemarch* and John Lewis in Kingsley Amis's *That Uncertain Feeling* as instances of (culpable) failure to exercise agentive powers in taking responsibility for one's commitments—an all too human possibility. Sartre begins to discuss the conditioning of the exercise of agentive powers in his discussion of seriality in his *Critique of Dialectical Reason*.

"a bloodsucker, fastened upon his daughter's flesh,"[10] determined to get his own way in matters of food, visits, after-dinner entertainments, and, especially, Emma's marriage, which he would block at all costs in order to secure his own care. How are we to make sense of cases of alienation from one's own motivations and actions—their dominating oneself rather than vice versa—such as this?

In his fine article on Jane Austen, Gilbert Ryle notes that Austen offers us

> an ample, variegated and many-dimensional vocabulary. Her descriptions of people mention their tempers, habits, dispositions, moods, inclinations, impulses, sentiments, feelings, affections, thoughts, reflections, opinions, principles, prejudices, imaginations, and fancies. Her people have or lack moral sense, sense of duty, good sense, taste, good-breeding, self-command, spirits and good humours; they do or do not regulate their imaginations and discipline their tempers. Her people have or lack knowledge of their own hearts or their own dispositions; they are or are not properly acquainted with themselves; they do or do not practice self-examination and soliloquy.[11]

---

10. Richard Jenkyns, *A Fine Brush on Ivory: An Appreciation of Jane Austen* (Oxford: Oxford University Press, 2007), 164. Like Emma, Elizabeth Bennet, too, must learn to see through the passive-aggressive manipulativeness of her father. See Richard Eldridge, *On Moral Personhood: Philosophy, Literature, Criticism, and Self-Understanding* (Chicago: University of Chicago Press, 1989), 168–172.

11. Gilbert Ryle, "Jane Austen and the Moralists," *The Oxford Review*, no. 1, 1966; reprinted in Ryle, *Critical Essays: Collected Papers*, Vol. 1 (London: Hutchinson, 1971), 286–301, at 299–300. Ryle traces this presentation of fully rounded characters to Austen's having an Aristotelian moral sensibility, more oriented toward flexible contextual judgments of character than to moral principle, transmitted and modified for a modern English context by Shaftesbury, in contrast with the implacable, intolerant, and implausible moral stance of eighteenth-century English Calvinism, which saw characters as entirely black or entirely white, entirely good or entirely evil, entirely elect or entirely damned.

This is surely right, and Ryle is correct to dwell on and to praise Austen's generosity and complex intelligence in eschewing simplistic moralizing and in being concerned with substantial self-knowledge. But Austen's authorial habits of complex, generous presentation and her overall moral sensibility do not yet explain, however, how a particularly alienated and un-self-knowing character might develop over time. Ryle suggests that "improper solicitude"—Emma's besetting vice—"is actuated by love of power, jealousy, conceit, sentimentality, and so on," that it fails to manifest "genuine good will," with the result that Emma "is not effectively self-critical."[12] This, too, is surely right. But how do *those* failings arise and develop over time?[13] What sorts of creatures are we in general insofar as we are subject to them, and how might they be overcome, to the extent that they can be?

At one level, the answers to these questions are straightforward. Emma's absent mother, weak father, and indulgent governess have given her, from childhood on, again "the power of rather having too much her own way, and a disposition to think a little too well of herself" (5). Her meddling and vanity are curbed both through the interventions of Knightley and through her experience, guided by him, of how she has misunderstood and wronged others. But these answers do not yet capture what one might call the phenomenology, texture, or psychodynamics of the experience of coming to a degree of increased self-understanding that the novel tracks in detail.

12. Ibid., 291, 297. Ryle's reference here to the need for "genuine good will" as a *central* virtue suggests both a compatibility with a flexible, naturalized Kantianism and the continuing influence of a broad-minded liberal Christianity in Austen's views, in addition to the Shaftesburyean Aristotelianism that he otherwise ascribes to her.

13. Richard Moran aptly suggests, especially in his discussion of Fred Vincy in *Middlemarch* that taking up a theoretical stance on one's own commitments and actions is itself motivated by a wish to evade responsibility for them (*Authority and Estrangement*, 188–192). That wish may be a natural one for beings freighted with reflective awareness. But exactly how does it arise and how does it take on force in one's conduct? Not everyone is as feckless in action as Fred.

In particular, how might one come to have some imperfect, agentive control over one's actions, so that one is significantly responsible for what one does, while also being alienated from one's commitments, unresponsive to others, and under the sways of motives that one has not adequately grasped or assessed? How, that is, can one both in some sense know what one is doing and yet also not know? And how, and how far, can one change?

In a nice piece of either influence or dramatic irony, the most useful general philosophical vocabulary for describing Emma's errors and subsequent development is provided by Ryle in his work on self-understanding.[14] Like Cassam, Ryle focuses on substantial self-knowledge, or what he calls "self-consciousness in [an] enlarged sense": that is, one's "estimates of [one's] own qualities of character and intellect"[15] that require skill and attention to form accurately, well beyond awarenesses of occurrent episodes of qualitative feeling. Like Cassam, Ryle also urges that "the sorts of things that I can find out about myself are the same as the sorts of things that I can find out about other people, and the methods of finding them out are much the same."[16]

Unlike Cassam, however, Ryle also notes at least five significant, interrelated differences between self-understanding and the understanding of others. (1) Self-understanding develops initially (when it develops) out of self-consciousness in the narrower sense, that is, out of experiences, especially in early adolescence, of embarrassment, anxiety, shyness, and affectation.[17] Hence the pursuit of apt self-understanding cannot be a dispassionate theoretical inquiry. One must confront and evaluate one's character or personality as it

---

14. Notoriously, when asked whether he ever read novels, Ryle is reported to have replied, "Oh, yes—all six of them, every year."
15. Ryle, *The Concept of Mind* (London: Hutchison, 1949), 157.
16. Ibid., 156.
17. Ibid.

is already in development, as one feels oneself to fall under the gaze of others, and as one must face up to responsibilities and possibilities for change. (2) "It is notorious," Ryle observes, "that people deceive themselves about their own motives"; and "there is one class of persons whose qualities and frames of mind are specially difficult to appreciate, namely . . . hypocrites and charlatans, the people who pretend to motives and moods and the people who pretend to abilities, that is, . . . most of us in some stretches of our lives and . . . some of us in most stretches of our lives."[18] One's own tendencies specifically to hypocrisy, charlatanry, and pretense must themselves be confronted and worked through. (3) Both pretense and candidness are learned from others. In the development of linguistic competence, ego-identity, and discursively structured point-of-view-having, "normal unstudied talk"[19] and imitation of it come first; a fall into pretense comes second, but is itself required in turn for being forthright as a matter of settled commitment. That is, there is a difference between the natural openness of expression of a young child whose linguistic behavior is less controlled and the specific, controlled sincerity of adult character: "a person could not be honest or candid who had never known insincerity or reticence."[20] (4) Learning to be forthright specifically involves the internalization of an authority figure and its skills of character assessment. Self-assessment depends upon the assessments of others, carried out by others, that one first imitates and participates in, and then only later comes to understand and to practice upon oneself.[21]

18. Ibid., 172.
19. Ibid., 182.
20. Ibid.
21. This is one reason why what contemporary psychology addresses under the heading of impression management, often involving pretense and prejudice, is unavoidable: we judge ourselves initially as others judge us.

At a certain stage the child discovers the trick of directing higher order acts upon his own lower order acts. Having been separately victim and author of jokes, coercions, catechisms, criticisms, and mimicries in the inter-personal dealings between others and himself, he finds out how to play both roles at once. He has listened to stories before, and he has told stories before, but now he tells stories to his own enthralled ear. He has been detected in insincerities and he has detected the insincerities of others, but now he applies the techniques of detection to his own insincerities. He finds that he can give orders to himself with such authority that he sometimes obeys them even when reluctant to do so. Self-suasion and self-dissuasion become more or less effective. He learns in adolescence to apply to his own behavior most of those higher order methods of dealing with the young that are regularly practiced by grownups. He is then said to be growing up.[22]

(5) Assessment of one's own motivations, character, and conduct is in principle never fully completed. The "I" suffers from what Ryle calls "systematic elusiveness," as we never fully succeed in understanding ourselves. "Self-commentary, self-ridicule, and self-admonition are logically condemned to eternal penultimacy," insofar as "my commentary on my performances must always be silent about one performance, namely itself."[23]

To these five points of Ryle's—the rootedness of self-consciousness in embarrassment and anxiety, the standing possibility of self-deception, forthrightness in avowal and assessment as a skill

22. Ibid., 193–194.
23. Ibid., 195. In *Nausea*, Sartre similarly criticizes the vain effort "d'attraper le temps par le queue [to catch time by the tail]" (*La Nauseé*, [Paris: Gallimard, 1938], 66), and the difference between self-knowledge, which is always incomplete and open to change, and knowledge of objects is a principal theme of *Being and Nothingness*.

learned from others, the role of others as internalized authorities, and the in principle incompleteness of self-assessment—we can add two further points that Richard Wollheim nicely makes. (6) There are typically specific occasioning circumstances for self-assessment. In various ways, the smooth formation of intentions to act on the basis of beliefs and desires and the subsequent smooth carrying out of these intentions can be disrupted. The relevant beliefs and desires may be incoherent, so that no intention is formed, or an occasion for action is missed, or an intention is executed but no satisfaction results. In such cases, as Wollheim puts it, a "person is required to ask himself a question about his desires and beliefs—a question which would never have arisen in the course of the unreflective life. . . . And this self-interrogation, once it has begun, has no natural termination."[24] (7) There is a particular danger that one's self-assessments may be distorted by what Wollheim calls crystallization—the tendency of a disposition to persist by reinforcing itself, as one rationalizes it and shrinks from change, as especially in experiences of "envy, hatred, superstition, and the love of gambling," though more happily also in love and friendship. In having motivational force, many occurrent emotional states tend "to reinforce the dispositions they manifest."[25] As a result, change is not easy, and it can require shocks or breakdowns to motivate active and more accurate self-assessment.

Critics have focused on Emma's path toward increased self-understanding, noting both its general character and its more specific occasions and contents. Karin Jackson describes the general progress of the novel as a matter of Emma's movement

---

24. Richard Wollheim, *The Thread of Life* (Cambridge, MA: Harvard University Press, 1984), 165–166. Compare also "A person leads his life at a crossroads: at the point where a past that has affected him and a future that lies open meet in the present" (31). The occasion for renewed assessment is when this moment of the crossing of past with future is also a moment of breakdown of smooth and successful action.

25. Ibid., 59.

from delusion to self-recognition, from illusion to reality; numerous images of sight and blindness reinforce this—the lack of sight, the necessity of insight. Emma's "blindness" to the real nature of Mr. Elton, of Harriet, Robert Martin, Jane Fairfax, Frank Churchill, Mr. Knightley, and of course herself, shows her unknowing errors of judgment, her fundamental lack of self-understanding. She is deceived as to the nature of the world around her, as well as to the nature of her own emotions. When the truth of human situations and feelings is not perceived accurately, disorder and unhappiness result.[26]

George Justice describes the class inflection of Emma's initial errors, noting she must "unlearn some of the vulgar categorizing of Mrs. Elton—[who cares only about money—] while preserving belief in the value of traditional social relations," wherein the upper classes, at least, "are judged on the basis of their contribution to the general well-being of the community."[27] What Emma must learn is a matter of not only content or standards for evaluation, but also of personal style as both object and manner of judgment. She must, as Justice notes, come to see "flirting and gallantry [as] aggressive tricks of the young that mark out their youth,"[28] while also preserving her imagination, spiritedness, and readiness in sympathetic feeling. In general, Emma's errors are a matter all at once of evaluative standards, misunderstandings of others, and failures of both personal style and self-understanding. As Jackson puts it, "her errors involve not only Harriet, but all the other major characters, including Mr. Knightley,

26. Karin Jackson, "The Dilemma of Emma: Moral, Ethical, and Spiritual Values," *Persuasions: The Jane Austen Journal Online* 21, no. 2 (Summer 2000), http://www.jasna. org/persuasions/on-line/vol21no2/jackson.html.
27. George Justice, "Introduction," in *Emma*, ed. George Justice, 4th ed. (New York: W. W. Norton, 2012), xvii.
28. Ibid., xxvi.

and most of all, and most unknowingly, herself. The result is chaos and confusion."[29]

What these apt summary characterizations of Emma's progress do not yet fully capture, however, are, first, the specific structure of the resistance to self-understanding that haunts Emma's character and, second, the complex process of confronting and working through this resistance that the novel unfolds.

The core of this resistance is, of course, Emma's wish to have her own way, coupled with her tendency to generate narratives for both herself and others that will bring about the states of affairs that she takes to be desirable. She has had, after all, the possibility and the habit of "doing just what she liked," with little in the way of parents or governesses to oppose her, and she has been in daily control of the considerable material resources of Hartfield (5). Joking with Mr. Knightley, she claims to see herself as "a fanciful, troublesome creature," (9), when in fact her view of herself is that she and only she is in a position to arrange the affairs of others most effectively and benevolently. The very fact that she makes this claim in jest is evidence of how her view of herself as benevolent, imaginative, perceptive, and effective has crystallized, forming a kind of center of her personality.

Hence it is no surprise that, immediately upon meeting the younger, fair, plump, sweet, but somewhat dim Harriet, Emma should resolve: "*She* [Emma] would notice her; she would improve her; she would detach her from bad acquaintance, and introduce her into good society; she would form her opinions and her manners. It would be an interesting, and certainly a very kind undertaking; highly becoming her own situation in life, her leisure, and powers" (20). Harriet is here little more than an occasion for Emma to fantasize about the worth and pleasantness of her own character and

---

29. Jackson, "The Dilemma of Emma."

powers.[30] This point about Emma's tendencies to fantasy and to approving self-regard is reinforced, as we find in the next paragraph that "[w]ith an alacrity beyond the common impulse of a spirit which yet was never indifferent to the credit of doing every thing well and attentively, with the real good-will of a mind delighted with its own ideas, did she [Emma] then do all the honours of the meal, and help and recommend the minced chicken and scalloped oysters with an urgency which she knew would be acceptable to the early hours and civil scruples of their guests" (20). Tellingly, the focus of this description is neither on what Emma does nor on whom (if anyone) she in fact benefits, but rather on Emma's attitudes and self-satisfactions in her own performance and its style. For Emma at this point, Harriet is less a being of independent worth or interest than she is an occasion for Emma to cultivate her own self-regard: "She [Harriet] would be loved as one to whom she [Emma] could be useful" (21).

Given that Emma's view of herself as benevolent, imaginative, perceptive, and effective has crystallized, it will not be easy for her to change, especially since she has, as Mr. Knightley observes, "no industry and patience" and, especially, no "subjection of the fancy to the understanding," having been "always quick and assured" and "mistress of the house . . . ever since she was twelve" (30). Her quickness and self-assurance lead her to fail to appreciate Robert Martin's merits and suitability for Harriet and to decipher Mr. Elton's *courtship* riddle but to misunderstand it as directed toward Harriet rather than herself (58). Emma is in fact determined to persist in her mastery of Hartfield and of those around her. She proclaims "very little intention of ever marrying at all," arguing explicitly that "a single woman, of good fortune, is always respectable" and that "mine is an active,

30. Here Austen's use of free indirect discourse puts us inside Emma's course of reflection, while her formulation "highly becoming" ironically highlights and criticizes Emma's vanity.

busy mind with a great many independent resources, and I do not perceive why I should be more in want of employment at forty or fifty than one-and-twenty" (68, 69). When John Knightley suggests that Mr. Elton may be interested in her and that she may inadvertently be encouraging him, she dismisses the thought and walks on "amusing herself in the consideration of the blunders which often arise from a partial knowledge of circumstances, of the mistakes which people of high pretensions to judgment are for ever falling into" (89).

When Emma learns she is wrong about Elton and that he has in fact been courting her, she admits her error as well as "pain and humiliation," but she also rationalizes her mistake and fails genuinely to question her own character and powers of judgment: "She looked back as well as she could; but it was all confusion. She had taken up the idea, she supposed, and made everything bend to it. His manners, however, must have been unmarked, wavering, dubious, or she could not have been so misled" (106). Here Emma primarily regards her mistake as, first of all, one of evidential judgment alone, rather than as also a function of the fantasies of authority and effect that have led her into error. She fails genuinely to question her own character, motives, or powers of judgment in general, casting the mistake as a kind of factual error made in light of misleading evidence. Austen's "she supposed" is an especially nice touch, in indicating that Emma is taking up a theoretical or exterior stance toward her own mistaken judgment, rather than taking responsibility for it as expressing her own genuine but flawed character.[31] While she forms the resolution "of being humble and discreet, and repressing imagination all the rest of her life" (112), she also imagines that carrying out this resolution lies in her immediate power, without any change of basic character

---

31. This passage is another striking example of the use of free indirect discourse for which Austen is justly famous, especially so in *Emma*, a novel about repeatedly compromised efforts at self-understanding.

or personality on her part. That she expresses this resolution hyperbolically as binding "all the rest of her life" shows that it and her self-image remain in the grip of a fantasy of superiority. She has, one might say, not yet been genuinely humbled, and her "youth and natural cheerfulness" (109), a good night's sleep, and her propping up of her image of herself through her fantasy-tinged resolution are enough to restore her spirits, without any fundamental change.

It is, then, no surprise when in Book II Emma continues to judge that Harriet and Robert Martin "must be separated" (147), even after Harriet has revealed her genuine feelings for him awkwardly and in an obvious rush of emotion, recounting to Emma her meeting with his mother and sisters. Moreover, Emma's fancy is now prompted by Frank Churchill, in whom she finds "nothing to denote him unworthy of the distinguished honour which her imagination had given him; the honour, if not of being really in love with her, of being at least very near it, and saved only by her own indifference" (162). Here Austen blends free indirect discourse, thus involving us in Emma's train of thought and calling attention to the fact that she sees herself yet again as an agent in awarding honors, with authorial commentary, in hinting via her double-negative and somewhat hyperbolic formulation "nothing to denote him unworthy of the distinguished honours" that there is something amiss in Emma's course of thought. Unsurprisingly, Emma then goes on, during a party at the Coles', not only to take delight in the thought that "she was [Frank's] object," but also that "every body must perceive it" (173), thus seeing herself as observed and admired by others for her attractiveness and command, rather than herself attending to and taking responsibility for her character and comportment. That Emma continues to see herself as seen and admired by others is especially marked in her imaginative rehearsal of Frank's courting her, wherein "the conclusion of every imaginary declaration on her side was that she *refused* him" (206), thus maintaining control of both her inner life and her external relations, untouched by others and confident in her power. Later, when her own flirtations with Frank have withered, Emma encourages what she misunderstands to be an attachment to Frank on Harriet's part, continuing to imagine that she might effectively and benevolently manage Harriett's affairs (268–269).

Emma's tendencies to self-centered, self-reinforcing fantasy about herself as the admired, benevolent, and effective manager of the affairs of others become explicit and are then explicitly challenged by Knightley at the party on Box Hill, when Emma insults Miss Bates by remarking archly that Miss Bates may have "a difficulty" in producing "only three [dull things] at once" rather than an unlimited number (291). Emma issues this insult in response to Frank's proposal to the party that they should each (besides Emma and himself) produce "either one thing very clever, be it prose or verse, original or repeated—or two things moderately clever—or three things very dull indeed" (291). About Frank's proposal and Emma's reaction to it, Mary Poovey insightfully observes that "the vanity Frank invites reawakens the 'original narcissism' of his auditors [—including, especially, Emma—], for implicit in his challenge is the opportunity to imagine, for just a moment, that every thought is as precious to one's listeners as to oneself, that one is, in short, the centre of a nonjudgmental little universe."[32] Indeed, the prompting of narcissistic fantasy is especially strong in Emma, for though she is not herself intended to produce a witty remark, she has already been fantasizing about others noticing and admiring her flirtatious command over Frank, she is herself to be the judge of whether any remark offered by another is suitably witty, and she is unable to resist the witty jibe at Miss Bates. Though she had just teased Frank about the importance of self-command (290), she here proves entirely unable to exhibit it herself.

---

32. Mary Poovey, "The True English Style," *Persuasions: The Jane Austen Journal* 5 (1983): 10–12, at 10.

Here Emma's failures of self-command and benevolent command over others are on full display, to others and to herself. Miss Bates blushes, those who care for her may be supposed to be quietly aghast—Mr. Weston recalls them to the contest, away from Emma's remark—and, after a short time, Mr. Knightley forcefully reproves her in private. Initially, "Emma recollected, blushed, was sorry, but tried to laugh it off" (294), but after Knightley presses the point and then hands her into her carriage, she finds herself, alone, filled with "anger against herself, mortification, and deep concern. . . . Never had she felt so agitated, mortified, grieved, at any circumstance in her life" (296). She has been forced—by the very figure whose judgment she most values—to confront the falsity, at least on this occasion, of her crystallized image of herself as benevolent, imaginative, perceptive, and effective.

Unsurprisingly, Emma resolves to do better and to call upon Miss Bates the next morning "in the warmth of true contrition" (296). Tellingly, however, she also in doing so imagines "that she might see Mr. Knightley in her way; or, perhaps, he might come in while she were paying her visit" (297). That is, even while she is remorseful, she still wishes to be seen—and especially by Knightley—as in appropriate command of her situation. Nonetheless, Emma does now manage to check her vanity and to retain her self-command. She remains calm and does not interfere as Harriet reveals her interest in marrying Mr. Knightley, despite her own sudden realization that "Mr. Knightley must marry no one but herself" (320). With composure, she tells Harriet "that Mr. Knightley is the last man in the world, who would intentionally give any woman the idea of his feeling for her more than he really does," so that Harriet may have some ground to think that her interest might be reciprocated (323).

Caught in contrition and disappointment, Emma finally fully confronts her own qualities of character as she reflects on what she has done:

With insufferable vanity had she believed herself in the secret of everybody's feelings; with unpardonable arrogance proposed to arrange everybody's destiny. She was proved to have been universally mistaken; and she had not quite done nothing—for she had done mischief. She had brought evil on Harriet, on herself, and she too much feared, on Mr. Knightley. (324)

Anticipating Harriet's marriage to Mr. Knightley, she then finds that

[t]he only source whence any thing like consolation or composure could be drawn, was in the resolution of her own better conduct, and the hope that, however inferior in spirit and gaiety might be the following and every future winter of her life to the past, it would yet find her more rational, more acquainted with herself, and leave her less to regret when it were gone. (332)

Matters are at last happily resolved only when Emma reveals to Knightley that while she had been flattered by Frank's attentions, she had never really loved him, whereupon Knightley proposes to her, having found, as he puts it, that "one sentiment" on his part— jealousy of Frank—had "probably enlightened him as to the other"— love for Emma (340).

What are we to make of this resolution? Has Emma changed and earned her match with Knightley? And what is the character of that marriage likely to be? Critics have been divided over this issue. There is general agreement that Emma embodies a number of qualities often thought to be interrelated and to be significantly shared among women: imagination, fancy, wit, a desire for male admiration, curiosity, and meddlesomeness. Lacking the possibility of making herself an independent socioeconomic identity apart from marriage or inheritance, her passions and intelligence have been channeled into the domestic and village spheres. As Tony Tanner puts it, in bearing imaginative energies that she cannot express otherwise, "Emma is a very active fantasist, . . . the central eccentric, who is the potentially most disruptive figure in the society. . . . She is the danger from within—if, that is—society itself is not beginning to seem like the danger from without."[33] From a traditionalist point of view, then, Emma deserves chastening and requires control, both of which are provided by Mr. Knightley, in order to fit appropriately into the regnant social order. In Alasdair Duckworth's formulation, "Emma in the end chooses society rather than self, an inherited order rather than a spontaneous and improvised existence."[34] Claudia L. Johnson adds that this choice "implicitly opposes and prefers the orderly, patriarchal, rational, masculine, and, above all, right, to the disorderly, subjectivist, imaginative, feminine, and self-evidently wrong."[35] Even more sharply, Maaja A. Stewart argues that Emma's "change [from sole mistress of Hartfield to Knightley's wife], like Elizabeth Bennet's, is marked by a loss of wit and autonomy, as she is disciplined to accept the male gaze. Reality, in the form of Austen's inscription of patriarchy in the novel, refuses to yield to Emma's desires as it educates and immobilizes this most independent of heroines firmly in the marriage plot."[36]

Other readers, however, have seen Emma as maintaining her independence and wit within the framework of the social order, as Mr. Knightley is induced to take up residence at Hartfield after marriage, in order to avoid requiring the querulous Mr. Woodhouse to move. Johnson argues that

33. Tony Tanner, *Jane Austen* (Cambridge, MA: Harvard University Press, 1986), 189.
34. Alasdair Duckworth, *Improvement of the Estate* (Baltimore, MD: Johns Hopkins University Press, 1971), 148.
35. Claudia L. Johnson, *Jane Austen: Women, Politics, and the Novel* (Chicago: University of Chicago Press, 1988), 122.
36. Maaja A. Stewart, *Domestic Relations and Imperial Fictions: Jane Austen's Novels in Eighteenth Century Contexts* (Athens: University of Georgia Press, 1993), 141.

the conclusion which seemed tamely and placidly conservative thus takes an unexpected turn, as the guarantor of order himself [—Mr. Knightley—] cedes a considerable portion of the power which custom has allowed him to expect. In moving to Hartfield, Knightley is sharing *her* home, and in placing himself within her domain, Knightley gives his blessing to her rule. Emma assumes her own entitlement to independence and power—power not only over her own destiny, but, what is harder to tolerate, power over the destinies of others—and in doing so she poaches on what is felt to be male turf. . . . In its willingness to explore positive versions of female power, *Emma* is itself an experimental production of authorial independence unlike any of Austen's other novels.[37]

Patricia Meyer Spacks adds that "Emma has kept herself alive while all around decayed, kept herself alive with the energies of gossip. . . . As a sub-text for the major line of narrative [gossip] supports the imaginative and improvisational, valuing the private, implying the saving energies of female curiosity and female volubility, celebrating the possibility and the importance of a narrative of trivia. It exemplifies the subversive resources of the novel as genre."[38]

Depending on which reading one favors, then, Emma either subordinates her imaginative energies to the requirements of social life (appropriately or not), or persists in them and retains some control over her affairs. Here the correct things to say are, first, that we just don't know which is decisively the case; second, that the novel ends by suspending us in this very uncertainty; and third, that Emma's achievements in self-understanding and in marrying Mr. Knightly are

37. Claudia L. Johnson, *Jane Austen: Women, Politics, and the Novel*, 143, 125, 126.
38. Patricia Meyer Spacks, *Gossip* (New York: Random House, 1985), 171.

best regarded as both genuine and partial.[39] The last sentence of the novel is, "But, in spite of these deficiencies—[viz. Mrs. Elton judged the wedding 'all extremely shabby, and very inferior to her own'—], the wishes, the hopes, the confidence, the predictions of the small band of true friends who witnessed the ceremony, were fully answered in the perfect happiness of the union" (381). As Poovey aptly notes, this last sentence "has the effect of robbing the future of its potential for change, for its temporal stasis freezes the Knightleys' marriage in an eternal repetition of their 'perfect happiness.'"[40] Or perhaps not: for this freeze-frame ending not only stops the dynamics of Emma's and Knightley's relationship, but also leaves their happiness slightly qualified. Just who composes "the small band of friends"? —Mrs. and Mr. Weston, perhaps; but how reliable is their judgment? Exactly what were their wishes, hopes, confidence, and predictions? Austen's art and genius here is to have presented character—that is, virtues and vices—as essentially existing in courses of their change and development, including experiences of humiliation and embarrassment,[41] and then to have cut that development off. This not only forces readers to speculate about the protagonists' futures and to entertain ambiguities, it also reminds us that character and self-understanding remain things for which these figures will be responsible, with nothing settled absolutely and with crystallization and emotion always in play.

39. James Austen-Leigh informs us, when asked about Emma's future, that Jane Austen would reply "that Mr. Woodhouse survived his daughter's marriage, and kept her from settling at Donwell, about two years," but we do not learn from her reports anything more than this. Austen-Leigh, *A Memoir of Jane Austen*, 119.
40. Poovey, 12.
41. Richard Simpson usefully notes that Austen "contemplates virtues, not as fixed quantities, or as definable qualities, but as continual struggles and conquests, as progressive states of mind, advancing by repulsing their contraries, or losing ground by being overcome.... A character therefore unfolded itself to her ... as a dramatic sketch, a living history, a composite force, which could exhibit what it was by exhibiting what it did." Simpson, "Jane Austen," *North British Review*, April 1870; reprinted in *Jane Austen: The Critical Heritage*, ed. B. S. Southam (London: Routledge, 1968), 249–250.

Philosophy typically seeks standing terms for assessment—here for describing and assessing the achievement of self-understanding and worldly success—from its own more dispassionate, spatialized, and generalization-seeking point of view. It offers useful standing terms for assessing which characters understand themselves and their situations and so act well, and which do not. In contrast, Austen's concern as a novelist for dramatic presentation over time rightly discloses complexities and responsibilities that attach to self-understanding as an ongoing, unclosed, and socially situated process that is suffused with feeling. Her presentation in free indirect discourse of Emma's streams of thought about herself and others, qualified by adverbial phrases that express ironic authorial evaluations ("highly becoming," "nothing to denote him unworthy") show the complexity, temporality, partiality, and elusiveness of self-understanding. Emma has somewhat curbed her tendencies to self-centered vanity and meddlesome plotting—she did not attempt to block Harriet's interest in Knightley, and she accepts the standing role of a wife—but she also retains her wit and her interest in self-management and the management of others. Philosophers would do well, like Emma, to register the complexities of self-understanding and self-management, without quite abandoning address to them. Even if self-understanding in general has standing appropriate objects or targets (motivations, temperaments, qualities of character, interests, desires, and so on), it is both a social and emotional process that we do not fully control as individuals and something also always to be achieved, as Austen compellingly demonstrates in the figure of Emma. Given the social situations, the emotion-laden characters, and the needs for imaginative narrative rehearsal that may always be structured by crystallized vanity that surround all exercises of agency, there is always a "danger at present unperceived."[42]

42. Unless, of course, social life becomes systematically and transparently just, with neither need nor occasion for the sort of impression management that is infused with pretense and prejudice—surely not a likely state of affairs.

REFERENCES

Austen-Leigh, James Edward. *A Memoir of Jane Austen,* edited by R. W. Chapman. Oxford: Clarendon Press, 1967.

Austin, J. L. "A Plea for Excuses." In Austin, *Philosophical Papers,* 3rd ed., 175–204. Oxford: Oxford University Press, 1979.

Boyle, Matthew. "Critical Study: Cassam on Self-Knowledge for Humans." *European Journal of Philosophy* 23, no. 2 (June 2015): 337–348.

Cassam, Quassim. *Self-Knowledge for Humans.* Oxford: Oxford University Press, 2015.

Duckworth, Alasdair. *Improvement of the Estate.* Baltimore, MD: Johns Hopkins University Press, 1971.

Eldridge, Richard. *On Moral Personhood: Philosophy, Literature, Criticism, and Self-Understanding.* Chicago: University of Chicago Press, 1989.

Jackson, Karin. "The Dilemma of Emma: Moral, Ethical, and Spiritual Values." *Persuasions: The Jane Austen Journal Online* 21, no. 2 (Summer 2000). http://www.jasna.org/persuasions/on-line/vol21no2/jackson.html.

Jenkyns, Richard. *A Fine Brush on Ivory: An Appreciation of Jane Austen.* Oxford: Oxford University Press, 2007.

Johnson, Claudia L. *Jane Austen: Women, Politics, and the Novel.* Chicago: University of Chicago Press, 1988.

Justice, George. "Introduction." In *Emma,* edited by George Justice, 4th ed., xvii. New York: W. W. Norton, 2012.

Moran, Richard. *Authority and Estrangement: An Essay on Self-Knowledge.* Princeton, NJ: Princeton University Press, 2001.

Poovey, Mary. "The True English Style." *Persuasions: The Jane Austen Journal* 5 (1983): 10–12.

Ryle, Gilbert. *The Concept of Mind.* London: Hutchison, 1949.

Ryle, Gilbert. "Jane Austen and the Moralists." *The Oxford Review,* no. 1, 1966; reprinted in Ryle, *Critical Essays: Collected Papers,* Vol. 1, 286–301. London: Hutchinson, 1971.

Sartre, Jean-Paul. *Being and Nothingness,* translated by Hazel E. Barnes. New York: Washington Square Press, 1993.

Sartre, Jean-Paul. *Critique of Dialectical Reason,* Vol. 1, translated by Alan Sheridan-Smith, rev. ed. London: Verso, 2004.

Sartre, Jean-Paul. *Existenialism is a Humanism,* translated by Carol Macomber. New Haven: Yale University Press, 2007.

Sartre, Jean-Paul. *La Nauseé.* Paris: Gallimard, 1938.

Scanlon, T. M. *What We Owe to Each Other.* Cambridge, MA: Belknap Press, 2000.

Simpson, Richard. "Jane Austen." *North British Review,* April 1870; reprinted in *Jane Austen: The Critical Heritage,* 249–250, edited by B. S. Southam. London: Routledge, 1968.

Spacks, Patricia Meyer. *Gossip*. New York: Random House, 1985.

Stewart, Maaja A. *Domestic Relations and Imperial Fictions: Jane Austen's Novels in Eighteenth Century Contexts*. Athens: University of Georgia Press, 1993.

Tanner, Tony. *Jane Austen*. Cambridge, MA: Harvard University Press, 1986.

Wollheim, Richard. *The Thread of Life*. Cambridge, MA: Harvard University Press, 1984.

Chapter 5

The Many Faces of Gossip in *Emma*

HEIDI SILCOX AND MARK SILCOX

"News! Oh! Yes, I always like news," exclaims Emma just before learning about Mr. Elton's marriage from Mr. Knightley (135). Throughout *Emma*, Jane Austen's eponymous heroine repeatedly betrays her intense love of gossip. As Austen's protagonist navigates her world and manipulates the various personalities that comprise her social set, gossip is central to the text as a means of both revealing essential information to the reader and charting Emma's moral and psychological growth.

Emma's own personal predilection for gossip in the novel causes arguments with Mr. Knightley. It also misleads Emma to the extent that she becomes deluded about those around her, causing her to misconstrue situations to her own detriment and the detriment of others. However, these temporary failures of conversational discretion are also key components in Emma's growth. Her participation in gossip often provides her with false information and caters to her prejudices, but it also supplies her with an indispensable basis for reasoned action. Personal growth through engagement with gossip is a principal catalyst for Emma's eventual success, and for the reader's sense that her final triumphs over the weaknesses in her own nature are more than merely fortuitous.

Austen's famous ambivalence toward the character, as expressed both in her own correspondence ("a heroine which no one but myself would like"[1]) and in a somewhat more paradoxical tone by the novel's narrator ("this sweetest and best of all creatures, faultless in spite of all her faults" [340]) has been a source of speculation for generations of critics.[2] We want to argue that this aspect of the novel is best understood as a reflection of the author's provocatively equivocal attitude toward the effects that gossip—especially the type that is perpetrated by and about the inhabitants of a relatively closed social group—can have on human nature in general. Austen exhibits a fascinating, consistently ambivalent attitude toward the information-rich chitchat of all of the work's main characters. Gossip is the social lifeblood of the entire community and finds its way into the conversational patterns of most other characters. Miss Bates and Mr. Knightley, for example, routinely indulge and rejoice in this style of conversation, as does the novel's own narrator. The novel's portrayal of how their relationships and motivations are transformed through talk reveals a sensitivity both to the moral dangers of gossip and to what recent evolutionary psychologists have identified as its fundamental role in the regulation of human societies.

Like all of Austen's novels, *Emma* is set in a closed social world that is subject to very little external impetus for change. This aspect of her work has been occasionally disparaged for its artificiality, perhaps most infamously by Vladimir Nabokov, who described the similar restrictive

1. James Edward Austen-Leigh, *A Memoir of Jane Austen*, ed. R. W. Chapman (Oxford: Clarendon, 1967), 157.
2. F. W. Bradbrook diagnoses the character as brilliantly witty, but emotionally barren; see F. W. Bradbrook, *Jane Austen: Emma, Studies in English Literature* (London: Edward Arnold, 1970), 4. For Wayne Booth, she is easily beloved, but excessively prideful; see Wayne C. Booth, *The Rhetoric of Fiction* (Chicago: University of Chicago Press, 1961), 244.

social milieu of *Mansfield Park* as "the game of a child."[3] But like the artificial worlds thought up by science fiction and mystery authors, as well as those found in certain sorts of historical fiction, the restricted social milieu of the Austen novel allows for the performance of some fascinating thought experiments that explore how the most fundamental features of human nature can develop under stable conditions. This is perhaps less easy to appreciate about Austen's novels than it is about similarly purposed works of sci fi or historical fiction because she devotes so much attention to individualizing her characters. But recent observations by psychologists and evolutionary ethologists about the importance of small-group behavior to our very identity as a species— and especially, as users of language—can help to bring this more speculative, anthropological aspect of Austen's craft to the fore.

The dominant contemporary view of the evolution of language among primatologists and evolutionary ethologists is that, while the physiological prerequisites of human speech had already been in place for perhaps as long as two and a half million years (having developed for the first time in *Homo erectus*), language itself developed among our evolutionary ancestors only about 200,000 years ago, as an aspect of social cognition. More specifically, many believe that the earliest instances of human languages developed to fulfill some of the social functions already performed by *grooming*. There is plenty of evidence that apes, monkeys, and early primates have used grooming to establish and cement social bonds and allegiances, to mitigate the effects of hierarchies, and to provide opportunities for the exchange of social information—in other words, to (wordlessly) *gossip*.[4] The need for a new medium to facilitate the performance of these functions became

3. Vladimir Nabokov, *Lectures on Literature* (Orlando, FL: Mariner Books, 2002), 10.
4. See D. L. Cheney and R. M. Seyfarth, *How Monkeys See the World: Inside the Mind of Another Species* (Chicago: University of Chicago Press, 1990), 68–69, and R I. M. Dunbar, *Primate Social Systems* (London; Sydney: Croom Helm, 1988), 253ff.

especially acute when our forebears, finding themselves excluded to the fringes of the forest and the savannah and constrained to rove more wildly in search of high-nutrient foodstuffs to sustain their large-brained, small-gutted physiologies, had to forge bonds with affinity groups larger than those of their own forest-dwelling, leaf-chewing forebears. The advantage of speech over grooming for this purpose is that it can reach a wider audience more efficiently and with less concomitant exclusivity. Other uses of language, from the articulation of scientific theories to the writing of mass-market novels, are according to this hypothesis best understood as latter-day deviations from the original functions that language served: to form mutually advantageous personal relationships, and to track the relative social status of other conspecifics as they pursue the same goals.

This early mode of speech is classifiable as gossip in the relatively narrow, content-specific sense of being concerned with social minutiae. But its derivation from the gentle business of caressing and plucking at the coats of a fellow primates at least suggests that it deserves to be regarded as a precursor to what we now refer to with the word "gossip" in its somewhat broader connotation—a linguistic practice distinguished not only by its subject matter, but by its characteristic "leisure, intimate revelation and commentary, ease and confidence."[5]

The account of the origins of language just provided has some fascinating axiological implications. Almost everyone has heard the weary old saw that "great minds discuss ideas; average minds discuss events; small minds discuss people."[6] There is a long tradition among philosophers (and others who aspire to serious-mindedness) of regarding gossip as one of the least valuable uses of our time and discursive abilities as a species. Such a view is not exactly falsified by

---

5. Patricia Meyer Spacks, *Gossip* (New York: Alfred A. Knopf, 1985), 3.
6. It is usually attributed to Eleanor Roosevelt (at least on the Internet) but we have been unable to discover a reliable citation.

the "grooming and gossip" (hereafter G&G) hypothesis about the earliest uses of human language. But to the extent that the hypothesis is plausible, one must acknowledge that whatever negative value is attributable to individual instances of gossip on account of its frequent triviality, partiality, or unkindness must be partially offset by the transcendental value that it bears—conceived of holistically—as a precondition for most varieties of social cohesion and for any other use of human languages whatsoever.

Such a view about the ambivalent nature of gossip is provocatively foreshadowed in Heidegger's *Being and Time* (of all places!), during his fascinating discussion of *Gerede* (which is usually translated as "idle talk" or "idle chatter"). In his 1924 lectures on Aristotelian philosophy, Heidegger had already playfully suggested that the Greek definition of the human as ζῷον λόγον ἔχον should be translated as "human being that reads the newspaper."[7] In his magnum opus, Heidegger aggressively denigrates *Gerede*, treating it in Div. One, Section Five as the principal impediment in everyday life to genuine, ontologically significant human reflection. *Gerede* arises as a result of the degeneration of "discourse" (*Rede*), and as such poses the threat of "not really keeping being-in-the-world open in an articulated understanding, but . . . closing it off and covering over inner-worldly beings." But at the same time (in the very same paragraph, in fact), he also characterizes *Gerede* itself as "the possibility of understanding everything without previous appropriation of the matter," which "develops an indifferent intelligibility for which nothing is closed off any longer."[8] Scholars have noted this provocative ambiguity in Heidegger's axiology of gossip, which has been taken to suggest that "the negative and positive aspects of *Gerede*" as represented in

7. Jesús Adrián Escudero, "Heidegger on Discourse and Idle Talk: The Role of Aristotelian Rhetoric," *Gatherings: The Heidegger Circle Annual* 3 (2013): 2.

8. Martin Heidegger, *Being and Time*, trans. Joan Stambaugh (Albany: State University of New York Press, 1996), 158.

Heidegger's work are "part of a continuum and not an all or nothing affair."[9]

In the following section of this chapter, we will examine Austen's own axiological ambivalence about gossip by considering how it is used to exhibit Emma's various moral failings, as well as the highly contagious foibles and moral blindnesses of some of the novel's other characters. We will then go on to take a look at the novel's depiction of gossip's positive influence on social cohesion and individual psychological development. In spite of their frequent descents into casual malice and irresponsible speculation, the characters of *Emma* are not mere perpetrators of what Martin Heidegger dismissed as "idle chatter." Often, even in talking about one another, they attain the specifically modern species of "eloquence" famously (albeit also somewhat equivocally) lauded by David Hume. What gradually emerges, it seems to us, is a depiction of the use of gossip in Emma's social circle that carefully balances considerations about the ethical dangers it presents against a sense of its fundamental and transcendent inevitability, in a way that interestingly mirrors broader accounts of the social and organic function of gossip provided by contemporary ethologists and intimated in the work of several philosophers.

In the chapter's final section, we will step back a bit to consider how Austen's depiction of gossip in *Emma* may also be read as recapitulating a philosophically suggestive (and evolutionarily plausible) account of the origins of language for human sociality. We will close by briefly defending the strategy of reading great works of fiction as proto-philosophy in this sort of way.

9. Escudero, "Heidegger on Discourse and Idle Talk," 13. See also Christina Lafont, "Was Heidegger an Existentialist?" *Inquiry: An International Journal of Philosophy* 48, no. 6 (2005): 5–6.

I. MALICIOUS/IDLE/SERIOUS

Patricia Meyer Spacks's 1985 monograph *Gossip* is the most eloquent, far-reaching, and philosophically informed critical study currently available of the uses of gossip in English literature. According to Spacks, gossip is a distinctive style of conversation that comes in multiple varieties, but that can be taxonomized without too much remainder into three distinct forms. First, it can be an expression of "distilled malice" that "plays with reputations, cumulating half-truths and falsehoods about the activities, sometimes about the motives and feelings, of others."[10] More common, however, is the type of "idle talk" that issues "from unconsidered desire to say something without having to ponder too deeply. Without purposeful intent, gossipers bandy words and anecdotes about people, thus protecting themselves from serious engagement with one another."[11] This type of gossip is perhaps best exemplified by Miss Bates, whose nonstop chatter frequently irritates other characters. Additionally, Mrs. Elton is easily dismissed because she is not only supercilious but talks a great deal about nothing of consequence.

Finally, however, there is a species of "serious" gossip that occurs during leisurely, intimate discourse and serves as a "crucial means of self-expression, a crucial form of solidarity."[12] As examples of the type of gossip she is talking about here, Spacks adverts to the conversations of Muslim women in harems, of Chaucer's Wife of Bath with her friends, and of the schoolgirl clique in Muriel Spark's *The Prime of Miss Jean Brodie*. She also places the intimacies between Nurse Rooke and Mrs. Smith that Anne Elliott witnesses in Chapter Seventeen of *Persuasion* within this category of morally salutary gossip. It is

10. Spacks, *Gossip*, 4.
11. Ibid., 5.
12. Ibid., 5.

somewhat startling that absolutely none of Spacks's literary examples involve women talking to men.[13] If the reading we will provide later of certain exchanges between Emma and Knightley is accurate, they would perhaps for this reason alone represent something of a rarity in the history of English fiction, at least based on the data provided by Spacks's extensive survey.

In Chapter Eight of *Emma*, Emma and Knightley have a heated exchange about Robert Martin, Harriet Smith, and their suitability as a couple. Emma explains to Mr. Knightley that "Mr. Martin is a very respectable young man, but I cannot admit him to be Harriet's equal; and am rather surprised indeed that he should have ventured to address her" (48–49). Emma betrays her prejudice against the gentleman farmer on the grounds of class. In the heat of disputation, she also goes too far in the opposite direction on behalf of her friend when she carelessly and erroneously speculates, "[t]here is little doubt that her father is a gentleman—and a gentleman of fortune.— Her allowance is very liberal; nothing has ever been grudged for her improvement or comfort" (49). Knightley responds by exaggerating Harriet's deficiencies in birth and abilities:

> [s]he is the natural daughter of nobody knows whom, with probably no settled provision at all, and certainly no respectable relations. She is known only as a parlor-boarder at a common school. She is not a sensible girl, and is too young and too simple to have acquired any thing herself . . . [s]he is pretty, and she is good tempered, and that is all. (49)

13. Late in the book, Spacks does advert to the possibility that "serious" gossip can play a benign role in a community's "myth-making," and cites as an example some of the "tales of supernatural deeds" that anthropologists describe as forming the background noise of life in small, self-enclosed communities. See Spacks, *Gossip*, 231.

He is overly harsh here, betraying, at best, carelessness about someone whom he knows very little.

The novel's first-time reader is placed in an interesting situation by these passages. With little information to go on about Harriet apart from an endorsement from her schoolmistress and vague suggestions of a nameless benefactor (19), and absolutely nothing about Martin, there are few points of reference against which the relative merits of Emma's and Knightley's claims can be measured. One's attention is thereby drawn away from the relative legitimacy of each character's claims on behalf of their respective friends, and toward the intensifying acrimony that gossiping causes between them. Yet the reader has surely already begun to guess that Emma and Knightley would be far more profitably occupied in mutual courtship or seduction.

Over-energetic participation in gossip also at certain points causes Emma to be seriously deluded about people and situations. When Mrs. Weston tells Emma about the cold, dark night during which Knightley offered Jane Fairfax the service of his carriage, she does not stop there, but explains at rather fatuous length her own reaction to the story: "I was quite surprised;—very glad, I am sure; but really quite surprised. Such a very kind attention—and so thoughtful an attention!—the sort of thing that so few men would think of" (175). While Mrs. Weston reads deeply into the situation, Emma initially tries to explain it as simply a case of "disinterested benevolence" (176). But Mrs. Weston will not let the subject drop: "[A] suspicion darted into my head," she pronounces, "and I have never been able to get it out again . . . I have made a match between Mr. Knightley and Jane Fairfax. See the consequence of keeping you company!" (176).

Here Mrs. Weston, who has been passively helpful up to now, is portrayed as taking a more active role in the status economy produced by gossip, as a direct result of Emma's personal example. And, her own example having been invoked, Emma's equanimity is disturbed.

Mrs. Weston cannot know the effect of her speech as she continues: "The interest he takes in her—his anxiety about her health—his concern that she should have no happier prospect. Such an admirer of her performance on the pianoforte, and her voice! I have heard him say that he could listen to her for ever" (177).

The spectacle of Mrs. Weston's enthusiasm ends up making a convincing case, even to the more experienced matchmaker. Emma broods at length and becomes greatly agitated at the thought of a union between Knightley and Jane. Her disposition toward Jane changes for the worse as a result, at least by her own lights. In the famous pianoforte scene in Chapter Twenty-eight, she uncharitably misconstrues Jane's blush at the mention of the mystery donor's "true affection" as a sign that the "amiable, upright, perfect Jane Fairfax was apparently cherishing very reprehensible feelings" (191). The passage is written in the free indirect style, but Austen's idiom here very cleverly mimics the verbal rhythms of pejorative gossip. Then later on, at the dinner party at Hartfield, Emma is complicit in Frank Churchill's silly scheme during the word game, and actively participates in causing Jane obvious pain. The game involves forming from alphabet tiles words that have significance for some participants while puzzling others. Frank chooses the word *Dixon* purposely to upset Jane with the implication of impropriety between her and her patron's son-in-law (274). Frank consults Emma before handing Jane the word, and Emma, "opposing it with eager laughing warmth," betrays her amusement and implicit approval. When Knightley later asks her about the incident, Emma knows full well that her actions do not bear scrutiny, and becomes "extremely confused" (275).

Neither of these small flickers of hostility causes any real harm, but it is striking that, in spite of the considerable and culpable extent to which she has been deceived by Frank and Jane, Emma's final verdict on her own behavior is that "I feel that all the apologies should be on my side" (361). Her qualms of conscience clearly have less to do with her public behavior toward Jane, and more with her entirely private errors in status-tracking, which only she and the reader have any reason to be aware of in the first place.

Observing the unsteady path that Emma takes in these episodes toward this final moment of enlightenment, the reader is also prompted to notice the kind of power that can be exercised by gossip itself, as it acquires a peculiar sort of authority over its participants that has nothing to do with the reliability of its originators. It is this very feature of "idle talk," in fact, that Heidegger seems to warn against when he makes the odd-sounding claim that *Gerede* "holds any new questioning and discussion at a distance because *it* presumes *it* has understood and in a peculiar way it suppresses them and holds them back."[14] A major theme of post-Heideggerian philosophy is the notion that language itself exerts a peculiar kind of agency that specifically works to undermine the authority of speakers as what they say is publicly propagated.[15] The hypothesis that language derives its essential features from the careful social positioning one engages in during gossip is helpful in demystifying these *prima facie* much less empirically defensible claims.

Understanding the tendency that gossip has to self-propagate, as well as to introduce new elements of ambiguity into established social distinctions, is absolutely crucial to parsing the psychological and moral subtext of the Box Hill scene. Critics have remarked upon the scene as a relatively rare display of class consciousness from Austen. For Jonathan H. Grossman, Emma's lot in life as a member of Highbury's leisured class is to maintain the standards of etiquette,

---

14. Heidegger, *Being and Time*, 158 (italics mine).
15. This is the central theme of the second half of Jacques Derrida's *Of Grammatology*, Fortieth Anniversary Edition, trans. Gayatri Chakravorty Spivak (Baltimore, MD: Johns Hopkins University Press, 2016); see esp. 153–178—as well as his later tour de force *The Post Card: From Socrates to Freud and Beyond*, trans. Alan Bass (Chicago: University of Chicago Press, 1987).

and her egregious breach in this case aligns her with Frank Churchill's *ethos* of callous disregard.[16] Lynda A. Hall avers that "Austen uses the character of Miss Bates not only to facilitate Emma's personal transformation, but also to shed light on the confining societal structures that can create both a ridiculous, pitiful spinster and a cruel, selfish heiress."[17] It is undeniable that the episode is meant to provoke the reader to empathize with the socially marginalized, helplessly prattling Miss Bates.

But it would be a subtle error to suppose that the inequity between the two characters is as gross and unmitigated as Knightley's speech after the incident makes it appear to be. "She is poor; she has sunk from the comforts she was born to; and, if she live to old age, must probably sink more. Her situation should secure your compassion" (295), Knightley himself gossips, in order to elicit Emma's contrition. But the unkindness Emma has just exhibited toward Miss Bates is itself an act of conversational ventriloquism. During the Box Hill outing, Frank Churchill proposes that everyone say something entertaining. In response, Miss Bates witters on in her usual style that she "shall be sure to say three dull things" (291). Emma's fatal remark— "Ah, Ma'am, but there may be a difficulty. Pardon me—but you will be limited as to number—only three at once" (291),—exhibits the same circumlocuitous, almost Joycean syntax as Miss Bates's own more lengthy deliverances, with which Austen has already teased the reader unto a certain degree of exasperation.

16. See Jonathan H. Grossman, "The Labor of the Leisured in Emma: Class Manners, and Austen," *Ninetheenth-Century Literature* 54, no. 2 (1999): 143–164. While Grossman has little to say about gossip itself, he does think that the most basic impetus of the plot is the attainment of status equilibrium. By marrying Mr. Knightley, "Austen depicts Emma finding not just her proper place but also her work" (156).

17. Lynda A. Hall, "Valuing the Superfluous Spinster: Miss Bates and the Struggle to Remain Visible," *Eighteenth-Century Novel* 9 (2012): 297.

And Miss Bates herself, while she often cannot seem to exercise re-
straint, does exhibit a degree of self-awareness about her own discursive foibles. Consider more closely how Austen's narrator frames her
remarks that immediately precede Emma's brief act of unkindness:

> "I need not be uneasy. 'Three things very dull indeed.' That will
> just do for me, you know. I shall be sure to say three dull things as
> soon as ever I open my mouth, shan't I? (looking round with the
> most good-humoured dependence on every body's assent)—
> Do not you all think I shall?" (291)

Bharat Tandon remarks upon the "extraordinary bracketed stage
direction" in the middle of this quotation, which he takes as an indication that Miss Bates has "partly pre-empted Emma's joke at her
expense." He appeals to this passage (among others) to support his
more general contention that

> Emma['s] ... adventures in social and amatory ventriloquism, to-
> gether with their attendant slip-ups, are the novel's motive force.
> Throwing the voice becomes, in the course of Austen's narrative,
> more than a stylistic device: indeed, it is the very medium within
> which she comes to apprehend how repentance might work in
> an atmosphere of polite conversation.[18]

Literary theorists have often spoken in a rather loosely metaphor-
ical way about how "language speaks us,"[19] in the sense that it can
itself exhibit a kind of agency that is independent of—perhaps,

18. Bharat Tandon, *Jane Austen and the Morality of Conversation* (London: Anthem Press,
2003), 146.
19. For a useful, albeit somewhat deflationary reading of this aphorism, see Timothy W.
Crusius, *Kenneth Burke and the Conversation after Philosophy* (Carbondale: Southern
Illinois Press, 1999), 246.

even, conceptually prior to—the agency of individual speakers and auditors. But here Austen provides a genuine example of a particular style of speaking (along with its associated affects) that should strike the reader as genuinely emergent from the collective dispositions of a particular social group at a particular, highly unstable stage in the development of their mutual relations. The reader is not prompted to let Emma off the hook for her mean jibe, but we should certainly take seriously Austen's observation that "Emma could not resist" (291).

But of course, Emma's culpable complicity with and intensification of Miss Bates's careless chatter ends up serving a higher purpose when it leads her to confront her own suppressed (and partly inherited) malice directly. Knightley's speech leaves her mortified and repentant, and she immediately sets to work for a return to their easy friendship, which she ironically enough manages to gain access to through the propagation of even more casual gossip.

More specifically, Emma makes amends with Miss Bates via a discursive exhibition of concern for Jane. When Emma visits her the next day, she notices "there was not the same cheerful volubility as before—less ease of look and manner. A very friendly inquiry after Miss Fairfax, she hoped, might lead the way to a return of old feelings. The touch seemed immediate" (297). The narrator explains that

> [h]er heart had been long growing kinder towards Jane; and this
> picture of her present sufferings acted as a cure of every former
> ungenerous suspicion . . . and the remembrance of the less just
> and less gentle sensations of the past, obliged her to admit that
> Jane might very naturally resolve on seeing Mrs. Cole or any
> other steady friend, when she might not bear to see herself. (298)

All of these subtle psychological observations are offered, not as a comment upon anything that Emma actually says herself, but as a gloss on yet another of Miss Bates's uninterrupted, bizarrely digressive monologues. The end result of the whole episode is that Austen's heroïne re-evaluates her formerly uncharitable attitudes and comes to an important moment of self-discovery. When Knightley learns of Emma's visit, he warmly approves, and the damage done at Box Hill is repaired. The narrator reports that Knightley "looked at her with a glow of regard. She was warmly gratified—and in another moment still more so, by a little movement of more than common friendliness on his part. He took her hand" (303).

It is surely not an accident that Austen chose this rare, wordless gesture to provide the first solid intimation of a blooming romance between the two characters. Knightley is subtly depicted throughout the novel (and much more explicitly in its film adaptations) as physically remote to the point of awkwardness. The surest sign that he disapproves of one of Emma's machinations is "rising and walking off abruptly" (53), and during a couple of Emma's more extensive perorations, he is depicted as "listening in perfect silence. She wished him to speak, but he would not," and as "silent; and, as far as she could judge, deep in thought" (335). These passages have a very gently satirical feel to them, an aspect of the text that is brought to the fore in the 1996 film by Jeremy Northam's playfully judicious portrayal of Knightley, with his preposterously high collar and his hands almost perpetually clasped behind his back.

Robin Dunbar, the most prominent among evolutionary ethologists who have argued for the G&G hypothesis, also entertains the following somewhat less rigorously testable conjecture:

> one of the more curious aspects of language [is] its complete inadequacy at the emotional level. It is a most wondrous invention for conveying bald information, but fails most of us totally when we want to express the deepest reaches of our innermost souls. We are so often "lost for words" in such circumstances. Language is a wonderful introduction to a prospective relationship. . . . But

when the relationship reaches the point of greatest intensity, we abandon language and return to the age-old rituals of mutual mauling and direct stimulation. At this crucial point in our lives, grooming—of all the things we inherit from our primate ancestry—resurfaces as the way we reinforce our bonds.[20]

It would not be out of line to cringe at the clichéd romanticism of Dunbar's remarks here. But like any good empiricist, he is ready with an alternate explanation of stereotypical masculine behaviors such as Knightley's. One controversial but well-supported elaboration of the G&G hypothesis about the origins of language is that "the earliest human females were the first to speak," a hypothesis entertained both on the basis of experimental data about contemporary female social bonding and genetic evidence that female kin groups among our evolutionary ancestors tended to remain closer together.[21]

Is Knightley's physical gesture better understood to be offering Emma a type of personal intimacy that "transcends language," or to be an attempt at gaining admittance into a restricted social circle? The point of suggesting alternate interpretations of his little piece of gestural communication derived from these two logically compatible but (in this instance) interestingly divergent accounts of the original functions of language is not, of course, to suggest that Austen was somehow anticipating debates in contemporary ethology. It is rather just to suggest that the ambiguity of such moments in the narrative can helpfully be understood as running deeper than merely to questions about the ephemeral motives of individual characters.

20. Robin Dunbar, *Grooming, Gossip, and the Evolution of Language* (Cambridge, MA: Harvard University Press, 1996), 147–148.
21. Dunbar, *Grooming, Gossip, and the Evolution of Language*, 149–150. The *locus classicus* of the "females first" theory of language origins (as acknowledged by Dunbar) is Chris Knight, *Blood Relations: Menstruation and the Origins of Culture* (New Haven, CT: Yale University Press, 1990).

At any rate, this moment of uncharacteristic intimacy with Knightley leaves a profound impression on Emma. In a subsequent, unusually meandering conversation full of exactly the sorts of intricate cross-referencing and meta-discursive digressions that the G&G hypothesis would have us treat as paradigmatic features of the earliest human speech, Harriet tells Emma, "I hope I have a better taste than to think of Mr. Frank Churchill, who is like nobody by his side." Emma asks, "Are you speaking of—Mr. Knightley?" to which Harriet responds, "To be sure I am. I never could have an idea of any body else—and so I thought you knew. When we talked about him, it was clear as possible" (319). These remarks prompt Emma to reach the apparently spontaneous conclusion that "Mr. Knightley must marry no one but herself!" (320) Having formerly eschewed all thoughts of marriage, Emma is led with a singular inexorability *via* gossip itself to conclude (with perfect reasonableness) that Knightley is her appropriate partner.

Note also the main theme of the speech that Knightley delivers when their courtship at last becomes explicit: "You hear nothing but the truth from me," he says. "I have blamed you, and lectured you, and you have borne it as no other woman in England would have borne it" (338). It is Emma's tolerance for the serious moral burdens imposed by Knightley's own relatively severe style of gossip that have assured her of his ultimate esteem.

There is other subtle, but significant evidence that Austen thought that gossip might sometimes be strictly indispensable as a prompt for reasoned action. Emma and Knightley are portrayed as changing their respective attitudes toward Robert Martin and Harriet Smith thanks to the slow, benign intercession of gossip. When Knightley tells Emma that her friend accepted Robert Martin's proposal, he worries at first that she is horrified. When Emma approves, Knightley remarks, "You are materially changed since we talked on this subject before." Emma responds that "at that time I was a fool" (373). Knightley confesses that he, too, is changed, and he explains the effects of having gotten to know Harriet better: "[F]rom all my observations, I am convinced of her being an artless, amiable girl, with very good notions, very seriously good principles, and placing her happiness in the affections and utility of domestic life" (373). The two characters' sober self-corrections in this conversation embody the "serious" type of gossip described by Spacks as an irreplaceable means to self-expression and solidarity. At the same time, though, Austen makes clear that a significant cause of their changes of heart is just what they have learned via previous, perhaps somewhat less ethically exalted, sessions of gossip about their friends' low social status. Knightley has already acknowledged about Robert that "[h]is situation is an evil—but ... His good sense and good principles would delight you," to which Emma has responded, "I think Harriet is doing extremely well. *Her* connections may be worse than *his*" (371). The effects of both idle and "serious" forms of gossip on their personal growth are profoundly interwoven here, but Austen makes it clear that the overall happiness of the community is increased thereby.

Eva Dadlez has observed that "Austen's novels all have a clear focus on intellectual development," especially that of their protagonists.[22] And (as Dadlez also points out) Emma herself exhibits awareness of a key aspect of her own character that allows for the eventually broadening of her sympathies: "to her great amusement, [she] perceived that she was taking the other side of the question from her real opinion, and making use of ... arguments against herself" (114). This image of psychological development as a gradual integration of conflicting inner "voices" has been elaborated in different ways by a diverse variety of figures throughout the history of Western philosophical psychology, from Socrates to Julian Jaynes. Advocates of

22. See E. M. Dadlez, *Mirrors to One Another: Emotion and Value in Jane Austen and David Hume* (Chichester, UK: Wiley-Blackwell, 2009), 143.

the G&G hypothesis also find a place for the idea in their explanation for why our language centers developed on the left side of the brain (along with the ability for gestural communication). According to Dunbar, this occurred because the right hemisphere was "already fully preoccupied" with "the processing of emotional information."[23] Thus the development of language via gossip produced a physiologically based asymmetry in how we read the emotional cues we receive from other speakers—a difficult legacy with which our species as a whole still struggles.[24]

Not all of Austen's characters come to their final wisdom via the give-and-take of conversation. Elizabeth Bennet's slow changes of mind come about mostly via introspection in the latter half of *Pride and Prejudice*, and the gossip and status judgments made by third parties are depicted as the main obstacle to insight and self-realization for Anne Elliot in *Persuasion*. There is, in fact, nothing quite like the long and remarkably sophisticated exchanges between Emma and Knightley in any of the other novels. Perhaps they may be taken as an example of the specifically modern type of "eloquence" that David Hume characterizes in his famous essay on the topic—a style of elevated speech based more upon "good sense, delivered in proper expression"[25] than the "sublime and pathetic" modes of speech favored by ancient orators, and a phenomenon better exemplified by "our writers" than "our public speakers."[26]

Insofar as they belong at the top of Spacks's hierarchy of gossip, the intense and high-minded exchanges had by Emma and Knightley toward the end of the book are the exception to the rule and are clearly meant to set the two characters apart from their relatively

23. Dunbar, *Gossip, Grooming and the Evolution of Language*, 136.
24. Ibid., 137–140.
25. David Hume, "Of Eloquence," in *Essays* (Dumfries; Galloway: Anodos Books, 2017), 70.
26. Ibid., 72.

THE MANY FACES OF GOSSIP IN EMMA

frivolous associates (with the exception of the near-silent Jane). But the arc of *Emma*'s moral universe—and of the gossip that serves as its lifeblood—bends toward positive psychological development and greater social integration for all of her characters. Like our ancestors who first ventured tentatively out of the forest onto the savannah, they learn to navigate the world by learning to trust and adjust to one another.

II. IN DEFENSE OF JUST-SO STORIES

In discussing a few of the various injuries and revelations afforded to Austen's characters via the medium of gossip, we have treated the G&G hypothesis (as well as the observations of some philosophers that seem to resonate therewith) as a potential source of illumination when it comes to understanding Austen's own attitudes toward this ethically and functionally ambivalent mode of human speech. We have thereby chosen to read *Emma* at least partly allegorically, as an analogue for an episode in our species' collective history that allowed us all to become more distinctively human. So what is the ultimate value of reading Austen's novel—or works of literary fiction more generally—in this way?

One aim that we wish to strenuously disavow is that of providing anything like a "scientific justification" of Austen's insights into human character. The very idea that there is a stable concept of character that does indispensable explanatory work outside of the interpretation of narrative has been forcefully questioned by several contemporary philosophers,[27] and nothing that we have said either about *Emma* or about the view of human nature implied by the

---

27. This type of character skepticism receives a detailed defense in Gregory Currie, *Narratives and Narrators: A Philosophy of Stories* (Oxford: Oxford University Press, 2010), 199–216.

G&G hypothesis provides any ammunition for participants on either side of this debate. More important, though, we also think that the usefulness of the G&G hypothesis as an aid to the interpretation of literature deserves to be evaluated at least partly *independently* of its ultimate scientific plausibility.

Without getting too embroiled in any of the very vigorous debates currently underway about the origins of language, we may identify two reasons for viewing the G&G hypothesis as an evolutionary just-so story. First of all (as we already mentioned), it is widely believed that *Homo erectus* had already developed all of the physiological mechanisms required for speech over a million years before the migratory events that caused human beings to have to associate in larger social units (i.e., groups of around 150 rather than twenty-five to fifty in size). These earlier physiological developments were adaptively quite expensive, and while it is unlikely that any future discoveries from the fossil record could decide the matter one way or another (since speech and writing leave no such traces behind them) it is at least problematic to suppose that the relevant traits (expanded chest cavities, the hyoid bone, etc.) could have lain dormant so long before anybody thought to strike up a conversation. And secondly, as even Dunbar very openly acknowledges, there is a central ambiguity in the G&G hypothesis itself. Supposing that the earliest language users first started to speak as a way to cultivate the sorts of intimacies they had earlier developed via grooming, was their aim in doing so simply to share information, or was it to induce social cohesion through something more like religious ritual, imitative play, or singing songs? "It still remains unclear," as Dunbar puts it, "whether the initial stimulus to language was provided by the emotional uplift of the Greek chorus or by the need to exchange information about other members of the alliance or group."[28] Once again, given the absence of fossils or

---

28. Dunbar, *Gossip, Grooming and the Evolution of Language*, 150.

a written record, how one answers this question is likely to depend more upon one's philosophical views about the nature of human language and society than it ever will upon delicate empirical questions of etiology.

Understanding this latter indeterminacy in the G&G hypothesis can, in fact, itself cast a little additional light on Austen's overall literary project. *Emma* is easily Austen's most casual-conversation-rich novel, and far fewer of its key scenes are acted out in the midst of social rituals such as dances, artistic performances, or formal social events than in her other works, especially *Mansfield Park* and *Pride and Prejudice*. In both of these other novels, the abilities that certain characters (e.g., Mary Bennet and Maria Bertram) exhibit at art, social ritual, and performance are windows into their personalities rather than sources of mystification, as is the case in *Emma* with Jane Fairfax's piano playing. Perhaps it is not too much of a stretch for us to regard Austen the ethologist as willing to countenance both variations on the G&G hypothesis, and for us to read her corpus as an attempt to tease out the implications of these very different views about the social function of language and communication.

While the epistemic status of evolutionary just-so stories will always be problematic—even when, as has long been the case with questions about the origins of language, scientists despair of ever finding a better mode of speculation—they should not for this reason be merely ignored as *loci* of intertextuality. The G&G hypothesis is a story worth telling because it taps into deep intuitions that thoughtful, empirically well-informed people have about the abiding properties of human nature and the most redoubtable functions of human speech. The type of support that it provides for the psychological insights of a novelist like Austen is bi-directional; if we have independent reasons to think that her work has survived in the public esteem because she grasps fundamental truths about human nature, then her representation of gossip and how it functions in the lives of her characters cannot but have at least some broader implications for how we view its overall place within the human drama.[29]

REFERENCES

Austen-Leigh, James Edward. *A Memoir of Jane Austen*, edited by R. W. Chapman. Oxford: Clarendon, 1967.

Booth, Wayne C. *The Rhetoric of Fiction*. Chicago: University of Chicago Press, 1961.

Bradbrook, F. W. *Jane Austen: Emma, Studies in English Literature*. London: Edward Arnold, 1970.

Cheney, D. L., and R. M. Seyfarth. *How Monkeys See the World: Inside the Mind of Another Species*. Chicago: University of Chicago Press, 1990.

Crusius, Timothy W. *Kenneth Burke and the Conversation after Philosophy*. Carbondale: Southern Illinois Press, 1999.

Currie, Gregory. *Narratives and Narrators: A Philosophy of Stories*. Oxford: Oxford University Press, 2010.

Dadlez, E. M. *Mirrors to One Another: Emotion and Value in Jane Austen and David Hume*. Chichester, UK: Wiley-Blackwell, 2009.

Derrida, Jacques. *Of Grammatology*, fortieth anniversary edition, translated by Gayatri Chakravorty Spivak. Baltimore, MD: Johns Hopkins University Press, 2016.

Derrida, Jacques. *The Post Card: From Socrates to Freud and Beyond*, translated by Alan Bass. Chicago: University of Chicago Press, 1987.

Dunbar, R. I. M. *Primate Social Systems*. London; Sydney: Croom Helm, 1988.

Dunbar, Robin. *Grooming, Gossip, and the Evolution of Language*. Cambridge, MA: Harvard University Press, 1996.

Escudero, Jesús Adrián. "Heidegger on Discourse and Idle Talk: The Role of Aristotelian Rhetoric." *Gatherings: The Heidegger Circle Annual* 3, no. 2 (2013): 1–17.

Grossman, Jonathan H. "The Labor of the Leisured in Emma: Class Manners, and Austen." *Nineteenth-Century Literature* 54, no. 2 (1999): 143–164.

Hall, Lynda A. "Valuing the Superfluous Spinster: Miss Bates and the Struggle to Remain Visible." *Eighteenth-Century Novel* 9 (2012): 281–299.

29. For a suggestive and fascinating discussion of how this relation of bi-directional evidentiary support might work between the interpretation of literature and another epistemically under-determined account of human psychology (Jungian psychoanalysis), see Francis Sparshott, "The Riddle of *Katharsis*," in *Centre and Labyrinth: Essays in Honour of Northrop Frye*, ed. Eleanor Cook (Toronto: University of Toronto Press, 1993), 14–37.

Heidegger, Martin. *Being and Time,* translated by Joan Stambaugh. Albany: State University of New York Press, 1996.

Hume, David. "Of Eloquence." In Hume, *Essays,* 132–148. Dumfries & Galloway: Anodos Books, 2017.

Knight, Chris. *Blood Relations: Menstruation and the Origins of Culture.* New Haven, CT: Yale University Press, 1990.

Lafont, Christina. "Was Heidegger an Existentialist?" *Inquiry: An International Journal of Philosophy* 48, no. 6 (2005): 5–6.

Nabokov, Vladimir. *Lectures on Literature.* Orlando, FL: Mariner Books, 2002.

Spacks, Patricia Meyer. *Gossip.* New York: Alfred A. Knopf, 1985.

Sparshott, Francis. "The Riddle of *Katharsis.*" In *Centre and Labyrinth: Essays in Honour of Northrop Frye,* edited by Eleanor Cook, 14–37. Toronto: University of Toronto Press, 1993.

Tandon, Bharat. *Jane Austen and the Morality of Conversation.* London: Anthem Press, 2003.

Chapter 6

The Reconstrual of Imagination and Romance

PETER KNOX-SHAW

When Sir Walter Scott characterized the novel as the "legitimate" child of romance, he was referring to the limits imposed on the writer's imagination by a form that ranged between what he described as the "concentric circles of probability and possibility."[1] A few previous novelists had set their sights on a more august descent, and some (with less concern for the benefit of clergy) had continued to embrace the incredible. But Scott's observation, made in the course of a review of *Emma*, led him to state that Jane Austen epitomized a new class of fiction that kept within the inner circle of realism by virtue of an exceptional fidelity to the "current of ordinary life."[2] The allocation had its drawbacks. So strongly linked was the idea of invention to the marvelous and heroic that a contemporary reviewer, clearly influenced by Scott, concluded that Austen's truth to experience exacted the sacrifice of romance and imagination.[3] Since *Emma*

---

1. "Unsigned Review of *Emma*," *Quarterly Review*, March 1816, in *Jane Austen: The Critical Heritage*, ed. B. C. Southam (London, 1968), 59, 61.
2. Ibid., 59.
3. "Unsigned Review," *British Critic*, March 1818, in *Critical Heritage*, 80–84.

manifestly does provide a critique of this time-honored coupling, it has often been approached as a late flowering of quixotic fiction, and with good reason—foremost among the many "errors of imagination" displayed by Austen's chief "imaginist," for instance, is the supposition that Harriet, being a pretty heroine of unknown birth, can only belong to the gentry. Was *Emma* then intended as a final nail in the coffin of imagination and romance?

The senses of "imagination" have always been many, and in the long eighteenth century, a period in which it was beginning to develop a fresh set of significances, the word was employed at times in almost antithetical ways.[4] While it could denote the faculty of genius in creating a new order or revealing an existent one, it had begun to refer to the entire gamut of mental resources that underlay all perception. It continued, at the same time, to signify the mistaken and delusory, and in this pejorative sense it was frequently coupled with the far-fetched extravagances of ancient literature, particularly of romance. When David Hume makes use of this coupling at the start of the *Treatise*, it is to insist, however, that "the liberty of imagination" is not only natural but irrepressible: "winged horses, fiery dragons, and monstrous giants" are to be expected from a power that is free, unlike memory, to transpose, or to fuse the ideas that issue from impressions, with the result that "nature there is totally confounded."[5] This was the first step in a discussion of imagination that was to prove formative not only to later philosophy, but also to other adjacent fields, including literary criticism.

Although imagination has, for Hume, all the epistemological unreliability of romance, there is no making sense of what is present

---

4. Michael Williams discusses *Emma* in relation to eighteenth-century ideas of imagination, but with reference chiefly to Samuel Johnson; see Williams, *Jane Austen: Six Novels and Their Methods* (London: Macmillan, 1986), Ch. 6.

5. David Hume, *A Treatise of Human Nature*, ed. David Fate Norton and Mary J. Norton (Oxford: Oxford University Press, 2002), 1.1.3.1, 12.

to the senses without it. Marvelously versatile ("a magical faculty in the soul") yet uncontrollable ("naturally sublime"), it is the means by which the "mind looks further than what immediately appears to it."[6] The point is elsewhere underlined when Hume asks his readers to envisage the confusion and bewilderment that would be the lot of a fully developed adult suddenly "transported into our world."[7] Cognition depends on a depth of mental resource, which spontaneously brings order to the atomism of present experience. And to this end the imagination, by linking up the discrete and discontinuous, produces a series of imperceived fictions—"natural beliefs" that include our sense of the continued and distinct existence of bodies, as well as the relation of cause and effect—without which survival would not be possible. For the most part, Hume's charting of the "empire of imagination" is devoted to metaphysical themes, but even in this arena his findings are replete with psychological implication.[8] Readers are likely to forget that he has the foundations of mathematics in mind when he remarks that the imagination is "apt to continue, even when its object fails it, and like a galley put in motion by the oars, carries on its course without any new impulse."[9] Inspired by such asides from the *Treatise*, William Smellie in his *Philosophy of Natural History* (1790) sketches the hypothetical case of a robustly imaginative man, whose life of reverie continually informs his daily

---

6. Hume, *Treatise*, 1.1.7.15, 21; Hume, *An Enquiry concerning Human Understanding*, ed. Tom L. Beauchamp (Oxford: Oxford University Press, 1999), 12.3.25, 208; *Treatise*, 1.4.2.4, 126.

7. Hume, "Of the Passions" in *Four Dissertations* (London: A. Millar, 1757), 156. Hume appears in this passage to be concerned chiefly with the power that social conventions exercise over perception, but his exemplum, borrowed from the fantasy with which Buffon concludes his section on the senses in his *Histoire Naturelle* (II, viii), has more general import.

8. Hume, *Treatise*, "Abstract," 416.

9. Hume, *Treatise*, 1.4.2.22, p. 132.

existence until given free rein in his dreams: this scientifically minded naturalist takes quixotism to be the norm.[10]

Immanuel Kant, whose notion of the synthetic imagination was much indebted to Hume, could get away with the claim, made in 1781, that "psychologists have hitherto failed to realize that imagination is a necessary ingredient of perception itself."[11] Both philosophers understood this largely unconscious power to be inherent in consciousness, but Hume gave imagination preeminence, also, in his account of the natural virtues, a place denied it by Kant in his duty-based ethics. So Hume speaks not only of imagination allowing us to "enter" into the feelings of another person, but also of its role as a "productive faculty" that conjures up moral approval through projection, a process that by "gilding or staining all natural objects with the colours, borrowed from internal sentiment, raises, in a manner, a new creation."[12] While stressing the all-pervasiveness of the imagination, Hume remains alert, however, to the perils posed by a "principle so inconstant and fallacious," and finds a sole corrective in the rational exercise of judgement.[13] If Hume provides, as one recent commentator has graphically put it, "a naturalistic conception of a creature afflicted by projective errors, but capable nonetheless of a reasonable grip on its real circumstances," some anti-realist proponents of his thought might quibble over the last clause.[14] But the far-reaching influence of his theory soon demonstrated that it transcended sectarianism. Coleridge was indebted to Hume as well as to German idealism when

10. William Smellie, *The Philosophy of Natural History* (Edinburgh: T. Cadell, G. G. and J Robinson, 1790), Ch. 5.

11. Immanuel Kant, *Critique of Pure Reason*, trans. Norman Kemp Smith (London: Macmillan, 1933), A 120n, 144.

12. Hume, *An Enquiry concerning the Principles of Morals*, ed. Tom L. Beauchamp (Oxford: Oxford University Press, 2004), App.1, 163.

13. Hume, *Treatise*, 1.4.7.4, 173.

14. Stephen Buckle, "Review of P. J. E. Kail, *Projection and Realism in Hume's Philosophy* (Oxford, 2007)," *Hume Studies* 34, no. 1 (April 2008): 163–165, at 165.

he famously declared in *Biographia Literaria*, published in the year of Jane Austen's death, that the divine "primary" imagination (differing from the literary form in degree rather than kind) was the familiar "living Power and prime Agent of all human Perception."[15]

If *Emma* typifies a new category of fiction by virtue of its fidelity to the "current of ordinary life," it shows the imaginary to be as intrinsic to that everyday stream (*pace* Scott) as oxygen is to water. Indeed, in this major work Jane Austen sets out to imagine the unconscious and everyday work of the imagination with all the conscious deliberation appropriate to a central theme. Before Emma ever meets Harriet Smith, we are led to explore the idea of projection through the comedy arising from her father's valetudinarianism. The feeling of loss stirred in Mr. Woodhouse by the marriage first of his older daughter and then of the much-loved Miss Taylor is obstinately transferred by him to them, as his customary attachment of the epithet "poor" to both their names signals, and the point is brought home when Mr. Knightley observes, "Poor Mr. and Miss Woodhouse, if you please."[16] The reader is reminded twice that Emma's father "could never believe other people to be different from himself," and is briefed on the style of his transference: "he had, in fact, though unconsciously, been attributing many of his own feelings and expressions" (7, 16, 85). Mr. Woodhouse's projection is of such a rudimentary kind as to be highly visible, since taking minimal account of the circumstances and feelings of others, he effectively projects onto a screen that is blank. And so transparent are his appeals to abstinence and celibacy that they prove disarmingly ineffectual. While he seeks to impose his dietary regime on others with a strength of will that rivals Emma's, his

15. Samuel Taylor Coleridge, *Biographia Literaria*, ed. J. Shawcross, 2 vols. (Oxford: Oxford University Press, 1973), I, 202.
16. *Emma*, ed. James Kinsley and Adela Pinch (Oxford: Oxford University Press, 2008), 9. Subsequent quotations from this edition will appear in text within parentheses.

wary guests—with the aid of her tactful interventions—manage for the most part to evade it. But at Hartfield the odds are against the famished or eligible being helped unconditionally to what they most want, and Emma's matchmaking is all the more formidable for being honed by her exceptional percipience.

Harriet's first meeting with her patron takes place at a supper punctuated by a patter of asides ("'a *small* half glass—put into a tumbler of water?'," 20) that serve as a reminder of Mr. Woodhouse's inability to suppose that other people could feel differently from himself. Emma is particularly attracted, however, by a feature that distinguishes her young guest from herself, a feature that she registers initially as "blue eyes," but which she modifies—as Harriet increasingly reveals her amiable and deferential disposition—to "those soft blue eyes," a formula that, on further repetition, opens a stimulating vista:

> She was so busy in admiring those soft blue eyes, in talking and listening, and forming all these schemes in the in-betweens, that the evening flew away at a very unusual rate. (19)

Remarking on the way a cryptic diagram can suddenly spring into representational relief, Wittgenstein noted that "it is as if an *image* came into contact, and for a time remained in contact, with the visual impression."[17] Emma's refining of blue to *soft* blue eyes registers an equivalent shift in perception, since it points to the enlivening presence of a highly charged stereotype, at once both literary and social, comparable in status to the dumb blonde of a later century. Those soft blue eyes put Emma under a spell that charms away illegitimacy (a stigma to which she is otherwise sensitive) and smooths the path to a prestigious marriage. Tellingly, as the relationship unfolds, and she proceeds to paint Harriet's portrait for Elton, she takes the

17. Ludwig Wittgenstein, *Philosophical Investigations* (Oxford: Blackwell, 1953), 207e.

opportunity to flesh out the fashion-plate more fully, attenuating her sitter's figure while framing the soft blue eyes with brows and lashes.

Emma's pictorial make-over of Harriet hardly rates as shape-shifting à la Quixote, but her plans for Harriet soon betray a kinship with popular romance when she attempts, once intimacy is established, to undermine Robert Martin's chances as a suitor by depicting him as uneducated and underbred. Harriet objects that "he has read a good deal—but not what you would think any thing of," and immediately proceeds, "He has never read the Romance of the Forest, nor the Children of the Abbey" (23). The heroines in both these works (which Emma evidently approves) arrive at high status from originally distressed circumstances: in Ann Radcliffe's *Romance of the Forest* (1791), Adeline—thought to be illegitimate—turns out to be the daughter of a marquis; and in Regina Maria Roche's *Children of the Abbey* (1798), both Amanda and Adeline are finally blessed with unforeseen connections. All three heroines belong to the blue-eyed prototype. Roche's Adeline has eyes that are "soft, blue," and the "soft eyes" of her Amanda suggest the "soft expression of a Madonna" while her "fine blue eyes [beaming] with modesty and gratitude" grace the "softest smile of complacence."[18] Radcliffe adroitly performs a similar service for her Adeline by quoting from James Thomson, "An eye / As when the blue sky trembles thro' a cloud / Of purest white," but prefers "captivating sweetness" to softness, possibly inspiring Mrs. Courtney, who writes of her protagonist in *Isabinda of Bellefield: A Sentimental Novel* (1795), "her mild soft eyes beamed with ineffable sweetness."[19] Such usage had become sufficiently hackneyed by the turn of the century to provoke satire. William Beckford in *Modern*

18. Regina Maria Roche, *The Children of the Abbey*, 4 vols. (London: Minerva Press, 1798), I, 182, 131, 96, 53.
19. Ann Radcliffe, *The Romance of the Forest*, ed. Chloe Chard (Oxford: Oxford University Press, 1991), 6–7, 29; Mrs. Courtney, *Isabinda of Bellefield: A Sentimental Novel*, 2 vols. (Dublin: P. Wogan, 1795), I, 169.

Novel Writing (1796), a skit on sentimental fiction, gives a "soft eye" to the moon, while Eaton Stannard Barrett in *The Heroine* (1813), a burlesque much admired by Jane Austen, has his Cherubina (formerly Cherry) picture herself "tall and aërial, tresses flaxen, my eyes blue and sleepy," before she cuts all ties with her father—a blue-eyed, flaxen-haired farmer whose features betray her legitimacy.[20]

By bracketing off the issue of reading, Jane Austen contrives to suggest that the image Emma projects upon Harriet has its source not simply in fiction but in a deep-seated cultural form that popular romance both drew upon and intensified. A clue to its identity and presence (long established before the sentimental or gothic novel got under way) is given by James Fordyce in his widely influential *Sermons to Young Women* (1766), the work used by Collins to vex the Bennet daughters in *Pride and Prejudice*. Taking as his text the apostle Paul's exhortation that "women adorn themselves with modest apparel and Shamefacedness" (which he glosses as "amiable reserve"), Fordyce contends that the fair sex was designed to be submissive, and points to the outward and visible sign of this subservience when Nature, in an inset speech, pronounces on the fate of fallen women: "Their eyes formerly soft, virtuous, and downcast; those very eyes that effused the soul of innocence, have learnt to stare."[21] Soft eyes achieve a welcome degree of definition from Fordyce's jeremiad since they are evidently eyes that are looked at, rather than eyes that do the looking. But, commenting on this particular speech as a whole, Mary Wollstonecraft provides a broader sense of what is involved in the stereotype: "A virtuous man may have a choleric or a sanguine constitution, be gay or grave . . . but all women are to be

---

20. William Beckford, *Modern Novel Writing*, 2 vols. (London: G.G. and J. Robinson, 1796), II, 95; Eaton Stannard Barrett, *The Heroine*, 2nd ed., 3 vols. (London: H. Colburn, 1814), I, 31, 43.

21. James Fordyce, *Sermons to Young Women*, 2 vols. (London: A. Miller, 1791), I, p. 101.

PETER KNOX-SHAW

levelled, by meekness and docility, into one character of yielding softness and gentle compliance."[22] Fordyce's portrait, she concludes, is that of a "house slave."[23]

It is with her "quick eye" that Emma rapidly solves the riddle on "courtship" that Elton inscribes into Harriet's collection of riddles but intends for her, and she instantly supposes that he is requesting Harriet to favor his advances, though the relationship pictured in the verse is not exactly an enticing one. For the duration of courtship, the courting male may sacrifice his freedom ("Lord of the earth and sea, he bends a slave, / And woman, lovely woman, reigns alone"), but lord of the earth he remains, his sovereignty on land and ocean in no way altered (57–58). Disconcerting, too, is Elton's theft of the last line from the *Vicar of Wakefield*, not only because it recalls Harriet's patient admirer Robert Martin, who is reported to have read the book, but because Goldsmith's line is sung by Olivia, the daughter whose glamorous wooing ends in a mock-wedding and the groom's desertion. With good reason, the idea that courtship displayed a reversal of the customary roles was widely aired during this period. In *Clarissa*, Samuel Richardson has his sprightly Anna Howe complain that women are "courted as Princesses for a few weeks, in order to be treated as Slaves for the rest of our lives,"[24] and Hume compares courtship among the beau monde to the controlled annual release of topsy-turvydom in the classical feast of Saturnalia at the close of his second *Enquiry*.[25] But the fullest treatment is offered by Mary Wollstonecraft, who argues that women have been inveigled out of their natural equality by the short-term allure of male gallantry, clinching the point with a quote from Anna Aikin:

---

22. Wollstonecraft, *Vindication of the Rights of Women*, in *Mary Wollstonecraft: Political Writings*, ed. Janet Todd (London: W. Pickering, 1993), 177.
23. Ibid.
24. Samuel Richardson, *Clarissa*, 7 vols. (Oxford: Blackwell, 1930), I, 191.
25. Hume, *Morals*, 191.

In beauty's empire is no mean,
And woman, either slave or queen,
Is quickly scorn'd when not ador'd.[26]

Providing the male perspective on this seesaw-like state of affairs, Elton's "gallant charade" holds out cold comfort for the addressee, whom he finally encodes in the language of romance:

Thy ready wit the word will soon supply,
May its approval beam in that soft eye.

Because Elton's shorthand for female desirability coincides so exactly with her own ("Soft, is the very word for her eye"), Emma feels able to overlook the difficulty of applying "ready wit" to Harriet, though she soon turns this phrase to good account—such is the opportunism of the imagination when fully engaged—by supposing it to result from Elton's blind love for her friend. On her behalf she is happy to accept the terms of Elton's courtship, urging her to make the most of her advantage while it lasts: "Your soft eyes shall chuse their own time for beaming" (62). Emma's own distance from the sort of romance she envisages for Harriet is well brought home by the extraordinary inappropriateness of Elton's choice of "soft eyes" for herself. More than her "hazle eye, the true hazle eye" establishes her as the antitype to the romantic heroines of the previous generation (31). As Austen's contemporary, the novelist Susan Ferrier put it, with a hint of mock nostalgia:

Formerly, in *my time*, a heroine was merely a piece of beautiful matter, with long hair and soft blue eyes, who was buffeted up and down the world like a shuttle-cock, and visited with all sorts

26. Wollstonecraft, *Vindication*, 130–132.

of possible and impossible miseries. Now they are black-haired, sensible women, who do plainwork, pay morning visits, and make presents of legs of pork; – vide "Emma."[27]

Jane Austen sees to it, however, that Harriet is no mere foil for Emma. Indeed, the outcome for both Elton and her protégée defies all her expectations. Elton, whose romantic pretences are a camouflage for his pursuit of status through marriage, finds himself in the tow of a domineering woman whose egotism masquerades as "knight errantry," while Harriet, who reveals an irrepressibly robust personality when asked by Knightley to dance at the Crown ("she bounded higher than ever, flew farther down the middle, and was in a continuous course of smiles") ends not as Emma's creature, but as her surprisingly assertive rival in love (221, 257).

Though the picture that Emma initially assembles of Harriet falls short of true likeness, the reader is left with the impression that the imaginative processes entailed in such construction are not only universal but inescapably fallible. One motif that contributes to this sense is supplied by the narrator's careful record of a seemingly irresistible urge in Highbury to speculate on the unknown. Before Frank Churchill makes his appearance, Emma congratulates herself on her "instinctive knowledge" of his character, and discourses at some length on her "idea of him" with Knightley, who has own opinions on the matter (97, 118). Miss Hawkins is widely agreed to be "highly accomplished, and perfectly amiable" before she steps foot in the village, and Miss Bates—who later mistakes a stranger at Box Hill for Mrs. Elton—confesses to picturing Mr. Dixon as another John Knightley, until forced to admit: "one never does form a just idea of any body beforehand. One takes up a notion and runs away with it"

27. In a letter of March 1816; see Lady Charlotte Bury, *The Diary of a Lady-in-Waiting*, ed. A. Francis Steuart (London: J. Lane, 1908), 260–261.

(142, 138). The same form of words is used by Emma when she scoffs at Mrs. Weston's mischievous hint of a serious attachment between Mr. Knightley and Jane, whose mysterious presence at Highbury soon proves to be the epicenter of all local preconception and conjecture (178). Indeed, when Emma playfully remarks that the feelings of her old acquaintance can only be surmised since her "sensations [are] known to no human being, I guess, but herself," she effectively puts the liveliest wits of the parish on trial (159).

While demonstrating that imagination is basic to the growth of relationships, and exposing the many hazards of this process, Jane Austen reminds her hapless readers of their own susceptibility to misreading. One model of this misprision is on display in the way Emma's thrall to an "animating suspicion" shuts down access to other eventualities (125). That she remains blind to Jane Fairfax's secret engagement for longer than Frank Churchill finds conceivable is owing to the fictions in which she has embroiled the principals, making Harriet over to Frank and bundling up Mr. Dixon with Jane. In the traditional quixotic novel, fantasy can safely be read as delusional, but in *Emma*—where perception is seen to rely absolutely on the incorporation of the non-actual—imagination can never be flagged as a red herring. Of Emma's many mental pairings, one does take effect (Miss Taylor and Mr. Weston), another proves as insubstantial as thistledown (Harriet and Frank), and some fail but have hurtful or unintended consequences (Harriet falls both for Elton, and— misunderstanding Emma's encouragement—for Knightley). A series of other couplings are entertained by the characters: Frank-and-Emma (by Mr. Weston, Mr. Knightley, and—in daydream only—by themselves), but also, as already mentioned, Jane-and-Knightley, and Jane-and-Dixon. These phantom alliances exercise some claim upon first-time readers who have to contend not only with a complex blend of the real and fanciful, but with direct evidence that the bias of plot does everything to conceal.

Three levels of representation can usefully be distinguished in *Emma*: the imaginary, the actual and observed, and the actual but hidden. Their interplay is especially well illustrated by the layered narrative of Frank Churchill's rescue of Harriet from the gypsies, an account given in the third person of what Frank himself has retailed of the incident to Emma. The scene unfolds in a wholly realistic way with plentiful social implication. Austen dwells elsewhere on the prejudicial effects of judging individuals according to rank or mode of living, and Harriet, who has dismissed Jane Fairfax's exceptional musicianship as a mere requirement of her position and who learns from Emma to know better than to care for Robert Martin, readily transforms the children she meets by the roadside into objects of terror, while the excessive fright of her companion serves as "an invitation for attack" (262). When Frank appears by "fortunate chance," and saves the situation by his mere presence, the ugly encounter undergoes a sea change, instantly taking on the aura of romance. Described at this juncture as an "imaginist," Emma thrills at the spectacle of a "fine young man and a lovely young woman thrown together," more particularly at the alluring role allotted to Harriet, who—true to her soft-eyed persona—shrinks, clings, and faints (263). She revels also in the uncanny timing of their convergence, and in its coincidence with her plans for a further match. Nor is she alone in being unable to resist shaping the affair into a gratifying fiction. In Highbury the event has an afterlife as an adventure story, whether adapted to those with a taste for the shocking, or pruned of all ornament to satisfy the hard-headed sons of John Knightley.

The episode reveals a further level, however, so unobtrusive as to provide a challenge to the reader's percipience. Beneath the realistic narrative, and the will-o'-the-wisp of fantasy that plays over it, there lies a buried scene that has more claim to true romance than Emma's beguiling fabrication. The economy of Frank and Jane's secret engagement depends on subterfuges such as private visits to the post office on her part, or on manufactured pretexts for their irregular meetings on his. Once Frank has mentioned, then, that he stopped at the Bates's to give back a pair of scissors that he had forgotten to return, the rest of his explanation for his presence in the country lane becomes suspect. His plan of walking a mile or two beyond Highbury to meet his horses on the London road is clearly made to draw less attention to a tryst of some duration rather than to inhale morning air. Emma, who has unwittingly foiled one of Frank's earlier attempts to drop in on Jane, and has overlooked his conspicuous lie on that occasion, is now too distracted by the confirmation of her "foresight" to guess at the bond that would annul her developing scheme.

But thanks to Frank's playful but tactical collusion, Emma's fiction of Jane's romantic attachment to Mr. Dixon has already done its work of obstruction. And here again, Emma's conviction is originally sealed by a tale of heroic rescue. Readers, too, are encouraged to give some respect to Emma's reading of the boating escapade at Weymouth by the account of a further rescue that immediately follows. Orphaned in infancy, Jane owes her adoption by Colonel Campbell and his family to the gratitude incurred by her father when he nursed the Colonel through a life-threatening fever on campaign. This deliverance, like so much else in Jane's career, is rich in the overtones of romance, and indeed the already cited *Children of the Abbey* provides a parallel episode, except that Regina Maria Roche's heroine owes her protection by a rural family to her father's intrepid saving of a humble musket-bearer on the battlefield.[28] Though Jane Austen patently sanctions the famous romantic archetype of the "preserver," she gives it a twist, placing Jane's father in the role of nurse rather than dauntless warrior. Nor was she entirely a pioneer in this respect. Scott permits himself a number of variations on the stock romance theme in *Waverley* (1814), where his hero is handsomely rewarded

28. Roche, *The Children of the Abbey*, I, 15–16.

for his brave rescue of an English officer at Preston, but only after
several undignified submissions to Highland rescuers of both sexes
have brought about his conversion to the Jacobite cause. True to her
brief, Austen refashions romance in line with her commitment to
a realism that foregrounds the generative power of imagination. In
Emma the accent falls differently from of old, not on high adventure,
nor even indeed on action itself, but rather on its subjective impact,
and so on ordinary events that have the capacity to stir the minds
of her characters deeply. Frank and Harriet's seemingly dramatic encounter proves to be as empty as it was haphazard, leaving Harriet
shocked but unmoved, and Frank "amused and delighted" (263).
It is further cut down to size by the complementary scene at the
Crown that immediately precedes it. Explaining to Emma the start
of her intense feelings for Knightley, Harriet reflects: "It was not the
gipsies ... I was thinking of a much more precious circumstance—of
Mr Knightley coming and asking me to dance, when Mr Elton would
not stand up with me and when there was no other partner in the
room" (319). What gives centrality to this scene, moreover, is not
simply its reworking of a standard motif, but its embodiment of several related ethical precepts that lie at the heart of romance.

So integral to the genre was the theme of rescue that some
historians of the period speculated that the medieval romance had
its origins in the relief of the Holy City, the official raison d'être of
the Crusades.[29] Others took the theme to be an appropriately con-
densed expression of the "spirit of chivalry" (a term approved by
Fanny Price),[30] the essence of which consisted in the impulse to safe-
guard the weak and distressed from oppression. Several characterized

29. William Robertson, *Charles V*, 3 vols. (London: Strahan and Co., 1796), I, 69; Richard
    Hurd, *Letters on Chivalry and Romance*, in *Hurd's Dialogues*, 3 vols. (London: T. Cadell,
    1765), 212. Both these sets were available to Jane Austen at Godmersham.
30. Austen, *Mansfield Park*, ed. James Kinsley and Marilyn Butler (Oxford: Oxford University
    Press, 1970), 190.

chivalry as a cultural antidote formed to redress or at least abate the evils (such as "rapine and anarchy") endemic to feudal society.[31] One popular historian—whose *magnum opus* Jane Austen had been reading shortly before embarking on *Emma*—contended that the partnership of chivalry and romance had "roused the human soul from its lethargy," principally by bringing about a revolution in the status of women, who "instead of being nobody in society . . . became its *primum mobile*."[32] The institution of courtly love looms large in William Russell's thinking at this point, but he also identifies an innately bellicose strain in romance, and warns against its "refinements in gallantry," urging that they be "excluded from the improvements in modern manners."[33] Jane Austen could rely on readers who were on the alert for any betrayal of the original spirit of the genre. These would have been ready to appreciate the deftness with which she showed up Elton's gallantry as a charade, and quick to distrust heroines whose passivity signified a surrender of will. Though the word "gallantry" takes on several senses in *Emma*, in the arena of courtship its use is invariably pejorative. While Mr. Knightley is found completely deficient in the trait, Frank Churchill reveals himself as its top exponent when he characteristically deploys a smokescreen of masculine charm to conceal a series of strategic manoeuvres.

Romance came so persistently under fire in the eighteenth century, particularly from the quarter of satirically minded novelists, that many critics felt obliged to insist that the genre had much of perennial value to offer. Though the historian William Robertson conceded that "romantic knights" provided an easy target for ridicule, he argued that the

---

31. Robertson, *Charles V*, I, 69; David Hume, *The History of England*, 6 vols. (Indianapolis: Liberty Classics, 1983), I, 487.

32. William Russell, *The History of Modern Europe*, 6 vols. (London, 1810), II, 170–171, also 172–173.

33. Ibid., I, 194–195. Hume also describes gallantry as an outmoded relic of romance; see *History*, I, 487.

long-term effects of chivalry, though largely unobserved, had been for the better, encouraging a humanitarian concern for the oppressed.[34] Even more vocal in defence was Richard Hurd who, in his *Letters on Chivalry and Romance* (1762), drew a graphic picture of ancient heroes restlessly wandering the world "to exercise their generous and disinterested valour, indifferently to friends and enemies in distress." Where, he demands, would modern society be without such "compassion, gentleness, and generous attachments to the unfortunate"?[35] Enlarging on the way the spirit of chivalry transcends divisions of rank, of gender, and even of enmity, he quotes Milton on the knightly virtue of courtesy:

> sooner found in lowly sheds
> With smoky rafters, than in tap'stry halls
> And courts of princes, where it first was nam'd,
> And yet is most pretended.[36]

Contemporary writers of romance invariably short-handed these egalitarian concerns as "benevolence," and a number of them gave serious attention to the theme. So Ann Radcliffe in the *Romance of the Forest* after showing, by way of warning, how easily the benevolent are duped by the wicked, devotes her third volume to a pastoral celebration of the virtue, alluding plentifully, with customary erudition, to Rousseau's exemplary Vicar of Savoy. Her novel ends with the evocation of an idyllic community centered in her married couple whose happiness, owing to their benevolence, is "diffused to all."[37]

Eagerly awaited by Emma, the ball at the Crown provides an apt setting for Mr. Knightley's informal rescue of Harriet from the

34. Robertson, *Charles V*, I, 70–72.
35. Hurd, *Dialogues*, III, 202, 235.
36. Ibid., III, 207. Milton, *Comus*, ll, 323–326.
37. Radcliffe, *The Romance of the Forest*, 152, 363.

social assault of the Eltons, and more particularly for the deliberation on "general benevolence" that frames his courteous act. The ball ranks as the largest assembly of identified characters in Jane Austen's work, and the names of the guests, mainly filtered through the benevolent Miss Bates (whose knowledge of Highbury resembles a dropped card index), include several new to the reader. In fact the choice of the Crown—a shabby inn that appears to resist gentrification—represents a defeat of the original scheme for a ball attended exclusively by the five couples who represent the cream of young local society. It is with some alarm that Emma yields to Frank Churchill's blithe disregard for a "want of proper families," and accepts his assurance that by the next morning all will have returned to "their proper place" (156). Though Emma's recoil from a "confusion of rank" is evidently deep-seated, it proves to be a trait that she overcomes to a considerable degree. She learns to recognize that enjoying the hospitality of the Coles is better than dining in solitary grandeur; and though her disdain for the Cox daughters may remain undiminished, she finally resolves that it would be a "great pleasure to know Robert Martin," whom she has for so long put beyond the pale (374). Her snobbery coexists paradoxically with a heartfelt commitment to charity (despite a tendency to pigeonhole its recipients), so that the ideal of perfection she silently articulates on being invited by Mr. Weston to preview the setup for the ball is fully characteristic: "General benevolence, but not general friendship, made a man what he ought to be.—She could fancy such a man" (251). Emma's exclusion of Mr. Weston from the company of the truly benevolent is prompted by the insensitivity he displays in asking the opinion not of herself alone but of several carriage loads of flatteringly appointed connoisseurs, and the relation between benevolence and percipience is to come under the spotlight later, as we shall see. But a context for Emma's half-expressed wish has already been prepared.

When Knightley arrives at the Coles's evening party in a carriage, rather than by foot as was his custom, Emma is pleasantly surprised, but her approval increases when she recognizes that his motive is to ensure a safe return journey for Jane, and that she is witnessing a characteristic "act of unostentatious kindness" (175). Mischievously, however, Mrs. Weston plants the idea that Mr. Knightley has a soft spot for Jane and that he should not be credited in this instance with a "simple, disinterested benevolence" (176). When Knightley performs his nameless, but much-remembered act of kindness at the ball, Austen devises a choreography that erases any suspicion of its disingenuousness. Because Emma is involved in a set that involves dancing with her back to Knightley, and can only take in the scene (which she has partly to imagine) through snatched backward glances, she avoids appearing to be the ulterior object of his attention. The notion that benevolence and self-interest, though often conjoined, are essentially contrary impulses is explored earlier when Emma and Knightley argue over the motives that have for so long prevented Frank Churchill from visiting Highbury. They agree that paternal respect dictates that Frank should stand up against the wishes of his aunt, but that to do so with effectual force might risk what he hopes to inherit. While Emma contends that Frank has a strong sense of what is right, even if he is unable to act on it, owing to the dependence inculcated by his upbringing, Knightley answers, "Then, it would not be so strong a sense. If it failed to produce equal exertion, it could not be an equal conviction" (117). The metaphor from mechanics, used to explain Frank's inertia, tallies precisely with the language employed by the philosopher Francis Hutcheson in a highly influential discussion of benevolence to which the novel later alludes.

When Mr. Weston responds to Emma and Frank's request at Box Hill for something clever from each of the company, he unwittingly contributes to a developing theme with his conundrum, "What two letters of the alphabet are there, that express perfection?" (292). The answer he spells out—"M. and A.—Em-ma"—is judged as no more than a "very indifferent piece of wit," but it invokes, as the critic Mark Loveridge has shrewdly pointed out, Hutcheson's mathematically expressed definition of benevolence in his *Inquiry*:[38]

Since then Benevolence, or Virtue in any Agent, is as $\dfrac{M}{A}$, or as $\dfrac{M \pm I}{A}$, and no Being can act above his natural Ability; *that must be the Perfection of Virtue where* M = A, or when the Being acts to the utmost of his Power for the publick Good; and hence the Perfection of Virtue in this Case, or $\dfrac{M}{A}$, is as Unity.[39] (my italics)

M and A stand, respectively, for "Moment of Good" and "Ability" in this pioneering venture into moral arithmetic, and Hutcheson arrives at the former concept through his quantitative understanding of beneficence, just as he has earlier treated Benevolence (B) and Self-Interest (I) as "two Forces impelling the same Body to Motion; sometimes they conspire, sometimes are indebted to each other, and sometimes are in some degree opposite."[40] Because Hutcheson, unlike Mandeville and others, takes benevolence to be entirely independent of self-interest (hence the addition of loss to the self, or the subtraction of gain to it from the overall force for good: M ± I), and takes it to be independent, too, of personal capacity (hence the division, $\dfrac{M \pm I}{A}$), it emerges as a supremely democratic virtue. Indeed, Hutcheson immediately proceeds to the maxim, "a Creature suppos'd Innocent, by pursuing Virtue with his utmost Power, may in Virtue

---

38. See Mark Loveridge, "Francis Hutcheson and Mr Weston's Conundrum in *Emma*," *Notes and Queries* 30 (1983): 214–216.

39. Francis Hutcheson, *An Inquiry into the Original of Our Ideas of Beauty and Virtue* (Indianapolis: Liberty Fund, 2004), 130.

40. Ibid., 104.

equal the Gods." These words find an echo when Harriet enlarges on the feelings inspired by Mr. Knightley's unostentatious rescue of her at the ball, forcing Emma, faced by a mirror image, into a sudden apprehension of herself:

> "That was the kind action; that was the noble benevolence and generosity; that was the service which made me begin to feel how superior he was to every other being upon earth."
> "Good God!" cried Emma, "this has been a most unfortunate— most deplorable mistake!" (319)

Though far from heroic, Mr. Knightley's sensitive act of rescue is enriched by the added touch of self-denial, since he has stubbornly opposed Emma's plans for Harriet vis-à-vis Mr. Elton. It owes much of its power, in fact, to the way benevolence was seen to undercut the heroic as traditionally conceived.

Mindful of the classical origins of the virtue, and of its linkage with ancient literature and romance, Francis Hutcheson concludes his section on the foundation of morals by insisting that benevolence is not the preserve of those "whose external Splendour dazzles an injudicious World" but rather a disposition natural to the humble, to "the kind Friend, the faithful prudent Adviser, the charitable and hospitable Neighbour."[41] This point is developed at some length by Hume in his second *Enquiry* when he calls attention to the relative modernity of the social or tender virtues (which he equates with benevolence) by contrasting them with the martial valor from which the concept of *virtue* originally derived. While benevolence is, in Hume's view, the fundamental principle of morals and thus built into the human frame, it is subject to historical vicissitude nonetheless: flourishing in times of comparative stability and peace, it proves

41. Ibid., 164–165, 134–135.

a ready casualty to the values of a militant state. Noting the difference between the ethics of Homer and Fenelon, Hume warns against the insidious influence of a heroic literature "recommended by parents and instructors, and admired by the public in general."[42]

Benevolence was to become a literary stock-in-trade during the age of sensibility, one often dulled by its formulaic use in heroic romance. In Jane Austen's hands, however, it underwent a conscious revival and kept its pristine edge. Indeed, it seems to have been a quality as much associated with her memory as with her work, which is hardly surprising considering the fullness of its expression in *Emma*.[43] Here, its paragon, George Knightley, is—despite his name—less than saintly, blunt rather than courteous, and (unlike Frank Churchill who rides a black mare) without a horse. His reason for keeping none is that he likes to walk and spend all he can on farming, the profession that rates, according to Barrett's starry-eyed heroine, as least acceptable in romance.[44] Less doughty still is the valetudinarian Mr. Woodhouse through whom the virtue is introduced. But what we observe in his case is a "general benevolence" annulled by an inability to enter the experience of even those in his immediate circle, who nevertheless willingly pay the tax of his goodwill out of respect for the "friendliness of his heart," a trait missed by many critics (6). Answering this shortcoming in Mr. Woodhouse is the exceptionally outgoing Miss Bates, "interested in every body's happiness, quick-sighted to every body's merit," whose benevolence is proportionately addressed to a real world, and fully reciprocated (17). Austen's emphasis on goodwill as the redeeming feature in the untoward circumstances of the aging spinster (who otherwise lacks the means to "frighten those who might hate her, into outward respect" [17]) echoes a remark made by

---

42. Hume, *Morals*, 7.13–9, p. 135.
43. See the "Biographical Note"; also Francis Austen on the "native benevolence of her heart," Deirdre Le Faye, *Jane Austen: A Family Record* (London: British Library, 1989), 247.
44. See Barrett, *The Heroine*, I, 43, and *Emma*, 167.

Hume in a passage from the second *Enquiry* in which he similarly presents benevolence as an absolving and sympathetic activity that results in a mutual transfusion of feeling.[45] So Miss Bates is described in an aptly self-reflexive way as a "woman whom no one named without good-will. It was her own universal good-will that worked such wonders" (17). To the truth of this statement, both Emma's anguish after her tactless repartee at Box Hill and Mr. Knightley's gruff warning ("Perfection should not have come quite so soon") abundantly testify (292).

Benevolence counts for little without perception, and the sharper the perception the more beneficial benevolence proves. Part of Austen's brief in *Emma* is to show how susceptible our perceptions are to the ubiquitous and capricious work of imagination, but the novel is equally concerned with the heuristic processes that act as a corrective to false judgment. And in this field Mr. Knightley, though by nature less sensitive than Emma, and quite as often wrong, comes to the fore, owing to his deep-seated respect for verification. This trait is exhibited early at the Westons, when he ventures out from the Christmas party to test the depth of snow and to report that all fear of being benighted is unfounded. The same reluctance to believe "without proof" characterizes his dealings with Frank Churchill, and inspires the detective-like acumen that puts him onto the trail of his supposed rival's secret attachment to Jane (114). It is in the course of this pursuit that he cautions himself to be on guard against illusion, quoting Cowper on the imaginary scenes conjured up by a winter fire ("Myself creating what I saw"), and takes pains to place himself "to see as much as he could" (270, 273). That the pedestrian Mr. Knightley has his feet on the ground has, again, everything to do with his profession,

45. Hume argues that benevolence can compensate "for the want [of talents], or preserve the person from our severest hatred, as well as contempt," and that the tender virtues "seem to transfuse themselves... into each beholder, and to call forth, in their own behalf, the same favourable and affectionate sentiments"; see *Morals*, 2.1, 79.

more particularly (witness talk of crop rotation and the latest in seed drills) with his reliance on new experimental trends in agriculture. That his benevolence, like his empiricism, is rooted in his situation as a farmer is borne out, furthermore, by a down-to-earth hospitality that extends from the Donwell strawberry beds to the sacrifice of his own apple hoard. A man concerned with satisfying the Bates's taste for dumplings is at far cry from the warrior heroes of current romance who repeatedly risk their lives in the belief that only the brave deserve the fair. But such bounty is a mark of Knightley's distance from the idealized heroes of Harriet's favorite reading, as sure an index of character as the gifts of pork that set Emma apart, in Susan Ferrier's view, from the "soft blue-eyed" heroines of romance.

In common with many of her contemporaries, Jane Austen understood romance to be a highly paradoxical genre. While it owed its origin and many of its features (duels, jousts, tournaments) to the ascendancy of feudalism, and was evidently prone to revival in times of strife, it emphatically championed the cause of those who suffered under such an ethos, or were effectively nullified by it. Written with the prospect of peace in view, *Emma* is unique among the six novels in its total avoidance of reference to war, or to the services.[46] But Jane Austen has more to hand than turning gun carriages into seed drills, for she undertakes, within her comedy, a critique of romance that salvages the virtue of benevolence, revealing the important role it has to play in moderating the inevitably self-interested ploys of a radically reconceived imagination. Choosing for her focus Highbury, rather than the more romantic and peripatetic story of Frank Churchill and Jane Fairfax, Austen implicitly accepts the challenge of making the apparently familiar more absorbing than the exceptional. But her success goes further. *Emma* spells out a farewell to arms by reconfiguring the sublime.

46. Captain Weston exchanged the militia for trade (13).

REFERENCES

Austen, Jane. *Emma*, edited by James Kinsley, introduction by Adela Pinch. Oxford: Oxford University Press, 2008.

Austen, Jane. *Mansfield Park*, edited by James Kinsley and Marilyn Butler. Oxford: Oxford University Press, 1970.

Barrett, Eaton Stannard. *The Heroine*, 2nd ed., 3 vols. London: H. Colburn, 1814.

Beckford, William. *Modern Novel Writing*, 2 vols. London: G. G. and J. Robinson, 1796.

Buckle, Stephen. "Review of P. J. E. Kail, *Projection and Realism in Hume's Philosophy* (Oxford, 2007)." *Hume Studies* 34, no. 1 (April 2008): 163–165.

Bury, Lady Charlotte. *The Diary of a Lady-in-Waiting*, edited by A. Francis Steuart. London: J. Lane, 1908.

Coleridge, Samuel Taylor. *Biographia Literaria*, edited by J. Shawcross, 2 vols. Oxford: Oxford University Press: 1973.

Courtney, Mrs. *Isabinda of Bellefield: A Sentimental Novel*, 2 vols. Dublin: P. Wogan, 1795.

Fordyce, James. *Sermons to Young Women*, 2 vols. London: A. Millar, 1791.

Goldsmith, Oliver. *The Vicar of Wakefield*, edited by Arthur Friedman. Oxford: Oxford University Press, 1974.

Hume, David. *An Enquiry concerning Human Understanding*, edited by Tom L. Beauchamp. Oxford: Oxford University Press, 1999.

Hume, David. *An Enquiry concerning the Principles of Morals*, edited by Tom L. Beauchamp. Oxford: Oxford University Press, 2004.

Hume, David. *Four Dissertations*. London: A. Millar, 1757.

Hume, David. *The History of England*, 6 vols. Indianapolis: Liberty Classics, 1983.

Hume, David. *A Treatise of Human Nature*, edited by David Fate Norton and Mary J. Norton. Oxford: Oxford University Press, 2002.

Hurd, Richard. *Letters on Chivalry and Romance* in *Hurd's Dialogues*, 3 vols. London: T. Cadell, 1765.

Hutcheson, Francis. *An Inquiry into the Original of Our Ideas of Beauty and Virtue*. Indianapolis: Liberty Fund, 2004.

Kant, Immanuel. *Critique of Pure Reason*, translated by Norman Kemp Smith. London: Macmillan, 1933.

Le Faye, Deirdre. *Jane Austen: A Family Record*. London: British Library, 1989.

Loveridge, Mark. "Francis Hutcheson and Mr Weston's Conundrum in *Emma*." *Notes and Queries* 30 (1983): 214–216.

Milton, John. *Comus and Other Poems*, edited by F. T. Prince. Oxford: Oxford University Press, 1972.

Radcliffe, Ann. *The Romance of the Forest*, edited by Chloe Chard. Oxford: Oxford University Press, 1991.

Richardson, Samuel. *Clarissa*, 7 vols. Oxford: Blackwell, 1930.

Robertson, William. *Charles V*, 3 vols. London: Strahan and Co., 1796.

Roche, Regina Maria. *The Children of the Abbey*, 4 vols. London: Minerva Press, 1798.

Russell, William. *The History of Modern Europe*, 6 vols. London: Charles and William Spear, 1810.

Scott, Sir Walter. *Waverley*, edited by Claire Lamont. Oxford: Oxford University Press, 2008.

Smellie, William. *The Philosophy of Natural History*. Edinburgh: T. Cadell, G. G. and J Robinson, 1790.

"Unsigned Review of *Emma*." *Quarterly Review*, March 1816, reprinted in *Jane Austen: The Critical Heritage*, edited by B. C. Southam, 59–61. London: Routledge & Paul, 1968.

Williams, Michael. *Jane Austen: Six Novels and Their Methods*. London: Macmillan, 1986.

Wittgenstein, Ludwig. *Philosophical Investigations*. Oxford: Blackwell, 1953.

Wollstonecraft, Mary. *Vindication of the Rights of Women*. In *Mary Wollstonecraft: Political Writings*, edited by Janet Todd. London: W. Pickering, 1993.

Chapter 7

Misreading Emma

DAVID DAVIES

Emma Woodhouse misreads the intentions, and the significance of the actions, of those around her in ways that reflect both her projects and her own acknowledged or unacknowledged desires. If the first-time receiver of *Emma* is aware of Emma's misreadings, or at least of some of them, such awareness is not predicated upon insights into such matters conveyed by an informative narrator. Rather, as a number of critics have stressed, *Emma* is innovative in its wide use of "free indirect style": we view the fictional events largely through a third-person narrative that is inflected by Emma's consciousness of these events, her manners of thinking and expressing herself. A consequence of this, for many critics, is that the first-time receiver will have considerable difficulty detecting Emma's misreadings. I shall argue, however, that, far from deliberately obscuring details of the narrative in this way, Austen's particular use of the free indirect style allows her to also furnish the receiver with the clues necessary to see Emma as the misreader that she is. Austen presents us with *both* the evidence available to Emma—reported actions of other characters and lengthy passages entirely in the form of dialogue—and the conclusions that Emma draws from this evidence. The reader who identifies misreadings infers something different from the very same evidence, and, I shall argue, does so under the very skillful guidance of Austen, who also in key places inserts narratorial hints. Contrary to what many critics have supposed, the intended first-time receiver is supposed to register Emma's misreadings, and one who *fails* to do so is him- or herself misreading *Emma*. I shall focus on Emma's most salient misreadings, examine Austen's narrative strategy in presenting these misreadings, and look at how we might think of the reader as "trained up" to be an interpreter.

I. THE ANATOMY OF MISREADING

Since the notion of misreading is central to this chapter and, so I argue, to Austen's project in *Emma*, I begin with some general remarks on the nature and varieties of misreading. To misread, in the broadest sense, is to fail to read correctly. It thus presupposes a norm that a reading fails to satisfy. The aim of a reading is to identify a meaning or sense rightly ascribable to a thing read. Things read, again in the broadest sense, include linguistic utterances and inscriptions, other signifying artifacts such as paintings, the intentional behaviors of individuals and the mental states implicated in such behaviors, and the social practices in which agents are involved. Purely natural phenomena can also be read—we can read a natural situation in terms of what it indicates. The object of a reading is thus a signifier, natural or conventional.

A *mis*reading ascribes to a signifier a meaning that it lacks. The norm that such a misreading fails to satisfy is the norm of truth or epistemic warrant. This carries by itself no implicit or explicit criticism of the misreader: the misreading may represent exactly what the signifier conveys to one possessing the background knowledge and interpretive skills of the misreader, where it would be unreasonable to demand superior knowledge and skills on her part. An English tourist stopping over briefly in an Italian airport who takes the remark of a flight attendant that she is "troppo sensibile" as an invitation to act more emotionally is misreading the remark, but not having internalized the information required to avoid this misreading is hardly a failing on her part. A student in an advanced Italian conversation class who misreads the same remark, however, *would* presumably be held responsible for her misreading because the background information required to read the signifier correctly is information that either (i) she possesses but has failed to properly apply, or (ii) she should have acquired but has failed to do so.

This suggests that misreadings can be assessed relative to a different kind of norm, one that bears upon the process of misreading rather than the product of that process. Sometimes, we may say, the misreader is *culpable* for her misreading. Two sources of such culpability are the failure to properly apply the skills and cognitive resources one possesses, and the failure to possess interpretive skills and cognitive resources that one should have possessed. The former source of culpability may itself take different forms. One may be culpable for one's misreading through failing to pay proper attention to manifestly salient aspects of the signifier, or one may fail to give proper weight to salient aspects of the signifier because one is predisposed by one's preconceptions, biases, desires, or interests to read the signifier in a particular way. In the latter case, we may talk of wishful thinking or self-deception.

As noted earlier, what Emma misreads are primarily the actions and motivations of other characters. Furthermore, with one possible exception, Emma's misreadings are clearly culpable, biased by her preconceptions, projects, and desires: her project for the betterment of Harriet, her perception of Frank Churchill as her possible future husband, and her dislike of Jane Fairfax, for example. Nor is Emma the only character who misreads these kinds of signifiers for these kinds of reasons—Mr. Knightley and Harriet are guilty to a lesser extent of such misreadings.

The culpable misreading of behavioral signifiers, where culpability resides in the inflection of hermeneutic activity by the interpreter's personal projects, interests, and desires, is one of the central themes in *Emma*. This is undeniable in the sense that it is Emma's culpable misreadings, and her actions consequent upon these misreadings, that structure the plot throughout. But I want to make a stronger claim: a central aim of the novel is to engage the reader in the detection of such misreadings. Before defending that claim, I shall briefly survey the established critical view that the nature and extent of Emma's misreadings are matters that Austen deliberately masks from the first-time receiver. On this account, it is only on a second reading that the receiver can begin to appreciate much of Austen's artistry in narrating the story in the way she does and its dramatic ironies. I shall argue to the contrary that a close analysis of the means whereby Austen presents the events misread by Emma testifies to Austen's efforts to make these misreadings evident to her intended receiver long before they are revealed to Emma as such. Such a receiver can appreciate the ironies on a first reading, and is intended to do so.

II. CRITICAL PERSPECTIVES ON EMMA'S MISREADINGS

When Jane Austen, writing as she began to work on *Emma*, said that she feared that the central character of the book was one that "no one but myself will much like,"[1] she presumably had in mind not

---

1. Cited by James Edward Austen-Leigh in *A Memoir of Jane Austen* (1870), reprinted in *A Memoir of Jane Austen: And Other Family Recollections*, ed. Kathryn Sutherland (Oxford: Oxford University Press, 2002).

only Emma's tendency to misread the motivations and interests of others, but also the sources of the culpability of those misreadings. As just noted, Emma's misreadings result from her tendency to understand others in ways shaped by her own preconceptions, prejudices, and projects. But, in addition, these preconceptions and projects are themselves often morally flawed. This applies most obviously to her attempts to "socially improve" Harriet, a project inflected by her very uncharitable readings of some (Robert Martin) and her naïve understandings of others (Mr. Elton). Her view of Jane Fairfax, which fuels her hypothesis about Jane's romantic attachment to Mr. Dixon, is explicitly characterized as "so little just" by the narrator.[2]

The receiver will surely register at least some of these more general moral failings in Emma. Of interest here, however, is the receiver's ability to detect the particular misreadings that are products of these failings. Three misreadings play a central role in structuring the narrative, in two senses: first, they largely determine which events are included in the narrative; and second, they operate as causal forces that shape the unfolding of these events. The first misreading is the central theme in Volume I: Emma misreads the object of Mr. Elton's romantic interest, and this informs her efforts to bring about Harriet's social improvement. The second and more complex misreading is of the motivations of Frank Churchill and Jane Fairfax, and Emma's subsequent failure to recognize the attachment between them. The third misreading is of the identity of the person whom Harriet describes as "infinitely superior" to any other human being. It is in discovering the third misreading that Emma becomes aware of a fourth misreading, this time a misreading of her own heart and of her feelings for Mr. Knightley.

2. Jane Austen, *Emma* (Oxford: Oxford University Press, 2003), 131. The novel was originally published in 1815. All subsequent references in the text are to the 2003 edition of *Emma*.

Critics have generally assumed that the first-time receiver of *Emma* will not detect many of these misreadings prior to their being revealed as such. Reginald Ferrar, writing in 1917, maintained that

> [o]nly when the story [of *Emma*] has been thoroughly assimilated, can the infinite delights and subtleties of its workmanship begin to be appreciated, as you realize the manifold complexity of the book's web. . . . In every fresh reading you feel anew that you never understood anything like the widening sum of its delights.[3]

And in a recent newspaper article, a contemporary Austen scholar, John Mullan, drawing upon views defended at greater length elsewhere,[4] maintains that

> the narration follows the path of Emma's errors. Indeed, the first-time reader will sometimes follow this path too, and then share the heroine's surprise when the truth rushes upon her . . . Frank is . . . so clever that it is easy to miss his tricks. Sharing Emma's perspective, we sometimes get fooled too.[5]

Mullan cites the very influential analysis by Wayne Booth[6] that sees the first-time receiver's blindness to Emma's misreadings as a

3. Reginald Farrer, "Jane Austen, *ob* July 18th 1817," *Quarterly Review* CCXXVIII: 24–28, reprinted in David Lodge, *Jane Austen: Emma, A Casebook*, revised ed. (London: Macmillan, 1991), 65–69, at 65 in the reprinted edition.
4. Mullan is the author of *What Matters in Jane Austen?: 20 Crucial Puzzles Solved* (London: Bloomsbury, 2012).
5. John Mullan, "How Jane Austen's *Emma* Changed the Face of Fiction," *The Guardian*, December 5, 2015.
6. Wayne Booth, "Control of Distance in Jane Austen's *Emma*," in *The Rhetoric of Fiction* (Chicago: University of Chicago Press, 1961), 243–266. Reprinted in Lodge *Jane Austen: Emma*, 137–156.

necessary consequence of both Austen's strategy in presenting an unattractive central character like Emma, and Austen's attempts to pursue two potentially conflicting goals in the novel. The challenge for Austen is to engage the sympathy of the receiver for a central character with serious character flaws that threaten the welfare of others, while still allowing for the receiver's negative judgment of these flaws. In responding to this challenge, Booth argues, Austen avails herself of a radically new narrative strategy not fully taken up by others until the twentieth century. This strategy is "primarily to use the heroine herself as a kind of narrator, though in third person, reporting on her own experiences."[7] Booth describes this as "the sustained inside view,"[8] but it has become more commonly known as the "free indirect style" of narration.[9] If this is to foster the receiver's sympathy for Emma, we must be denied a similar presentation of the "sustained inside view" of other characters whose judgments of Emma might be highly negative. But Booth thinks that denying us insights into the perspectives of the other characters is also essential for Austen's further aim of "mystifying" the reader. Since Austen surely wishes the receiver to enjoy the dramatic ironies resulting from Emma's misreadings, this creates a conflict between two strongly desired effects: "On the one hand she cares about maintaining some sense of mystery as long as she can. On the other, she works at all points to heighten the reader's sense of dramatic irony, usually in the form of a contrast between what Emma knows and what the reader knows."[10] It is Austen's decision to give mystery greater weight than irony that explains why she must intend that the first-time reader not detect Emma's misreadings.

7. Booth, "Control of Distance," 138.
8. Ibid, 139.
9. For an informative discussion of free indirect style, see Kathleen Stock, "Free Indirect Style and Imagining from the Inside," in *Art, Mind, and Narrative*, ed. Julian Dodd (Oxford: Oxford University Press, 2016), 103–120.
10. Booth, Ibid., 145.

As a result, "we all find that on second reading we discover new intensities of dramatic irony resulting from the complete loss of mystery."[11] This decision on Austen's part might be viewed as a flaw in the work, although Booth tries to reserve judgment.

Others broadly sympathetic with Booth's account have defended on independent grounds Austen's supposed decision to mystify the first-time reader rather than provide authorial insight into Emma's interpretive failings. W. J. Harvey,[12] for example, claims that that the mystification is required by the very nature of the fictional world represented, so that even on rereading the novel, "our attention is so diversified by the thick web of linguistic nuance that we do not concentrate single-mindedly on the ironic results of the mystification." Austen's choice of mystification becomes "the main structural agent and narrative strategy of the novel,"[13] and this choice is necessary to prevent an overly ironic depiction of Emma. Graham Hough also takes the mystification of the reader to be a necessary consequence of the role that it plays in motivating the receiver's engagement with the narrative: "Half the energy of the book would be gone if the reader did not share in [Emma's] mistakes. . . . The structure of the work depends on mysteries and tensions that must not be prematurely released."[14]

A contrasting interpretation suggests that the receiver's failure to detect Emma's misreadings, far from being an unintended consequence of the mystification necessary to realize Austen's directly intended ends, is in fact directly intended by Austen and indeed is part of the very purpose of the novel. Adena Rosmarin maintains that "Austen meant the reader to be mystified, to make many of the

11. Ibid.
12. W. J. Harvey, "The Plot of *Emma*," *Essays in Criticism* XVII (1967): 48–63.
13. Harvey, "The Plot of *Emma*," 48.
14. Graham Hough, "Narrative and Dialogue in Jane Austen," *Critical Quarterly* XII (1970): 201–29. The cited passage is on 211–212.

same interpretive errors or, as Booth aptly puts it, many of the same misreadings that Emma makes. . . . The reader not only watches Emma's education, but re-enacts it, learning from his misreading and the subsequent rereading it makes possible."[15] This represents another way in which the reader can overcome any feelings of condescension toward Emma. But to ensure that she shares in Emma's misunderstandings, the receiver must be put into a similar state to that of Emma at the beginning of the novel, sure of the superiority of her own interpretive skills. The purpose of the events in Volume I, when Emma schemes toward the attachment of Harriet and Mr. Elton, is "to inflate our confidence both in the text and in our ability to read,"[16] something accomplished by providing us with numerous clues to Emma's misreadings and also with narratorial interventions to guide our diagnoses. However, so Rosmarin maintains, this is done so that the receiver can be more easily led to follow Emma in the later misreadings. The narrative becomes "hermeneutically oblique," "dense with . . . meticulously ambivalent incident," and this leads the receiver into error: "the growing subtlety of Emma's misreadings interestingly challenges and thus develops our reading competence, our misreadings and Emma's become increasingly alike, both in kind and degree, till our reading of Churchill's letter takes them to be one."[17]

Rosmarin's interesting take on Austen's intentions for the receiver makes the latter's failure to detect Emma's errors a conscious end of the work rather than a necessary evil. She nonetheless agrees with other commentators that Austen's purposes in the novel require that the first-time reader fail to detect those of Emma's misreadings that occur in the final two volumes of the novel. In the following section,

15. Adena Rosmarin, "Misreading *Emma*: The Powers and Perfidies of Narrative History," *English Literary History* 51 (1984): 315–342. Reprinted in Lodge, *Jane Austen: Emma*, 213–241. The cited passage is on 220.

16. Ibid, 221.

17. Ibid, 222–225.

I shall call this assumption into question by looking in much more detail at how Austen embeds Emma's misreadings in her text.

III. AN ANALYSIS OF THE NARRATORIAL PRESENTATION OF EMMA'S MISREADINGS

Emma's First Misreading

Emma's first misreading, we may recall, concerns the object of what she rightly takes to be a romantic interest on the part of Mr. Elton. Her growing conviction that Mr. Elton is falling ever deeper in love with Harriet is based on a number of pieces of evidence presented to the reader in the narrative. She initially takes certain of Mr. Elton's positive remarks about Harriet as indicative of his interest in her, and sees clear proof of the flourishing of this interest in further remarks and actions on his part during and after the painting of Harriet's portrait. She then takes Mr. Elton's charade with the solution "courtship" to be strong confirmation of the depth of his love for Harriet, and assures Harriet that it will soon be followed by "the completest proof" (59). Emma is aware of other evidence that might seem to throw doubt on these conclusions, but she offers reasons to discount this evidence. She dismisses Mr. Knightley's reports of Mr. Elton's talk, in male company, about his intention to socially better himself through marriage. Passion, she insists, can outweigh the calculations of rational self-interest, and the strength of Mr. Elton's passions is clearly evidenced in his manner (53). Mr. Elton fails to take advantage of the opportunities she affords him, in the encounter near and in the vicarage, to provide the promised "completest proof" of his intent toward Harriet because he is "very cautious" (73). When, on the evening of the party at Randalls, Mr. Elton obviously wishes to attend the party rather than seize the opportunity extended by Emma to absent himself for Harriet's sake, she reasons that single men are by nature so attracted to parties that they cannot resist invitations, however strong their reasons to do so (88). When, observing Mr. Elton's behavior in this context, Mr. John Knightley, knowing nothing of Emma's own reading of matters, suggests that Mr. Elton seems "to have a great deal of goodwill" (89) toward her, she takes this suggestion as indicative of Mr. John Knightley's hermeneutic failings, "amusing herself in the consideration of the blunders which often arise from a partial knowledge of circumstances, of the mistakes which people with high pretensions to judgment are for ever falling into" (89). Even when Mr. Elton's solicitousness at the party makes her think that Mr. John Knightley's suggestion might actually have some truth, she still assumes that Mr. Elton has indeed been courting Harriet: what is happening represents a *change* in his romantic interests.

Emma is therefore completely unprepared for Mr. Elton's profession of love, and his claim to have never had any romantic interest in Harriet, in the carriage ride from Randalls to Hartfield. But does the same apply to Austen's intended audience? I suspect that by the time we arrive at the party at Randalls, even a minimally competent reader will have doubts as to Emma's readings. But, more significantly, a receiver who only comes to such a conclusion at this juncture in the narrative will have missed numerous clues provided by Austen that call Emma's understandings of such matters into question much earlier in the proceedings. These clues reside both in the narrator's more detailed description of the events that ground Emma's own understandings, and in Emma's reasons for discounting things that might seem to run counter to these understandings. In missing these clues, the receiver will also have missed much of the artistry and irony in Austen's presentation of Emma's misreading. That Austen intends this artistry to be appreciated on even an initial reading is, I think, apparent from the care she takes to provide such ample clues as to what is actually going on. Let me note some of those clues in more detail:

(1) The idea of Mr. Elton as a potential partner for Harriet Smith initially presents itself to Emma as a *desirable* state of affairs, given her wish to prevent any renewed interest on Harriet's part in Robert Martin (28). Initially, we are told only of some (unspecified) positive things he has said about Harriet's beauty, but when, immediately after, we are given some concrete examples of the remarks taken by Emma as evidence of Mr. Elton's "growing attachment" (34) to Harriet, they all seem to concern not Harriet herself but Emma's skill in bringing about an improvement in Harriet's manners and general demeanor. The receiver should not, I think, miss this—it is flagged by Mr. Elton's repeated insistence on praising the one who has worked the transformation, rather than the one transformed (34). The receiver already keyed to the ambiguous nature of Mr. Elton's praise will not miss this dimension in all of Mr. Elton's subsequent remarks about Emma's portrait of Harriet—his praise of "so charming a talent" (35) manifested in the portrait. Emma puzzles over his interest in her skill as a painter rather than in the subject of the portrait, but she takes this to be mere gallantry. Similarly, when Mr. Elton, volunteering to take the portrait of Harriet to London to have it framed, terms it a "precious deposit" (39), Emma assumes the "deposit" is "precious" because of its subject and marvels at his "sighing," which she takes to be aimed at Harriet, although "I come in for a pretty good share as a second." But again she discounts Mr. Elton's praise for her as merely gratitude on Harriet's account (39), and understands in the

same way Mr. Elton's reported remarks to Mr. Perry when leaving for London (54–55).

(2) Austen, in describing the events that ground Emma's reading of Mr. Elton's intentions, presents the receiver with exactly the same "evidence" upon which Emma herself draws, without (here at least) raising any narratorial doubts about her interpretation of that evidence. But the attentive receiver, taking this "evidence" in the context of Emma's professed project for the social improvement of Harriet, will at least suspect that Emma is misreading the situation. Such a receiver will then be more moved than Emma by Mr. Knightley's subsequent observation that Mr. Elton, seeking social elevation of his own, would not make "an imprudent match" (53). And such a receiver will have serious doubts about Emma's understanding of the intentions behind Mr. Elton's charade. Mr. Elton says it is not for Harriet's collection but that "you" [Emma] might like to look at it. Emma notes that his speech is more addressed to her and that Mr. Elton "found it easier to meet her eye than her friend's," (57) but interprets this as further evidence of the depth of his love for Harriet. Emma solves the charade immediately, but it is made abundantly clear that Harriet has no idea what it means or how to go about solving it (58–59). Emma nonetheless insists that the real intended audience for the charade is Harriet: she tells Harriet that "there can be no doubt of its being written for you and to you" (59).

(3) By this time, I suggest, the attentive receiver will believe that Emma is misreading Mr. Elton's intentions and that his romantic interest is in her rather than in Harriet. Furthermore, I think this is precisely what Austen intends her reader to conclude. Such a receiver can then appreciate

how Emma's own projects and desires are affecting her
judgment as the evidence against her reading increases.
Emma's attempt to dismiss, as a result of his extreme
caution, Mr. Elton's failure to pursue his presumed romantic interest in Harriet when left alone with her at the
vicarage will ring false, as will Emma's attempts to make
sense of his conduct on the night of the dinner party at
Randalls. Nor will the rich irony of Emma's criticisms of
Mr. John Knightley's hermeneutic failings be lost on such
a receiver. What is again striking here is that the receiver
is presented with exactly the same evidence as Emma—
none of the details that, for the reader, undermine Emma's
reading of Mr. Elton are unobserved by Emma, but their
salience is discounted in the ways I have described. The
receiver's ability to read correctly the same "evidence"
that Emma misreads is only once assisted by the narrator,
but this is late in the day, when the reader should already
be in a position to appreciate the narrator's description of
Emma, as she struggles to understand Mr. Elton's strong
desire to come to Randalls, as "too eager and busy in her
own conceptions and views to hear him impartially, or see
him with clear vision" (88).

Emma's Second Misreading

Those inclined to question the first-time receiver's ability to discern the nature and extent of Emma's misreadings might grant that
an attentive receiver will be able to diagnose the misreading of Mr.
Elton's romantic intentions. But, it might be claimed, the reader will
not be so fortunate in the case of the second and third misreadings
identified earlier. Here, it might be said, there are none of the kinds
of clues in the details of the narrative that I have identified in the case

of the first misreading. Indeed, as we saw, this is the central contention in Rosmarin's interpretation of the work. Furthermore, it might
be argued, it cannot be part of Austen's intention that the first-time
receiver identifies *these* misreadings on Emma's part, since (as Booth
and Hough maintain) this receiver's ignorance of the facts she would
need to know to diagnose these misreadings is crucial to her continued interest in and engagement with the narrative. It is the revelation of Emma's second and third misreadings that brings about the
successful disentangling of the different threads in the plot that will
have been the focus of the receiver's interest.

I shall suggest otherwise. While diagnosing the second and third
misreadings indeed calls for the greater hermeneutic skill noted by
Rosmarin, Austen, contrary to what Rosmarin contends, provides
the receiver with the necessary clues, relying in part on the fact that
the receiver has already been "trained up," so to speak, through her
diagnosis of the first misreading. The receiver already knows that
Emma's exercises in social hermeneutics are heavily inflected by her
projects, desires, and prejudices, and is given early warning of the
specific subjective colorings that are in play in the second and third
misreadings. Given the structure of the narrative, it is again plausible
to think that Austen intends that the receiver be able to detect and
correct Emma's misreadings, and thereby be capable of enjoying the
rich dramatic ironies in Austen's presentation. These ironies would be
invisible to a receiver who shares Emma's ignorance of what is going
on. I offer the following observations in support of these claims.

(1) Before either Frank or Jane are formally introduced to
the denizens of Highbury, we are made very aware of
Emma's prior affective dispositions with respect to each
of them. When Emma receives news of Frank Churchill's
impending visit, we are informed that she has always
been interested in him, and that, since the marriage of

Mr. Weston and Miss Taylor, she has often thought that Frank would be the ideal person were she ever to marry (94). The receiver, aware of the inflection of Emma's perceptions of the conduct and motives of others by her preconceptions, will expect her interpretation of Frank's actions to focus on things favorable to his interest in her and to overlook things militating against this idea. The news of Jane Fairfax's imminent arrival, on the other hand, leads Emma to reflect on why she has always disliked Jane (130–131). The receiver is therefore on her guard when Emma immediately, and with little apparent reason, fixes on the idea that Jane's coming to Highbury rather than going to Ireland with the Campbells is the result of some romantic dalliance between her and Mr. Dixon. The narrator promptly gives the receiver two further reasons to distrust Emma's reading of the situation. First, the narrator states that Jane's explanations of her reasons for not going to Ireland were "nothing but truth, though there might be some truths not told" (130). Second, the narrator describes Emma's dislike of Jane as "so little just" (131). The receiver, alerted to the general causes of Emma's misreadings, is hereby motivated (i) to discount Emma's speculative hypothesis about Jane and Mr. Dixon, and (ii) to assume that this hypothesis may itself color Emma's reading of anything else relating to Jane's conduct and motives.

(2) The receiver, forearmed with this knowledge of Emma's hermeneutic predispositions in respect to Frank and Jane, is primed to see significance in the following details:

First, in Emma's initial conversation with Jane (132), she finds the latter reticent on the topics of her time at Weymouth and the personality and appearance of

Mr. Dixon. Emma takes this to simply confirm her hypothesis about why Jane is in Highbury, and she dismisses Jane's own explanation: "Emma saw its artifice, and returned to her first surmises." Jane's equal reticence to say anything about her meeting with Frank Churchill in Weymouth, however, is accorded no significance by Emma.

Second, in Emma's later discussion with Frank about the same topics (156ff), he is equally reticent about his meetings with Jane in Weymouth, and seems unwilling to say anything until Emma reports that Jane has been completely uninformative on such matters. This conveys the sense that he is uncertain what Emma has already learned from Jane, and it is only "rather hesitatingly" that he does say something. Emma, eager to try out on Frank her hypothesis about Jane and Mr. Dixon, fails to draw any conclusions from this, but the alert receiver will.

(3) The receiver in whom such suspicions have been awakened will not miss a crucial detail that is accorded no deeper significance by Emma. Frank suddenly decides to ride up to London for a haircut (161), something taken by Mr. and Mrs. Weston and Emma to be completely out of character. Emma, noting that he appears completely unashamed of having done this, quickly forgives him on the grounds that "silly things do cease to be silly if they are done by sensible people in an impudent way" (166). The receiver, however, will feel there is something here in need of explanation, and will therefore be in a position to bring this unexplained visit to bear upon the mysterious and unexpected arrival of the pianoforte for Jane. The piano is delivered from Broadwood's (168), which, as Austen's intended receiver would know, was a famous piano manufacturer located in Great Pulteney Street in the Soho

district of London. The general consensus that the piano is a gift from Colonel Campbell is unsatisfying both to the receiver and to those sharing in this consensus—Jane was told nothing in her recent letter from the Colonel, and someone else was needed to act as his representative in London. Emma is untroubled by these considerations because she takes the new data to be "decisive" (171) evidence for her reigning hypothesis and concludes that the piano is a gift from Mr. Dixon. When she conveys this to Frank, he agrees that the piano must be viewed as "an offering of love" (172), an assertion whose true meaning will be quickly grasped by the receiver who has applied the hermeneutic lessons of Emma's misreading of Mr. Elton's heart to the current situation in something like the manner suggested earlier.

(4) Such a receiver is then well placed to appreciate perhaps the most delicious dramatic irony in the novel (190–191) when, during the visit by Frank and Emma to the Bates', Jane is invited by Frank to play the piano. Trading on his knowledge of Emma's convictions concerning Jane and Mr. Dixon, Frank engages in verbal flirtations with Jane in plain view of everyone. He gallantly invites Jane to play a tune they had danced to the previous evening at the Coles, but Jane blushes deeply and changes what she is playing when Frank suggests that they had danced to this piece in Weymouth. He then remarks that the donation of the piano must be a product of "true affection." Emma takes this remark to be a veiled allusion, for her benefit, to her hypothesis that the donor is actually Mr. Dixon. This hypothesis further informs Emma's judgment when she notes the "remains of a smile" of "secret delight" on Jane's face: she takes this to be a sign of Jane's "very

reprehensible feelings" for Mr. Dixon. Emma then chides Frank for making fun of Jane on the grounds that "[y]ou speak too plain. She must understand you," to which Frank replies "I hope she does. I would have her understand me. I am not in the least ashamed of my meaning." Rosmarin, I think, in describing the complexities of this exchange as beyond the grasp of the first-time receiver, seriously underestimates the resources and abilities of Austen's intended audience.

(5) As with the first misreading, we are presented with evidence that might have alerted Emma to her errors were she not "too eager and busy in her own conceptions and views to . . . see . . . with clear vision" (88). At the Coles' party, for example, Emma catches Frank looking intently across the room at Jane. He says this is because of her odd hairstyle and he is going to talk with her about it. Emma tries to observe her response but cannot because Frank "had improvidently placed himself exactly between them, exactly in front of Miss Fairfax," so that "she could absolutely distinguish nothing" (174). Emma accords no significance to this, nor to the fact that, when the music is about to begin, she notices that Frank "had found a seat by Miss Fairfax" (178). Again, when Frank has to return to Enscombe because of Mrs. Churchill's illness, he attempts to confide something to Emma who, he says, "can hardly be quite without suspicion" (204). Emma, however, assumes that he wishes to confess his love for her, and prevents him from continuing. She reads his subsequent embarrassment as an indication of how deeply he is in love with her. Third, Emma rightly concludes from Jane's insistence that she cannot consent to an arrangement whereby Mrs. Elton picks up her

mail, that Jane is expecting letters of an intimate nature, but assumes, in line with her hypothesis, that such correspondence from "someone very dear" will come via "the Irish mails" (233). Finally, Emma is so convinced of her readings of the nature of Frank's affections and of the truth of his expressed disinterest in Jane that she puts no stock whatsoever in Mr. Knightley's suspicions of intimacy between Frank and Jane, apparent in the "blunder" about Mr. Perry's carriage (270–276). In all of these cases, the receiver who has drawn the conclusions that I think are both merited and intended from the earlier evidence will be aware once again of how Emma's preconceptions are coloring her vision of things, and will grasp the dramatic ironies.

Emma's Third Misreading

The third misreading (268–269) relates to the identity of the person whom Harriet describes as possessing "infinite superiority to all the rest of the world" (268). This follows her expressed vow, to Emma, that she will never marry, on the day following the dance and Harriet's subsequent encounter with the gypsies. When Harriet talks of the "gratitude, wonder, and veneration" that she properly feels for this person, Emma assumes this relates to "the service he rendered you." Harriet redescribes it as creating an "inexpressible obligation," and talks of when she "saw him coming—his noble look, and my wretchedness before. Such a change! In one moment such a change! From perfect misery to perfect happiness!" Emma urges caution as to whether the preference is returned, and counsels Harriet to be "observant" of him and "let his behaviour be the guide of your sensations." Emma, thinking of the consequences of her earlier advice, says she will counsel no further and that "no name" should ever "pass our lips," but adds that there have been "matches of greater disparity."

Emma takes it that Harriet is speaking of Frank Churchill. This is a misreading, since, as is revealed later, she is actually speaking of Mr. Knightley. But is this a *culpable* misreading? Harriet's description of her "change" fits equally well Mr. Knightley's action in intervening when Mr. Elton refuses to ask Harriet to dance, and Frank's action in intervening to save Harriet from the gypsies. The latter action, however, is more recent, more a matter of general conversation, and more dramatic. To take Harriet's referent to be Frank Churchill is not in itself culpable. But the culpability of a misreading, as we noted earlier, resides not in the judgment itself, but rather in the manner in which the judgment is formed and maintained in the face of further evidence. Here we find clear culpability on Emma's part, and, indeed, a culpability grounded in her preconceptions and predispositions, as in the earlier cases. For Emma never even considers the alternative possible referent of Harriet's remarks. She leaps immediately to the conclusion that accords with her existing idea of a romantic attachment between Frank and Harriet, an idea formed when she sees Harriet being supported by Frank when he brings her to Hartfield after rescuing her from the gypsies. The narrator writes revealingly: "Such an adventure as this, a fine young man and a lovely young woman thrown together in such a way, could hardly fail of suggesting certain ideas to the coldest heart and the steadiest brain. So Emma thought, at least. . . . How much more must an imaginist like herself, be on fire with speculation and foresight? especially with such a groundwork of anticipation as her mind had already made" (263). This presents Emma's inference in a manner that at the same time calls it into question. Indeed, just before Harriet speaks to Emma about the "infinitely superior" being, Emma muses, in response to Harriet's declaration that this is "an end, thank Heaven, of Mr. Elton," "and when will there be a beginning of Mr. Churchill?" (267).

Perhaps more significantly, Emma fails to consider Mr. Knightley as Harriet's possible romantic interest in the face of subsequent evidence that casts doubt on her original judgment. She takes Harriet's calmness on the death of Mrs. Churchill—something that removes the most obvious obstacle to an attachment to Frank—as simply evidence of how well Harriet is now able to control herself: "Harriet behaved extremely well on the occasion—with great self-command. Whatever she might feel of brighter hope she betrayed nothing. Emma was gratified to observe such a proof in her of strengthened character . . ." (305). Nothing else in Harriet's conduct, however, would suggest any such change in her emotional dispositions. Emma also ascribes no significance to Harriet's lengthy conversations with Mr. Knightley during the visit to Donwell Abbey, viewing it merely as "an odd tete-a-tete" (283). But, when she learns of her third misreading, Emma takes her failure to see this as an unforgivable blindness on her part to evidence that was there for her to see (322–323).

If we hold Emma culpable for this third misreading, is the receiver also guilty of misreading *Emma* if she fails to detect this misreading? This is undoubtedly the most difficult of the three misreadings to detect, since the receiver herself, if taking Harriet's remarks in the context of the narrated events, might read them in the same way that Emma does. But if the receiver takes Harriet's remarks in the context of *the narrator's presentation* of the narrative, we find the same kinds of indications of what is actually going on, as in the case of the two prior misreadings. In particular, as just noted, we are alerted to Emma's prior disposition to favor anything that might be evidence of a romantic interest in Frank on Harriet's part.

There is one further clue that I have not yet mentioned, one which resides in the most profound misreading on Emma's part—her misreading of her own heart. Once she becomes aware of Harriet's interest in Mr. Knightley and of the possibility of its being reciprocated, she sees "her conduct, as well as her own heart . . . with a clearness which had never blessed her before": "A few minutes were sufficient for making her acquainted with her own heart; . . . she touched, she admitted, she acknowledged the whole truth. Why was it so much worse that Harriet should be in love with Mr. Knightley than with Frank Churchill? Why was the evil so dreadfully increased by Harriet's having some hope of a return? It darted through her with the speed of an arrow that Mr. Knightley must marry no-one but herself" (320–321). She chides herself for "the blunders, the blindness of her own head and heart," and claims that, in persuading herself that she had an interest in Frank Churchill, "she had been entirely under a delusion, totally ignorant of her own heart" (324). So described, Emma's misreading of her own heart seems to be a form of self-deception, to be contrasted with the wishful thinking that grounds her misreadings of others.

I described this as a "further clue" to the receiver in detecting Emma's culpable misreading of Harriet's intentions, since it might explain why the thought of a romantic attachment between Harriet and Mr. Knightley did not occur to her. But this can be a further *clue* only if the receiver might reasonably be expected to have diagnosed this fourth misreading prior to Emma's own epiphany. Where, it might be asked, are the narrator's clues to *this* misreading? There is no doubt that the kinds of qualities in Mr. Knightley that Emma cites *after* her epiphany are ones that are manifest earlier in the narrative—her respect for Mr. Knightley's intelligence and judgment, her wish that he think well of her, and her long-standing affection for him. But these by themselves would be insufficient to alert the receiver to the true nature of Emma's heart in the absence of one noteworthy scene.

Emma is not the only character in the novel who engages in culpable misreadings whose culpability is made apparent to the receiver. Mr. Knightley's uncharacteristically uncharitable feelings toward Frank Churchill, and his subsequent misreading of Frank's conduct,

strike the reader as stemming from his concern for Emma's welfare, whether or not that concern be motivated by jealousy, as Mr.
Knightley later confesses it to be (340). The receiver may also agree
with Emma's judgment that Harriet has misread Mr. Knightley's
kindness and attention to her. These misreadings are culpable because
they result from the preconceptions and projects of the misreaders.
But there is a further misreading that is puzzling in three respects:
(1) it seems not to be so culpable, but simply a result of innocent
curiousity; (2) the misreader seems to be acting completely out of
character; and (3) the scene in which the misreading occurs plays
no obvious role in advancing any of the tangled narrative threads in
the novel. I refer to Mrs. Weston's unexpected suggestion to Emma,
at the Coles' dinner party, of "a match between Mr. Knightley and
Jane Fairfax" (176). Emma immediately responds that little Henry
must inherit Donwell and that therefore Mr. Knightley must not
marry. The oddness of this response—asking not for evidence of the
proposed liaison but simply opposing the liaison itself—is apparent
to Mrs. Weston, who insists that the future of little Henry would not
be a reason to oppose Mr. Knightley's marrying. Emma, however, ve-
hemently disagrees. The strangeness of Emma's response may suggest
to the reader that Emma's opposition to Mr. Knightley's marrying is
grounded more in her feelings for her own welfare than for that of
little Henry. It also seems plausible that this is the principal purpose
of this otherwise rather unmotivated interruption in the general development of the narrative.

IV. READING AND MISREADING AUSTEN'S
AUTHORLY INTENTIONS

I have claimed that Austen intended that the receiver detect Emma's
misreadings. This distinguishes my interpretation from those canvassed

earlier. Even Booth admits that a particularly astute reader might on a first reading grasp those things that Emma does not—in particular, the true nature of the relationship between Frank and Jane. But for Booth and those sharing his general approach, such a reader would be acting to frustrate Austen's narrative intentions, central to which is the intention that the receiver be mystified. However, it might be asked, what evidence is there to prefer my reading of Austen's intentions over that of Booth, or, indeed, over that of Rosmarin?

If I sought biographical evidence of authorial intentions to this effect, I might begin with Austen's much-cited remark in a letter to her sister Cassandra that she only wrote for those who had "a great deal of ingenuity themselves."[18] But the evidence I have offered thus far is neither biographical nor grounded in authorial pronouncements. Rather, I have argued that my interpretation makes much better sense of the text of the novel—and, in particular, of the manner in which the narrator presents the details of the unfolding events and reflects on those events. These features of the text, I have suggested, are most plausibly taken to be clues for the receiver, which can function as such because, as Rosmarin also maintains, the receiver has been "trained up" through her engagement with the first misreading. But whereas Rosmarin sees this as instrumental in our being taken in by the later misreadings, I maintain that its objective is to provide resources enabling the receiver to *detect* the later misreadings. This makes better sense of the intricacy of the exposition and the consequent dramatic ironies that all critics take to be central to the novel's value. On standard readings, these ironies are only there for the re-reader, most being opaque to the first-time receiver. But, if Austen intends the first-time receiver to detect Emma's misreadings, then appreciation of these ironies

---

18. Letter to Cassandra Austen, dated January 29, 1813. Letter 79 in *Jane Austen's Letters*, ed. Deirdre Le Faye, 4th ed. (Oxford: Oxford University Press, 2011).

will reward the receiver's hermeneutic efforts and motivate her continued reading.

This allows us to address some of the reasons offered for the standard readings. Central to these readings, we have seen, is the belief that Austen intended the mystification of the first-time reader, and that this was essential if other aims of the novel were to be achieved. For Booth, mystification is required to complement the use of the free indirect style in establishing sympathy with Emma, which would be forfeit if other demystifying perspectives on the events were provided to the reader. Mystification is required for both Harvey and Hough to motivate the receiver's continued engagement with the text, either through the hermeneutic density of the plot or through its complex narrative structure. And for Rosmarin, only a mystified receiver can be chastened for her hubris in thinking that she has hermeneutic powers that Emma lacks.

But if Austen intends that the reader see through Emma's misreadings, these reasons for mystification are undermined. In using the free indirect style to provide us with Emma's perspective while also providing us with the resources to critically assess that perspective, Austen's reason for withholding insights into the perspectives of the other characters is not to prevent detection of the misreadings, but rather to enable the receiver to discover them for herself. And it is through her ironic but nonetheless sympathetic grasp of the events making up the narrative that the first-time receiver's attention is engaged. There is no need for the mystification of a receiver who can appreciate the delicious ironies in Austen's narrative and the clever entanglements in the plot. Such a receiver differs from the second- or third-time receiver not in kind but in degree.

One reason for thinking that Austen *does* intend the mystification of the first-time receiver is the presence near the end of the novel of a device familiar from works that *do* work through mystification. It is crucial to works of detective fiction, for example, that the receiver not be provided with authorial clues that might undercut the fictional sleuth's readings of the evidence. If the receiver can reason her way to an understanding, before the denouement, of what is actually going on, her reading experience is spoiled and the work is flawed. The task for the author of works in this genre is to mislead the receiver, to inject false leads and red herrings into the plot such that, when all is finally revealed, we marvel at the skill of the investigator who can see through these obfuscations. The clarifications presented at the end of such works—where the investigator reveals the truth to the assembled company of potential suspects—usually serve a purpose external to the diegesis. They are primarily for the benefit of the reader, who needs to understand how she has been diverted from the truth if she is to appreciate the skill with which this has been done.

One might think that Frank Churchill's letter to Mrs. Weston near the end of *Emma* serves a similar purpose. It is standardly read in this way by those who see Austen's aim to be to mystify the receiver. Thus read, its function is again external to the diegesis, and its intended audience is the first-time receiver who shares Emma's misreadings. But, if, as I claim, Austen intends the first-time receiver to detect what is actually going on in the plot long before this is revealed to Emma, then what is the narrative purpose of Frank Churchill's letter? Its purpose, I think, is to enlighten not the reader but the characters themselves, and in particular Emma. The demand for such enlightenment is internal to the demands of the narrative, rather than external. Emma needs to be enlightened on these matters so that she can forgive the conduct of Frank Churchill and Jane Fairfax, thereby making possible the harmonious triple marriage with which the novel concludes.

J. M. Q. Davies draws a similar contrast between *Emma* and detective mysteries.[19] While it is crucial to the latter that the reader be

---

19. J. M. Q. Davies, "*Emma* as Charade and the Education of the Reader," *Philological Quarterly* 65 (1986): 23–42. Reprinted in David Monaghan, ed., *Emma* (London: Macmillan, 1992), 77–88. References are to the reprinted edition.

mystified until the denouement, "Jane Austen furnishes enough information for the active, critical reader to perceive the true state of
affairs as the story unfolds."[20] For Davies, a crucial signal of Austen's
intent is her incorporation into the novel of the charade and other
kinds of verbal puzzles. This suggests that Austen thought of *Emma*
as a kind of extended charade whose aim is to strengthen the reader's
power of judgment. Davies also agrees that the novel "[confronts]
the reader with successively more complex puzzles."[21] He is less opti-
mistic than I am, however, about the first-time receiver's ability to rise
to this challenge in the case of the second misreading: "its successful
solution on a first reading is in practice to some degree contingent
on the reader's having perceived the rules of the game established in
the Elton sequence."[22] He further observes, in line with Rosmarin,
that "Frank's confessional letter . . . confronts readers with their own
deficiencies of judgment."[23]

Davies's talk of "the education of the reader" echoes Rosmarin
in ascribing an edificatory purpose to the novel. Let me conclude by
suggesting that these kinds of readings of *Emma*, like my own, provide a response to one of the more notorious assaults on the cognitive
claims of literature. Jerome Stolnitz[24] has argued that the "truths" that
we can supposedly learn from great literature are trivial, imprecise in
their scope, and empirically unsupported. To illustrate the first charge,
he cites Austen's *Pride and Prejudice*, the cognitive "yield" of which,
he opines, might be the trivial and vague assertion that "stubborn
pride and ignorant prejudice keep attractive people apart." A parallel
charge against *Emma* would ascribe the equally trivial meaning that

20. Ibid, 78.
21. Ibid, 80.
22. Ibid, 83.
23. Ibid, 85.
24. Jerome Stolnitz, "On the Cognitive Triviality of Art," *British Journal of Aesthetics* 32
     (1992): 191–200.

"one's understanding of the actions and motives of other people can be distorted by one's preconceptions and prejudices." For Stolnitz, the value of literature lies not in what we can learn from it, but in the pleasures that attend our imaginative engagement with the fiction.

One who understands *Emma* as intentionally engaging the hermeneutic powers of the reader, however, can distinguish what is right from what is wrong in Stolnitz's charge. He is right in thinking that the value of literature resides not in any extractable thematic meaning, but rather in the kinds of experiences elicited in the suitably attentive and intelligent reader. But he is wrong in thinking that these experiences themselves cannot have a kind of cognitive value crucial to the artistic value of some literary works. The reader's experience in detecting Emma's misreadings can help to foster valuable hermeneutic dispositions. This kind of cognitive value evades Stolnitz's charge against standard forms of literary cognitivism, since it resides precisely in those qualities of our imaginative engagements with fictions celebrated in his own account of literary value.

But what, more precisely, are these valuable "hermeneutic dispositions"? Those who find an analogous cognitive value ascribed to tragic literary works in Aristotle's *Poetics*[25] point to the directions provided therein for constructing a dramatic work that can fulfill the "proper function" of tragedy by producing a "catharsis" of the emotions of pity and fear elicited in the receiver. The well-designed tragic plot not only elicits these emotions, but does so in accordance with Aristotle's own views about the cognitive value of the emotions. Where our emotions are aroused by all and only those things that are the proper objects of such emotions, they promote rational agency by tracking the relevant dimensions of situations encountered in experience. The "catharis" produced through our engagement with the

25. See my discussion of this in *Aesthetics and Literature* (London: Continuum, 2007), 133–134.

well-formed tragic work is the shaping of our emotional dispositions to conform with reason in this way.

Can we provide an analogous account of the shaping of our *hermeneutic* dispositions by a literary work like *Emma*? Two brief observations may suggest how such an account might go. First, the culpable misreader of *Emma* is not obviously culpable for the same reasons as Emma herself. The receiver's misreading is presumably culpable because she pays insufficient attention to the kinds of narratorial clues that I have identified. Emma's culpability, however, is the result of her partiality and preconceptions. So if the misreading receiver learns anything, it is not what Emma learns through *her* misreadings. This presents a problem for Rosmarin, who thinks that the edificatory potential in *Emma* depends upon the reader's sharing in Emma's deception. On my account, however, the cognitive value for the reader lies in her correctly assessing the motives of the various characters based on the same evidence that Emma misreads, through an attentive reading assisted by narratorial guidance. Thus what is strengthened in the reader is the care and attention to actual details that is crucial in all of our readings of behavioral signifiers, something stressed by Iris Murdoch in her own defense of the cognitive value of reading fictions.[26] Second, while obviously not sharing in the desires and preconceptions that fuel Emma's misreadings, the receiver may form parallel desires or expectations *for* Emma. Once it is clear that Emma's potential love-match in the story is Frank Churchill, the receiver may share at least the expectation that romance will blossom between the pair. It is also likely that the receiver will favor some kind of romantic liaison between Frank and Harriet. We have a parallel between Emma's fictional desires and the receiver's desires that certain things be true in the fiction. In detecting the misreadings, the receiver

26. See Iris Murdoch, *The Sovereignty of Good* (Cambridge: Cambridge University Press, 1967), 84–90.

is not misled by her desires. This again accords with Murdoch's defense of the cognitive value of literature, which stresses how literary experience can foster "unselfing" in our hermeneutic judgments concerning the conduct of others.[27]

REFERENCES

Austen, Jane. *Emma*, edited by James Kinsley. Oxford: Oxford University Press, 2003.

Austen, Jane. Letter to Cassandra Austen, dated January 29, 1813. Letter 79 in *Jane Austen's Letters*, 4th ed., edited by Deirdre Le Faye. Oxford: Oxford University Press, 2011.

Austen-Leigh, James Edward. *A Memoir of Jane Austen* (1870), reprinted in *A Memoir of Jane Austen: And Other Family Recollections*, edited by Kathryn Sutherland. Oxford: Oxford University Press, 2002.

Booth, Wayne. "Control of Distance in Jane Austen's *Emma*." In Booth, *The Rhetoric of Fiction*, 243–266. Chicago: University of Chicago Press, 1961. Reprinted in *Jane Austen: Emma, A Casebook*, revised ed., edited by David Lodge, 137–156. London: Macmillan, 1991.

Davies, David. *Aesthetics and Literature*. London: Continuum, 2007.

Davies, J. M. Q. "*Emma* as Charade and the Education of the Reader." *Philological Quarterly* 65 (1986): 23–42. Reprinted in *Emma*, edited by David Monaghan, 77–88. London: Macmillan, 1992.

Farrer, Reginald. "Jane Austen, *ob* July 18th 1817." *Quarterly Review* CCXXVIII: 24–28. Reprinted in *Jane Austen: Emma, A Casebook*, revised ed., edited by David Lodge, 65–69. London: Macmillan, 1991.

Harvey, W. J. "The Plot of *Emma*." *Essays in Criticism* XVII (1967): 48–63.

Hough, Graham "Narrative and Dialogue in Jane Austen." *Critical Quarterly* XII (1970): 201–229.

Mullan, John. "How Jane Austen's *Emma* Changed the Face of Fiction." *The Guardian*, December 5, 2015.

Mullan, John. *What Matters in Jane Austen?: 20 Crucial Puzzles Solved*. London: Bloomsbury, 2012.

Murdoch, Iris. *The Sovereignty of Good*. Cambridge: Cambridge University Press, 1967.

27. I would like to thank Eva Dadlez and Nina Penner for helpful comments on an earlier draft of this chapter.

Rosmarin, Adena. "Misreading *Emma*: The Powers and Perfidies of Narrative History." *English Literary History* 51 (1984): 315–342. Reprinted in *Jane Austen: Emma, A Casebook*, revised ed., edited by David Lodge, 213–241. London: Macmillan, 1991.

Stock, Kathleen. "Free Indirect Style and Imagining from the Inside." In *Art, Mind, and Narrative*, edited by Julian Dodd, 103–120. Oxford: Oxford University Press, 2016.

Stolnitz, Jerome. "On the Cognitive Triviality of Art." *British Journal of Aesthetics* 32 (1992): 191–200.

Chapter 8

The Dilemma of *Emma*

Substance, Style, and Story

PETER KIVY

Why, Sir, if you read Richardson for the story, your impatience would be so much fretted that you would hang yourself. But you must read him for the sentiment, and consider the story as only giving occasion to the sentiment.

—Samuel Johnson

A work of art must not be a task or an effort; it must not be undertaken against one's will. It is meant to give pleasure, to entertain and enliven. If it does not have this effect on a reader, he must put it down and turn to something else.

—Thomas Mann

I. THE DILEMMA

In the Penguin Classics edition of Jane Austen's *Emma*, the editor of the volume, Fiona Stafford writes: "From its first appearance, late in December 1815, *Emma* has been criticized for its lack of action while being eulogized for its accurate description of everyday life."[1] Walter Scott declared that it had "even less story" than *Sense and Sensibility* or *Pride and Prejudice*.[2] And Stafford continues, "Almost two centuries later, similar attitudes are to be found. . . ."[3] These are harsh words indeed for a *novel*: lack of action; lack of a story. Is *Emma* then a *failed* novel?

But, to the contrary, one of the advertising blurbs on the back cover of the Penguin Classics edition describes the novel in glowing terms as "a brilliant, sparkling comic masterpiece." And it *is* published in a series called Penguin *Classics*. In other words, *Emma* belongs in the Western literary canon. That hardly spells "failure."

It appears to me that *Emma* presents a kind of informal paradox or dilemma for the philosophy of art: in particular, that part concerning itself with the genre of narrative fiction we know as the novel. For, after all, whatever else we expect from a novel that is a "masterpiece," a "classic," an artwork belonging in the Western literary canon, we surely expect it to tell us a whopping good story. (More of *that* anon.)

But *Emma*, although it is agreed on all hands to belong in the canon, far from telling a whopping good story, is agreed on all hands to be sadly deficient in the storytelling department. It is this seeming dilemma which *Emma* presents that is the subject of the present essay, and that I hope to resolve.

My first order of business, however, as prelude to the dilemma and its resolution, must be a thumbnail sketch of, if you will, my "philosophy of the novel." So to that I now turn my attention.

1. Jane Austen, *Emma*, ed. and intro. Fiona Stafford (London: Penguin Random House, 2015), vii.
2. Ibid.
3. Ibid.

II. A NOVEL PHILOSOPHY

I intend now, as briefly as possible, to offer an outline, in the form of a set of propositions (more or less without argument, but argued for at length elsewhere) that constitute what can, loosely speaking, be termed a "philosophy of the novel."

First, then, novels can be a source of knowledge about the world and its inhabitants. Furthermore, the pleasure we experience in gaining such knowledge from novels is a legitimate part of the novel-reading experience: part of the art-relevant pleasure that novels—at least some novels—are intended by their authors to elicit in their readers.

Philosophers of art do not deny the claim that we can and frequently do acquire factual knowledge from novel-reading, for example, knowledge of whaling in the nineteenth century from *Moby Dick* or knowledge of everyday living in Victorian England from the novels of Charles Dickens. What almost all deny is that gaining such knowledge and the satisfaction in so doing are relevant to the appreciation of the novel *qua* novel: it is not, so it is almost universally claimed, a part of the novel's legitimate function.

To the contrary, although I will not make an argument for it here, I contend, and general practice and lay opinion I think support my contention, that the imparting of factual knowledge is a legitimate function of the novel, *qua* novel, *qua* artwork, as is the pleasure we take in so acquiring it. But how important this is to the novel remains to be seen.

Second, novels frequently, but not by any means universally, convey, let us say, "theses" concerning issues of broad human concern. Many of them can be characterized, loosely speaking, as "philosophical" theses. They do not convey these theses directly but, rather, by informal implication or suggestion. Furthermore, as I have argued elsewhere, such theses are intended to be thought about by the reader as a legitimate part of the novel-reading experience, in what I termed the "gaps" and "afterlife" of novel reading, which is to say, the intervals between the time you put down the novel to attend to other matters and the time you pick it up again (since one seldom reads a novel at one go), and the time after you have finished the novel, when it is still fresh in your mind.

Third, novels, to a varying degree, possess what we can loosely characterize as "aesthetic" qualities of language, style, structure, and so forth. Or perhaps they can more appropriately be termed "literary" qualities of the work.

Fourth, and I shall urge, most important, there is, of course, *the story* that the novel tells. It is my strong conviction, supported, I think, by common sense, common experience, and common practice, as I have argued at length elsewhere, that it is the deep, insatiable desire of us all *to be told a story* that has kept the novel alive and has made it—second only, I imagine, to movies and television drama—the most popular, most widely consumed genre of art in the Western world. Novels do not, I trow, sell millions of copies because of our appetite for philosophical knowledge or our delicate aesthetic sensibilities, although, needless to say, some cater to both. They sell— and their sellers know this—because they are page-turners, which is to say, books "we cannot put down" because we are enthralled by the tale being told.

The subtitle of the present chapter is "Substance, Style, and Story." I have, in the preceding four claims, covered them all. Thus the claim is that any novel can be experienced and evaluated as to its substance (claims one and two); its style (claim three); and its story (claim four). And with these three aspects of the novel in tow, we can now turn to the novel, Jane Austen's *Emma*, which is the subject of the present exercise.

III. SUBSTANCE

Samuel Johnson is quoted by Boswell as having responded to the complaint that "[s]urely, Sir, Richardson is quite tedious" with the following: "Why, Sir, if you read Richardson for the *story*, your impatience would be so much fretted that you would hang yourself. But you must read him for the sentiment, and consider the story as only giving occasion to the sentiment."[4]

The first important point one gleans from this comment of Dr. Johnson's is that he assumes from the get-go—and I think quite rightly—that the primary, *prima facie* motivation for reading a novel is to be told an engrossing story. And *that* is why he must chide one who finds Richardson's novels "tedious" for reading Richardson for the *story*. He takes it as a given that if one finds Richardson "tedious," it *must* be because one finds the story tedious. So it follows that if he is not to find Richardson tedious, he must read him for something else: namely, the sentiment.

But now the question arises as to what Dr. Johnson meant by "sentiment." For in the eighteenth century, as now, it could mean feeling, which is to say, emotion, or it could refer to opinion. However, the answer is not far to seek. For he writes, "there is more knowledge of the human heart in one letter of Richardson's than in all of 'Tom Jones.'"[5] And by a "letter" of Richardson's Johnson obviously means one of the letters that make up Richardson's novels; for both *Pamela* and *Clarissa Harlow* are of course epistolary novels.

It is important to note, as well, that Dr. Johnson writes of *knowledge* of the human heart. In other words, when he urges that one

4. James Boswell, *The Life of Samuel Johnson, L.L.D.* (New York: The Modern Library, n.d.), 413 (April 6, 1772). My italics.
5. Ibid., 412.

must read Richardson for the sentiment, he is not urging that we be aroused by the sentiments expressed, that we take an emotional bath, but that we learn about them. Richardson's novels, Johnson is claiming, are the source of a certain kind of knowledge, that is, knowledge of the human heart, knowledge of the nature of human emotions.

And that brings us, at last, to *Emma*. Should we take a leaf from Dr. Johnson's book and say, "Why, Sir, if you read *Emma* for the story, your impatience would be so much fretted that you would hang yourself. But you must read it for the sentiment, and consider the story as only giving occasion to the sentiment." The directive would be to read *Emma* for "knowledge of the human heart." It is the imparting of such knowledge, not the story, that is the merit of *Emma* and places it in the canon. The dilemma of *Emma* is thus resolved.

Well, not so fast. Here is why. I think one of the problems many people who find *Emma* disappointing have with it is that the characters lack psychological depth and interest, unlike, for example, those of Dostoyevsky and Dickens, and, for that matter, Elizabeth and Darcy. Thus I do not think knowledge of the human heart gained through a reading of *Emma* is enough to sustain its place in the canon. Nor, by the way, can that status be sustained by our having acquired from the novel knowledge of the historical period in which Jane Austen flourished, although, as we have seen, it was "eulogized for its accurate description of everyday life."

But all is not lost. If knowledge of the human heart, which is to say, knowledge of the human emotions, is not to be found in *Emma*, and knowledge of everyday life in the early nineteenth century, which *can* be gained from it, is not enough to sustain its place in the canon, perhaps some other kind of knowledge might be found in the novel that does warrant its being denominated a "classic." And what might that "other" kind of knowledge be?

Not surprisingly, an answer comes readily to mind: some kind of "philosophical knowledge," broadly conceived. And again, not surprisingly, moral philosophy seems a likely candidate. At least so it seemed to Gilbert Ryle, when he penned the essay "Jane Austen and the Moralists."[6] It behooves us, then, to consider what Ryle had to say about the moral content of *Emma*. Perhaps *that* will turn out to be its redeeming feature. In *Emma*, so Ryle claims, Austen was raising the following moral question:

> Jane Austen's question here was: What makes it sometimes legitimate or even obligatory for one person deliberately to try to modify the course of another person's life, while sometimes such attempts are wrong? Where is the line between Meddling and Helping? Or, more generally, between proper and improper solicitude about the destinies and welfares of others?[7]

To be sure, Ryle has suggested a moral problem that *Emma* might plausibly be thought to be proposing to the reader by Emma's bungling but well-meaning attempts to arrange what she perceives to be appropriate marriages for her female friends and acquaintances. Generalized, the problem, as Ryle poses it in the preceding quotation, is, "What makes it sometimes legitimate or even obligatory for one person deliberately to try to modify the course of another person's life, while sometimes such attempts are wrong?" The worry, however, that I have, in the present context, is whether proposing such a, shall we say, less than profound moral problem would give enough substance to *Emma* to sustain it in the canon: to make it a Penguin *Classic*.

6. Gilbert Ryle, "Jane Austen and the Moralists," *The Oxford Review*, no. 1 (1966).
7. Gilbert Ryle, "Jane Austen and the Moralists," reprinted in Ryle, *Critical Essays: Collected Papers* (London: Routledge, 2009), 290.

Now this is not to say that the question, as Ryle alternatively puts it, of "Where is the line between Meddling and Helping?" cannot be projected onto a broader landscape than Emma's attempts at matchmaking. For, after all, one might well describe the question in ethics and political philosophy of "benevolent paternalism" as, colloquially put, "Where is the line between Meddling and Helping?" And the question of benevolent paternalism is surely a nontrivial one. Should smoking be outlawed to save human lives? After all, it *is* a killer. Would it be Meddling or Helping on the part of the government if it outlawed cigarettes? And if it *would* be Meddling, why is not the prohibition of "recreational" drugs? And so on.

Surely, though, most would find it quite a stretch to go from Emma's matchmaking to such profound moral problems as that of benevolent paternalism, and all of the socio-political issues it implies. If that were really the moral substance of *Emma*, what the novel was really "about," one wonders whether it would fall afoul of Thomas Mann's warning that "[a] work of art must not be a task or an effort." One wonders if Mann would not "put it down and turn to something else."[8]

Furthermore, the question of author's intention surely presses itself upon us here. It seems to me eminently reasonable to suppose that the moral question Ryle discerns in *Emma* is one that Jane Austen intended to convey. But it is not, I think, a question substantial enough to vouchsafe the novel as canonical, as the literary classic that it manifestly is.

Contrariwise, the question generalized to that of benevolent paternalism makes it, perhaps, a moral question of some considerable weight, which might well be considered worthy of a work in the canon. But unless one is willing to disregard authorial intention,

8. Thomas Mann, "The Making of *The Magic Mountain*," afterword to Thomas Mann's *The Magic Mountain*, trans. H. T. Lowe-Porter (New York: Alfred A. Knopf, 1993), 724.

or, rather, lack thereof, which many philosophers, not the present one, are inclined to do, it appears highly improbable to interpret Emma's matrimonial machinations as raising a moral issue as fraught and contentious as that of benevolent paternalism. That horse will not run.

Where, then, does that leave us? Neither story nor substance seem able to explain the solid position Jane Austen's *Emma* maintains in the canon. That leaves us with the second "S" in my subtitle, which is to say, *style*.

IV. STYLE

I can well imagine Samuel Johnson saying: "Why, Sir, if you read *Emma* for the story, your impatience will be so much fretted that you would hang yourself. But you must read it for the *style*, and consider the story as only giving occasion to the style." For, after all, what novelist in the English language is more admired for their style than Jane Austen? And *Emma* surely is no exception.

Indeed, the opening sentence of *Emma* has been described as the most perfect sentence in English prose fiction. It reads: "Emma Woodhouse, handsome, clever, and rich, with a comfortable home and happy disposition, seemed to unite some of the best blessings of existence; and had lived nearly twenty-one years in the world with very little to distress or vex her."[9]

The sentence, of course, is beautifully "composed." The musical term seems to force itself upon us; but I will not be so bold as to try to explain what it is in the sentence that makes it so. One thing,

---

9. For purposes of consistency in this anthology, the editor has converted all references to the text of the novel to the following edition. Jane Austen, *Emma*, ed. James Kinsley, introduction by Adela Pinch (Oxford: Oxford University Press, 2008), 5.

however, that no one can miss is how much information about Emma the author has, with such seeming ease, been able to pack into the opening sentence of her novel, and how trippingly off the tongue it falls. A lesser stylist would take a paragraph to do what Austen does in a sentence, with no feeling at all of crowding it in.

Emma, like Jane Austen's other novels, is, of course, full of such stylistic wonders. And our reincarnated Dr. Johnson is telling us to read the novel not for the story, which would fret our patience, but for the stylistic wonders for which it is merely the occasion. What would such a manner of reading be like? I think we can get a pretty good idea thereof by turning briefly to Peter Lamarque's recent book, *The Opacity of Narrative*.

Here, in brief, and in Lamarque's words, is what I take to be the manner in which we would read *Emma* not for the story but for the style. "When we know that a narrative is a work of fictional literature," Lamarque writes, "we know that attention to its formal structure is especially appropriate and potentially rewarding. . . ."[10] In other words, "the fictive stance involves foregrounding of the formal features of narrative."[11]

Now I want to make it perfectly clear that I am far from rejecting Lamarque's characterization of how we read fictional literature, just as long as we understand it is not *the* way we read or ought to read it. To be sure, it is *one* of the valid ways we read the novels of the canon. But I want to insist, as I already have in the preceding, that what has kept the novel alive, what has sold bestselling novels in the millions of copies, what put the complete works of Dickens on so many bookshelves, is the *story*, not the style. We may read fictional literature, in the manner Lamarque describes, in the English seminar

10. Peter Lamarque, *The Opacity of Narrative* (London; New York: Rowman & Littlefield, 2014), 59.
11. Ibid., 48.

room, and, no doubt, sometimes in the living room. That I do not deny. However, what sells the novel to the "masses," whether it is the classics or the latest bestseller, is prowess of the author as a teller of tales. The story's the thing.

So we seem to be back where we began. I am not claiming that there are no cases in which substance or style or both together can sustain a novel in the canon, in the absence of a compelling story to sweep the reader up. But *Emma* is not, I have argued, such a work. Neither its substance nor its style nor both together can explain its firm position in the canon. Yet occupy that firm position it does.

Perhaps such musings, then, should cause us to reconsider that with which we began, that *Emma* is weak in story. How might such a *volte face* be justified? For justified I think it is. So I will be occupied in the rest of this chapter with defending *Emma* as, received opinion to the contrary notwithstanding, *not* deficient in story but, for reasons that shall now become apparent, consisting in a story the enjoyment of which presents obstacles, but surmountable ones, to the past as well as the contemporary reader.

V. STORY

To say that there is no story to speak of, in *Emma*, would be literally false, and an obvious instance of hyperbole. But there *are* many readers by no means unsophisticated in their literary sensibility, and there are enthusiastic consumers of literary fiction (including the classics), who find *Emma*, not to put too fine a point on it, "an utter bore." The whole plot, so the dissatisfied go on, is simply a matter of who will marry whom. And one simply can't find that of enough moment to sustain interest. "Who *cares* who marries whom?"

In short, "nothing *happens*" in *Emma* to excite one's interest, as, for example, does what happens in *Great Expectations* or *Moby Dick*.

Such is the case against *Emma* as a story. But I think the challenge can be met.

To meet the challenge, I am going to appeal to what I shall call "reader resistance." It is a version of a phenomenon that has gone under numerous names, and has been presented in numerous versions.[12] I have no intention of exploring the complexities and controversies surrounding this phenomenon in detail and depth. There is, fortunately, no need to do so. What I hope to appeal to— perhaps a vain hope for a philosopher to entertain—is the phenomenon I am calling "reader resistance," considered in such a way as to be uncontroversial and readily acceptable.

As far as I know, and many others agree, the phenomenon I am calling "reader resistance" has its origin in David Hume's much commented upon essay, "Of the Standard of Taste," where he wrote, "We may observe, that every work of art, in order to produce its due effect on the mind, must be surveyed in a certain point of view, and cannot be fully relished by persons whose situation, real or imaginary, is not conformable to that which is required by the performance."[13] Thus Hume's point is, in modern terms and present context, that we must, in fictional works, assume "a certain point of view" in which we can take certain things as "fictionally true," for example, that Holmes and Watson lived on Baker Street, in London.

But Hume further observed, and this is crucial for our purposes, that certain points of view—Hume here singled out moral sentiments—were impossible for us to entertain, *as if they were*

---

12. For a careful examination of the numerous philosophical issues involved, see Derek Matravers, *Fiction and Narrative* (Oxford: Oxford University Press, 2014), Chapter 9. And see also Shaun Nichols (ed.), *The Architecture of the Imagination: New Essays on Pretence, Possibility, and Fiction* (Oxford: Clarendon Press, 2006), section III.
13. David Hume, "Of the Standard of Taste," in Hume, *Essays Moral, Political and Literary* (London: Oxford University Press, 1963), 244.

true, if they were too at odds with our own moral convictions. In Hume's words,

> Where errors may be found in the polite writings of any age or country, they detract little from the value of those compositions. There needs but a certain turn of thought or imagination to make us enter into all the opinions which then prevailed.... But a very violent effort is requisite to change a judgment of manners, and excite [moral] sentiments of approbation or blame, love or hatred, different from those to which the mind from long custom has been familiarized.[14]

And as Kendall Walton puts what I take to be Hume's point, in contemporary terms, there are limits to what we are able to take as even *fictionally* true. Thus, for example, we are able to accept such fictional truths as "that bloodletting cures disease, that the sun revolves around the earth, that people think with their hearts ... but not that the only good Indian is a dead one or that slavery is just and torture in the service of tyranny humane."[15] The latter, those that we cannot accept as fictionally true, elicit what I am calling "reader resistance." And with that concept to hand, I turn now to employ it in my effort to resolve what I am terming the "dilemma" of *Emma*.

Let me begin with some obvious assumptions. First of all, I take it that the story *Emma* tells is a story told from the point of view of a woman by a woman. Furthermore, I take it that the woman telling the story is the author herself, namely, Jane Austen. It matters not, I think, if my reader prefers to construe the story as being told by a fictional narrator, or an implied author. For what I have to say anon

14. Ibid., 253.
15. Kendall Walton, *Mimesis as Make-Believe* (Cambridge, MA: Harvard University Press, 1990), 154.

is consistent with both, although I just want to be up front with my own, if you will, storyteller ontology.

I take it, as well, that *Emma* belongs to the genre known as the "realistic novel," which is to say, a realistic fictional representation of the world as it was or, perhaps, in some respects, as it was falsely believed to be. (The characters in *Emma*, as to the latter, are, for example, obsessed with the fear of catching colds caused, they believe, by bad climate or getting caught in the rain.) Which is to say, the world projected by *Emma* is a world whose events and characters never did exist, but is an accurate, "realistic" depiction of Jane Austen's world in early nineteenth-century England.

We must now get an idea of what exactly *Emma*'s world, which I am assuming was Jane Austen's world, was like, in the respects relevant to the story Jane Austen is telling us. So here are some important points to note.

One thing seems apparent right from the get-go. Working for a living, in the social class that the characters in *Emma* occupy, was decidedly *declasse*. An eligible bachelor usually, as an essential mark of his eligibility, possessed a "fortune," which provided the income on which he subsisted. And if you were a woman, working for a living was the fate worse than death: a vital point to remember in understanding the story of *Emma*, and, I should add, in understanding reader resistance.

A man's "career," if I may so describe it, in *Emma*, in Emma's social class, seems to have been collecting interest on his fortune. What might a woman in this social class look forward to as her "career"? Emma's career had been, as the novel opens, looking after a widower, a valetudinarian father and self-made invalid—someone convinced that the only nourishing and healthy food for a human being was gruel. What could her future career be?

The point that becomes very clear in the novel is that a woman had, in the world of *Emma*, two career paths open to her (apart from a perpetual dependence on her relations): a good marriage to a man of financial independence, a teacher, or, *horibile dictu*, a live-in governess, the fate worse than death.

A woman's situation in the world of *Emma* is presented most vividly by Austen in the person of Emma's protégé, Harriet Smith, "the natural daughter of somebody. Somebody had placed her, several years back, at Mrs. Goddard's school, and somebody had lately raised her from the condition of scholar to that of parlour-boarder" (19).

Harriet Smith, early on in *Emma*, appears on the verge of being saved from the fate worse than death by a proposal of marriage from Mr. Martin, who, while "not born to an independence" (24), nevertheless "had a very fine flock . . ." and "had been bid more for his wool than any body in the country" (23). He is represented by the narrative voice, it would seem, as an altogether worthy young man, very much in love with Harriet, and ideally suitable as a prospective spouse, given her situation.

But Emma does not find him so, because, as she remarks, "He will be a completely gross, vulgar farmer—totally inattentive to appearances, and thinking of nothing but profit and loss." Furthermore, "And I have no doubt he *will* thrive and be a very rich man in time—and his being illiterate and coarse need not disturb *us*" (27). Class snobbery has reared its ugly head. And the narrative voice, which I take to be Jane Austen or her creation, leaves no doubt that she is registering disapproval of it.

The meddlesome Emma does, indeed, have another, far more suitable bridegroom, as she sees it, for Harriet, with all the correct social credentials. In the event, however, he turns out not to be so inclined, nor is a second prospect Emma chooses. And Harriet, now without any marital prospects at all, seemingly faces the fate worse than death, and is obliged to follow the only career besides matrimony open to a woman in the world of *Emma*. She faces the fate of governess, which Emma describes in this wise, when another apparent victim of the permanently unmarried state, Jane Fairfax, seems to embrace it. "Jane actually on the point of going as governess! What could he mean by such horrible indelicacy? To suffer her to engage herself—to suffer her even to think of such a measure!" (313).

Of course, as events happily transpire, all of the eligible ladies whose fortunes we follow in *Emma* achieve the goal of matrimony, even Emma herself to (we are supposed to be surprised?) her critic and adversary throughout the novel, Mr. Knightley. They embrace, in other words, the appropriate and most desired career in the world of *Emma*, that of wife and homemaker, and manage to avoid the only other alternative, if they do not possess an independent fortune, the fate worse than death, governess and/or schoolmarm.

Now the point I want to make here is that the world of *Emma* is a very different world from ours as regards the status and career prospects for women. And I mean of course by "our world" the world of the West. We have passed through the suffragette movement, the age of Rosie the Riveter, to an age in which a woman can be a candidate for president of the United States. I am not, by any means, suggesting that the women's liberation movement has completely and successfully run its course. Numerous inequalities still exist. But if we compare the career options for women in our world with those in the world of *Emma*, there are surely differences by an order of magnitude. What were the career prospects in the world of *Emma*? Well, as I have argued, there were two: the most highly desired career of matrimony and the fate worse than death, governess or schoolmarm. And in our world? To cut to the chase, I was operated on by a female surgeon, flown across the continent by a female pilot, and so on.

The status of women in the professions has, of course, only slowly evolved since the publication of *Emma*, but was given a giant boost during World War II by the need for women in the workplace to do the jobs of the men who were otherwise occupied. Be that as it may, it has been a long time during which career options for women were far wider than the few available in the world of *Emma*. And that being the case, two forms of what I have denominated earlier as "reader resistance" might be in play when we hear or read it said: "There just is no *story* in *Emma*. The whole bloody thing is about who will marry whom or whether someone will marry at all. And I just couldn't care less who marries whom or whether someone will marry at all. A story must depict events more significant than merely the event of marriage to be a story that will not so fret your impatience that you would hang yourself."

It appears to me that this common response to *Emma* may exhibit two possible forms of reader resistance, already, as we have seen, recognized by Hume: what I shall call "fact-in-fiction reader resistance" and "morality-in-fiction" reader resistance. The reader who makes the preceding negative response to *Emma* may be under the influence of one, or the other, or both.

Fact-in-fiction reader resistance is resistance to one or more of the things that may be fictionally true in the fictional narrative. For example, it is fictionally true in H. G. Wells's novella *The Invisible Man* that a man makes himself invisible by rendering himself completely transparent: that is to say, he does not reflect light, reflecting light being what makes physical objects visible, but light passes right through him, as light through perfectly transparent glass. In this invisible state, Wells's invisible man then performs various disruptive acts that a visible man could not perform or get away with. When I first read *The Invisible Man* I had no problem accepting these fictional truths and thoroughly enjoying the story. In other words, I had no reader resistance to the fictional truths as stated in the preceding. However, some years ago it was pointed out to me that Wells's invisible man would be blind, because we see by virtue of light striking our optic nerve and causally interacting with it. However, if the invisible man was transparent, every part of him would have to be, including his optic nerves. So light would not strike his optic nerves, but would pass right through them. He would, therefore, be sightless, and unable to do any of the things he is represented as doing in Wells's novella. Now if, prior to my first reading of *The Invisible Man*, I had been aware of these facts about how we see, and put two and two together, I might very well have been unable to "get into" the story because I would not be able to accept as fictionally true that a man made invisible by making himself transparent could do the things the invisible man does in the story, since a transparent man would be blind. In this regard I would be experiencing what I call "fact-in-fiction reader resistance."

What I call "morality-in-fiction reader resistance" is undoubtedly what Hume had in mind when he averred that "a very violent effort is requisite to change a judgment of manners, and excite [moral] sentiments of approbation or blame, love or hatred, different from those to which the mind from long custom has been familiarized." Thus, to take an example from America's deplorable past, the fictional truth, in *Uncle Tom's Cabin*, that slavery is grossly immoral, a cruel injustice, was met by antebellum Southern slaveholders with extreme reader resistance, which obviously kept them from "appreciating" the novel, as their minds, "from long custom," had been "familiarized" with the belief that slavery is a thoroughly moral institution. In this regard, they were exhibiting what I call "morality-in-fiction reader resistance."

The groundwork is now laid for resolution of what I have termed the "dilemma" of *Emma*. And I turn to that task now in the concluding two sections of this chapter.

VI. RESOLVING THE DILEMMA

Let me, then, make a beginning to my ending by reminding the reader what I have construed the "dilemma" of *Emma* to be. A formal dilemma or paradox, I take it, consists in a pair of propositions, both of which seem *prima facie* to be true, but cannot both be true because they are contradictory.

The dilemma of *Emma*, as I stated at the outset, does not lend itself to quite so concise a statement, in but two conflicting propositions, without awkwardness. So here it is as concisely as it can be put.

First, *Emma* belongs to the Western literary canon. In other words, it is a classic, one of the acknowledged literary masterpieces.

Second, *Emma* is a novel.

Third, it is a necessary (but not a sufficient) condition for a novel's belonging to the Western literary canon, being a classic, an acknowledged literary masterpiece, that it tell a whopping good story.

Fourth, *Emma* is sadly deficient in its story. Far from telling a whopping good story, its story is an utter bore about nothing more than who marries whom.

Thus the "dilemma" of *Emma*. And I intend to resolve it by denying the fourth statement. *Emma* is *not* sadly deficient in its story.

My argument, in brief, is simply that *Emma's* story elicits strong reader resistance, of the fact-in-fiction and the morality-in-fiction kind, as I have already hinted at in the preceding, from many readers. And when this reader resistance is overcome, the *Emma* story ceases to seem trivial and boring but, rather, emerges as a story of interest and moment. This of course requires spelling out.

Let me begin with fact-in-fiction reader resistance. It is fictionally true in the world of *Emma* that a woman's career choices were two in number: a suitable marriage to a man of financial independence, or the unrewarding lot of a governess or schoolmarm. It is not a fictional world as radically distinct from ours as are worlds in which it is fictionally true that a man makes himself invisible or travels in a time machine. But, nevertheless, the world of *Emma* is very different from our own, and has been for a long time, the status of women having become considerably more comparable to that of men in regard to career choices, among other things.

The contemporary reader, and the reader (say) at least since World War II, in order to find the story of *Emma* interesting, even enthralling and important, must overcome his or her reader resistance to what is fictionally true about the status and prospects of women in the world of *Emma*. When that suspension of disbelief is achieved (*if* it is achieved) and the reader "internalizes," as it were, the world of *Emma* and the status of women in it, then "who marries whom" and who fails to marry at all, where the "who" is a woman, emerges as a momentous, life-determining set of events: as momentous, for instance, as whether or not Marie Curie decides to become a scientist.

How does one overcome this fact-in-fiction reader resistance to the story of *Emma*? I think it clear that the most effective and indeed the mandated way of doing it is to come to realize, and correctly so, that Jane Austen was not weaving the world of *Emma* out of whole cloth but accurately representing *her* world; as Fiona Stafford puts it, creating "lifelike characters and situations . . ." such that "critics of a historical bent . . ." can "turn to her novels for information on how people lived in the early nineteenth century."[16] *Emma*, in short, belongs to the artistic genre of the realistic novel. When read as such, fact-in-fiction reader resistance is overcome, and who marries whom becomes profoundly important as the subject of the narrative. And thus is resolved the dilemma of *Emma*. The story *is* worthy, when so read, of belonging in the canon.

"But hold on," the skeptic may rightly object. "You have showed how to overcome fact-in-fiction reader resistance. What about

16. Jane Austen, *Emma* (London: Penguin Random House, 2015), vii.

morality-in-fiction reader resistance? How can we overcome reader resistance to the perceived immorality in the world of *Emma*, which surely manifests itself in the low status of women, who are consigned to the alternatives of a suitable marriage to a man of property or the fate worse than death: live-in governess or teacher?" Fair enough! We must now face the problem of morality-in-fiction reader resistance the world of *Emma* might elicit.

I take it that the modern reader—and by the modern reader I mean the reader from as far back as World War II, if not well before—would take the subservient status of women in *Emma's* world to be highly immoral, unless the reader is a confirmed sexist or misogynist. Thus, *if* Jane Austen or the fictional narrator were presenting the world of *Emma* in a positive moral light, morality-in-fiction reader resistance would be overpowering. It would fall under Hume's dictum that "a very violent effort is requisite to change a judgment of manners, and excite [moral] sentiments of approbation or blame, love or hatred, different from those to which the mind from long custom has been familiarized."

There are, it appears to me, three possibilities here. Jane Austen is presenting the status and prospects of women in *Emma's* world, Austen's world, as completely justified morally. Or, contrariwise, she is presenting the status and prospects of women in *Emma's* world, Austen's world, as morally unjustified. Or, finally, she is presenting the status and prospects of women in *Emma's* world, as well as Austen's own, in a completely disinterested manner, as an observer simply telling the reader "this is the way it is—no further comment."

It is a certainty, I believe, that Austen was not presenting the status and prospects of women in her own world and that of *Emma* as morally right and proper: hers was far too advanced and enlightened an intellect for that. And recall, a propos of this, that Mary

Wollstonecraft had published *A Vindication of the Rights of Women* in 1792. Austen is certain to have read it and, I am certain, was in sympathy with its message.

That leaves us with the two remaining possibilities: that Austen was presenting the career options in the world of *Emma*, her world (namely, marriage to a man of property or the dire fate of becoming a live-in governess or schoolmarm) with moral disapproval or with observer disinterest. Perhaps it is wishful thinking, but I plump for the former.

Now Jane Austen was far too subtle and stylish a writer of prose fiction to give any suggestion of preaching or didacticism in *Emma*. So if there is a moral stance on the part of the narrator, she does not wear it on her sleeve. It must be teased out. And the narrator, even if you do not take her to be Austen herself, surely *is* a "she," and I assume that, no argument necessary.

I derive my conjecture as to how the narrator conveys disapproval of the status of women, and their limited career opportunities in *Emma*'s world, from an advertising blurb on the back cover of the Penguin Classics edition, quoted earlier, which describes the novel as a "comic masterpiece." I rather think that the reader of *Emma*—certainly this reader—should be more than somewhat surprised at the term "comic" being applied to it and particularly surprised by the seeming implication that its comic qualities are what make it a "masterpiece." *The Importance of Being Earnest* is a comic masterpiece, and, indeed, a masterpiece in virtue of its comic attributes. But *Emma*? Hardly a side-slapper.

Perhaps, though, there is another way to read "comic masterpiece" as a description of *Emma* that makes more sense, namely, that it *is*, in certain respects, comic, and that it is, in truth, a masterpiece, but not mainly on account of its comic aspects. And, furthermore, it is its comic aspects that, I think, suggest a moral stance on the part of the narrator. To cut to the chase, I think the narrator exhibits a kind of "irony," not the only kind, which my *Webster's Illustrated Dictionary* defines as "humor implying the opposite of what is expressed."[17]

So let me now suggest that the comic aspects of *Emma*'s plot, in particular, the somewhat comic ways in which Emma and the other female characters behave, are, if you will, comic but not comic; laughable but don't laugh; in other words, ironically comic. "T'ain't funny McGee!"[18] It is sadly comic that they *must* behave the way they "comically" do. And they must behave that way because their career prospects are unjustly confined to marrying a man of property or becoming underpaid and underappreciated governesses and schoolmistresses. Finally, if you read *Emma* this way, morality-in-fiction reader resistance is overcome, as the "correct" moral stance to the world of *Emma* is expressed and invited.

But one further point in this regard. Perhaps some of my readers may be unable to accept my interpretation of the narrator as expressing moral disapproval of the world of *Emma*. Perhaps they are more comfortable with the third option: that the narrator is just disinterestedly presenting what is fictionally true of the status of women in the world of *Emma* and passing no moral judgment upon it. "Make up your own mind" is the message.

Well, *pas de problème*. If the reader is left to make up his or her own mind in the matter, there is no morality-in-fiction reader resistance to overcome. The limited career prospects open to women in the world of *Emma* will be judged unjust by the right-thinking modern reader, which is perfectly consistent with the intention of a disinterested narrator who desires you to reach a moral conclusion

---

17. For an examination of irony in its various forms, see Gregory Currie, "Why Irony Is Pretence," in *The Architecture of the Imagination: New Essays on Pretence, Possibility, and Fiction*, ed. Shaun Nichols (Oxford: Oxford University Press, 2006) 111–133.
18. For those who remember radio!

by reaching rather than preaching. (I presume there is no doubt about what moral conclusion Jane Austen wanted the reader to reach.)

Thus, to sum up the conclusion we have thus far reached, the dilemma of *Emma*, which is to say, how the status of the novel as a classic, as a canonical masterpiece, in the absence of a compelling, interesting, engaging story, has been resolved by demonstrating that the story is far from deficient if the modern reader succeeds in overcoming fact-in-fiction and morality-in-fiction reader resistance. But the skeptic may, it appears, have another string to his bow. And I conclude with a consideration of that possibility.

VII. BACK FROM THE FUTURE

Here, then, is how the skeptic might respond to my supposed resolution of *Emma*'s dilemma. "You have explained how the modern reader, if he or she overcomes fact-in-fiction reader resistance and morality-in-fiction reader resistance, can find the story in *Emma* important, engrossing, and thereby worthy of the status *Emma* is agreed on all hands to possess. But you make clear at the outset of your essay that the story of *Emma* was found wanting right from the get-go, witness the negative judgment made upon it by Jane Austen's contemporary, Sir Walter Scott. And *these* readers had neither fact-in-fiction nor morality-in-fiction reader resistance to the story of *Emma*. On the contrary, the world of *Emma* was *their* world, both fictionally and morally. They had, therefore, no reader resistance to the story to overcome and *still* found it virtually a non-story. So your resolution of *Emma*'s dilemma will not wash for a vast number of the novel's readers."

The point is well taken. I shall frame my answer in two parts, corresponding to the two groups of readers in question, namely—and obviously—the two sexes. For is it not obvious that women would have had a different reaction to *Emma* from that of men?

So let me begin with two historical conjectures. First, women readers of *Emma*, from its publication in 1815, until our times, women's suffrage and the "women's liberation movement," had, as opposed to men readers, little trouble being taken up in the story of *Emma*, and finding it both enthralling and of import. It *did* matter to *them* who marries whom and who does not marry at all because that was what their lives were all about.

Second, our historical source for the view that *Emma* is a bore, a defective story, no story at all, is *men*, starting, as we have seen, with Sir Walter Scott. Because, of course, it was mostly *men*, in the age of *Emma*, and for a long time thereafter, who occupied positions in the literary world that allowed *them* to make their assessments of literary works such as *Emma* known to the public through their critical writings. Women, for the most part, could not.

And of course, to continue the thought, men during the age of *Emma*, and for a long time thereafter, found the trials and tribulations of the women in *Emma*, in other words, the story in *Emma*, an utter bore: no story at all. They were, from our point of view and to put it bluntly, male chauvinists. Thus, they couldn't care less about the trials and tribulations of the women in *Emma*'s world, which is to say, who marries whom, and who suffers the fate worse than death, given the low status of women in their social structure.

But if I am correct in my interpretation of *Emma*, Jane Austen was not merely disinterestedly presenting the world of *Emma*, her world, to us; she was passing an adverse moral judgment on the status of women in her world. That being the case, it was, like so many great works of art, ahead of its time and, like the late Beethoven quartets, written for future generations (as Beethoven put it).

So here ends my answer to the skeptic and my defense of the story in *Emma* as fully worthy of its position in the Western literary canon. No doubt the Janeites will find my discussion of *Emma* naïve in the extreme. I am no literary critic or literary historian—merely a philosopher who rushes in where angels fear to tread. But at least it can be said that my naïveté has ended in a favorable judgment of the work whose heroine Austen described as a character "whom no one but myself will like."[19] I hope I have proved her prediction mistaken.

REFERENCES

Austen, Jane. *Emma*, edited by James Kinsley, introduction by Adela Pinch. Oxford: Oxford University Press, 2008.

Austen, Jane. *Emma*, edited by Fiona Stafford. London: Penguin Random House, 2015.

Austen-Leigh, James Edward. *A Memoir of Jane Austen*, edited by R. W. Chapman. Oxford: Clarendon, 1967. Originally published in 1870.

Boswell, James. *The Life of Samuel Johnson, L.L.D.* New York: The Modern Library, n.d.

Currie, Gregory. "Why Irony Is Pretence." In *The Architecture of the Imagination: New Essays on Pretence, Possibility, and Fiction*, edited by Shaun Nichols, 111–133. Oxford: Oxford University Press, 2006.

Hume, David. "Of the Standard of Taste." *Essays Moral, Political and Literary*. London: Oxford University Press, 1963.

Lamarque, Peter. *The Opacity of Narrative*. London; New York: Rowman & Littlefield, 2014.

Mann, Thomas. "The Making of *The Magic Mountain*." Afterword to Mann, *The Magic Mountain*, translated by H. T. Lowe-Porter. New York: Alfred A. Knopf, 1993.

Matravers, Derek. *Fiction and Narrative*. Oxford: Oxford University Press, 2014.

Nichols, Shaun, ed. *The Architecture of the Imagination: New Essays on Pretence, Possibility, and Fiction*. Oxford: Clarendon Press, 2006.

Ryle, Gilbert. "Jane Austen and the Moralists." *The Oxford Review*, no. 1 (1966). Reprinted in Ryle, *Critical Essays: Collected Papers*, 286–303, 290, (London: Routledge, 2009).

Walton, Kendall. *Mimesis as Make-Believe*. Cambridge, MA: Harvard University Press, 1990.

19. Austen-Leigh, James Edward. *A Memoir of Jane Austen* [1870], ed. R. W. Chapman (Oxford: Clarendon, 1967), 157.

INDEX

aesthetics, xiii–xvi, 211–212, 214–215
agency and action, 8, 86, 92–93, 100–102, 108, 131, 144, 146–147, 212
Aristotle, 7–8, 21, 25–27, 31–33, 35–37, 43–45, 47–48, 53–54, 56–63, 79–83, 212
   Nicomachean Ethics, 4, 7, 25, 31, 33, 53–54, 57–58, 83
   Poetics, 212–213
Austen-Leigh, James Edward, 110, 130, 132, 135, 156, 187, 214, 241
Austin, J.L., 111, 113, 132
autonomy, 8–9, 85, 87, 89–91, 94, 128

Badhwar, Neera K., 32–33, 37, 45, 48, 53–54
Barrett, Eaton Stannard, 165, 179, 182
Beckford, William, 164–165, 182
benevolence, 11, 142, 174–181
Booth, Wayne, 100, 108, 135, 156, 189–192, 198, 208–209, 214
Boswell, James, 220, 241
Boyle, Matthew, 112, 132
Bradbrook, F.W., 135, 156
Brewer, Talbot, 37, 54
Broadie, Sarah, 32, 54
Buckle, Stephen, 161, 182
Burnyeat, Myles, 57–63, 83
Bury, Lady Charlotte, 168, 182

canon, 12, 15, 217, 221–226, 234–235, 241
Cassam, Quassim, 111–112, 116, 132

character (moral). *See also* virtue
   assessment, 20, 22–23, 67, 74, 117–118, 130, 151, 153, 168, 181
   development, 4, 7, 29, 41, 98, 104, 110–111, 114, 116, 205
   equality of, in friendship, 49–52
   flaws, 26, 36, 121–126, 190
Cheney, D.L., 136, 156
class, 1, 29, 35, 43, 76, 82, 95, 98, 117, 120, 141, 144–145, 156, 229–230
Cocking, Dean, 45–46, 54
cognitive value of literature, 4–13, 211–214
Coleridge, Samuel Taylor, 161–162, 182
comedy, 20–21, 24, 162, 181, 217, 237–238
communication, 10, 149, 152, 155
conversation, 25, 28–29, 31, 34, 43, 52, 134–135, 140, 145–146, 151–157
Cooper, John, 37, 54, 83
Crusius, Timothy, 146, 156
crystallization, 119, 130
Currie, Gregory, 153, 156, 238, 241
Curzer, Howard J., 59–62, 83

Dadlez, E.M., 21, 24, 49, 54, 87, 92, 108, 151, 156, 214
Davies, David, 214
Davies, J. M. Q., 210–211, 214
defective action, 9, 84, 86, 90–91, 95, 102
Dennett, Daniel, 3, 24
Derrida, Jacques, 144, 156

INDEX

development, cognitive/intellectual, 7, 11, 12, 151
empathetic, 6
linguistic/communicative, 10, 117, 152
moral, 4, 7, 8, 57–58, 60, 82–83, 110, 116–117, 130, 139
psychological/social, 139, 151, 153–154
Duckworth, Alasdair, 128, 132
Dunbar, Robin, 136, 148–149, 152, 154, 156

Eldridge, Richard, 114, 132
embarrassment, 71, 116, 118, 130, 202
emotion, 1–2, 4–6, 8, 21, 23, 25, 56–57, 110–111, 119–120, 130–131, 135, 148, 152, 154, 212–213, 220–221
empathy, 2, 4–6, 145
empiricism, 14, 181
epistemic bias, 26, 47–48
equality (of character/ability), 7, 25, 27, 44, 48–52, 67, 82, 101, 107, 166
Escudero, Jesús Adrián, 138–139, 156
ethics, 3–4, 7, 25, 31–33, 37, 47–48, 53–54, 57–58, 79, 83, 161, 179, 223. See also character; virtue
evidence (consideration of), 1–2, 12, 23, 41–42, 47, 112, 123, 169, 184–185, 193, 195–197, 201–205, 207–208, 210, 213
evolutionary ethnology, 136, 148
evolutionary psychology, 10, 135

fantasy, 10, 39, 68, 96, 109–110, 122–125, 160, 169–170
feminism in Austen, 7–8, 17–20, 27, 48–53, 81–83, 236–238, 240
Ferrar, Reginald, 49, 189
Ferrier, Susan, 167, 181
Fordyce, James, 165–166, 182
Frankfurt, Harry, 100–102, 108
free indirect style/discourse 5, 10, 12, 63, 122–124, 131, 143, 184, 190, 209, 215
friendship, 4, 7–8, 25–27, 31–35, 37, 40, 44–50, 52–54, 65, 82–83, 89–90, 94, 96–97, 99, 103–104, 119, 147, 175

Gerede (idle chatter), 138, 144
Goldman, Alan, 101, 108
Goldsmith, Oliver, 166, 182

gossip, 10, 129, 133–145, 147, 149–157
Grenberg, Jeanine, 37–44, 54
grooming, 136–138, 149, 152, 154, 156
grooming and gossip hypothesis (G&G), 138, 148–150, 152–155
Grossman, Jonathan, 144–145, 156

Hall, Lynda, 145, 156
happiness, 4, 25–27, 39–40, 43, 53, 78, 92, 130, 151, 174, 179, 203
Harvey, W. J., 96, 100, 108, 191, 209, 214
Heidegger, Martin, 10, 138–139, 144, 156–157
Hough, Graham, 191, 198, 209, 214
human nature, 23, 44, 48, 135–136, 153, 155, 159, 182
Hume, David, 3, 10–11, 14, 23, 182
benevolence, 178–180
courtship and marriage, 27, 49, 50–54, 166
eloquence, 139, 152, 157
Enquiry Concerning the Principles of Morals, 161, 178–180
imagination, 159–161
"Of the Standard of Taste" 227–228, 232–233, 236, 241
Treatise of Human Nature, 159, 182
Hurd, Richard, 172, 174, 182
Hutcheson, Francis, 176–178, 182
hypocrisy, 117

idle chatter, 10, 138–139
imagination, 1, 3–7, 10–11, 13, 15–16, 48, 109, 114, 120, 123–125, 127–129, 131, 158–162, 167–170, 172, 176, 180–181, 204, 227–228, 241
imaginative engagement, see reader engagement
imaginative resistance 15–16, 227–239. See also resistance
intellect
development, 7, 151
equality of, 7–8, 25–27, 29, 33–35, 49, 51
intellectual solitude/isolation, 7, 28, 52
and morality, 57, 61
in reader response, 3–4
self-estimate, 116
as virtue, 7